THE ORIGINS OF VĪRAŚAIVA SECTS

THE ORIGINS OF VĪRAŚAIVA SECTS

A Typological Analysis of Ritual and Associational Patterns in the *Śūnyasampādane*

R. BLAKE MICHAEL

MOTILAL BANARSIDASS PUBLISHERS
PRIVATE LIMITED . DELHI

First Edition: 1992

ISBN: 81-208-0698-0

Also available at:
MOTILAL BANARSIDASS
41 U.A., Bungalow Road, Jawahar Nagar, Delhi 110 007
120 Royapettah High Road, Mylapore, Madras 600 004
16 St. Mark's Road, Bangalore 560 001
Ashok Rajpath, Patna 800 004
Chowk, Varanasi 221 001

PRINTED IN INDIA
BY JAINENDRA PRAKASH JAIN AT SHRI JAINENDRA PRESS, A-45 NARAINA INDUSTRIAL AREA, PHASE I, NEW DELHI 110 028 AND PUBLISHED BY NARENDRA PRAKASH JAIN FOR MOTILAL BANARSIDASS PUBLISHERS PVT. LTD., BUNGALOW ROAD, JAWAHAR NAGAR, DELHI 110 007

For Molly

CONTENTS

PREFACE

Several years ago, when we had first moved to Ohio, my wife began employment with an insurance company. In the company cafeteria, she met a woman from India and began a casual conversation. My wife related the joyful year we had spent in India and explained that I was engaged in the study of an obscure Hindu sect which even many Indians had never heard of—a group called the Liṅgāyatas. "But", exclaimed her companion, "I *am* a Liṅgāyata!"

Such a coincidence may be rare, but it illustrates the size of the parish in which we dwell on late-twentieth-century planet earth. My own spiritual mentor, John Wesley, justified his evangelical activities by proclaiming, "The world is my parish!" Today we might note that each parish has become a world, filled with persons of various religious backgrounds and following divers spiritual paths. No longer are the old boundaries between religious traditions defined by distant borders across unknown seas. Rather religious traditions which historically had been geographically, ritually, and theologically quite distinct now rub elbows in the workplace, in the marketplace, and in the neighborhood. Furthermore, individuals who work carefully at developing their faith lives, those who take seriously the spiritual component of human existence, can no longer do so in blissful ignorance of religious traditions which formerly could have been ignored as alien and obscure.

What is becoming apparent is that obscurity is in the eye of the beholder. My wife was surprised to find a Liṅgāyata in a central Ohio company cafeteria; but that event should be no more surprising than that I, a Methodist, have often been found dining at the Mysore Indra Bhavan. There are, after all, approximately equal numbers (around ten million each) of Methodists and Liṅgāyatas dwelling on planet earth. Seen in this light, effective living on planet earth requires an understanding of our Vīraśaiva brothers and sisters no less than of our Methodist ones.

Hence it is timely and appropriate that Westerners attempt to understand religion globally by trying to understand religious traditions such as Vīraśaivism. It is also appropriate that

Vīraśaivas listen, though not uncritically, to what a Westerner such as I sees within their tradition. Where I have been able to provide insight, I hope they will use it; where I have misunderstood, I hope they will (gently) correct me. Of such conversation is made progress in the field of religious understanding.

That such progress is possible I am confident because I have already learned a great deal about my own religious tradition and about myself by listening to what Vīraśaivas have to say. Some of those interlocutors have been the great *vacana* writers of the twelfth-century. Others have been the *svāmiji*-s, *jaṅgama*-s, scholars, et al. who preserve and promote the Vīraśaiva heritage. Still others have been unpresupposing but insightful individuals encountered on the by ways of rural Karnāṭaka. And most recent have been the members of the Vīraśaiva Samāj of North America, particularly the Ohio chapter, who have warmly received me within their fellowship and friendship. To them all, I am indebted for their perspicacity and patience in helping me understand about human religiousness—theirs and mine.

I hope that nothing said in this work will obscure the profound appreciation I feel toward those individuals and the sincere respect I hold for their religious tradition. Certainly my motivation in writing it has been to enhance understanding of the Vīraśaiva tradition both within and without. I can only hope that it will, to some small extent, succeed in that goal.

Among the individuals to whom special thanks are due are Professors John B. Carman of Harvard and A. K. Ramanujan of Chicago; Lecturers Liṅgadevaru Haḷemane of Mysore and Ravi Hiremath of Dharwar; and editor N. P. Jain of Delhi, perhaps the most patient man I know. Also due very great thanks for abiding my pecularities are my family—Molly and Meredith.

R. Blake Michael
Delaware, Ohio
18 June 1991

TRANSLITERATION

Kannada	Devanagari	Roman	Kannada	Devanagari	Roman	Kannada	Devanagari	Roman
ಅ	अ	a	ಕ	क्	k	ಧ	ध्	dh
ಆ	आ	ā	ಖ	ख्	kh	ನ	न्	n
ಇ	इ	i	ಗ	ग्	g	ಪ	प्	p
ಈ	ई	ī	ಘ	घ्	gh	ಫ	फ्	ph
ಉ	उ	u	ಙ	ङ्	ṅ	ಬ	ब्	b
ಊ	ऊ	ū	ಚ	च्	c	ಭ	भ्	bh
ಋ	ऋ	ṛ	ಛ	छ्	ch	ಮ	म्	m
ೠ	ॠ	ṝ	ಜ	ज्	j	ಯ	य्	y
ಌ	ऌ	ḷ	ಝ	झ्	jh	ರ	र्	r
ೡ	ॡ	ḹ	ಞ	ञ्	ñ	ಱ	—	ṛ
ಎ	ए	e	ಟ	ट्	ṭ	ಲ	ल्	l
ಏ	—	ē	ಠ	ठ्	ṭh	ವ	व्	v
ಐ	ऐ	ai	ಡ	ड्	ḍ	ಶ	श्	ś
ಒ	ओ	o	ಢ	ढ्	ḍh	ಷ	ष्	ṣ
ಓ	—	ō	ಣ	ण्	ṇ	ಸ	स्	s
ಔ	औ	au	ತ	त्	t	ಹ	ह्	h
ಂ	ं	ṃ	ಥ	थ्	th	ಳ	ळ्	ḷ
ಃ	ः	ḥ	ದ	द्	d	ೞ	—	ḻ

ABBREVIATIONS

Basava 800*th*.	[*Śrī*] *Basavēśvara: Eighth Centenary Commemoration Volume.*
BG.	[Bombay] *Gazetteer of the Bombay Presidency*
BP (K).	*Basavapurāṇa* (of Bhīmakavi). Murughā Maṭhta, Dharwar edition. In Kannaḍa.
BP (K-E).	"The Basava Purāṇa of the Lingaits." G. Würth translation. *Journal of the Bombay Branch of the Royal Asiatic Society* 8.24 (1865-66): 65-97.
BP (T-E).	"Account of the Basava Puran—the principal Book used as a religious Code by the Jangams." C.P. Brown paraphrase. *Journal of Literature and Science* (Madras) 12 (1840): 271-291.
BV (E).	[Basava] *Vacanas of Basavaṇṇa.* L.M.A. Menezes and S.M. Angadi translation. Annana Balaga edition.
BV (K).	*Basavaṇṇanavara Vacanagaḷu.* Karnatak University edition. In Kannaḍa.
CBP (K-E).	"Channa-Basava Purāṇa of the Lingaits." G. Würth translation. *Journal of the Bombay Branch of the Royal Asiatic Society* 8.24 (1865-66): 98-221.
EC.	*Epigraphia Carnatica.*
EI.	*Epigraphia Indica and a Record of the Archaeological Survey of India.*
ERE.	*Encyclopedia of Religion and Ethics.*
JKU (*H*).	*Journal of the Karnatak University—Humanities.*
JKU (*SS*).	*The Journal of Karnataka University—Social Sciences.*
KHR.	*Karnāṭaka Historical Review.*
LDC.	*Liṅgadhāraṇacandrikā* (of Nandikeśvara). Kāsī edition. In Sanskrit.
MAV.	[Mahādeviyaka] *Vacanas of Akkamahādēvi.* Armando Menezes and S.M. Angadi transla-

	tion. Shri Manohar Appasaheb Adke edition. With Kannaḍa text.
PAIOC.	*Proceedings and Transactions of the All-India Oriental Conference.*
PLL (sam).	*Prabhuliṅgalīleya Saṃgraha* [of Cāmarasa]. Mysore University edition. In Kannaḍa.
RTR.	*Realencyklopādie für protestantische Theologie und Kirche.*
SBE.	*Sacred Books of the East.*
SiŚi.	*Siddhānta Śikhāmaṇi* [of Śivayogi]. Śrī Kāśīnātha Śāstri edition. In Sanskrit.
SPV.	*Sakalapurātanara Vacanagaḷu.* Karnatak University edition. In Kannaḍa.
SRV.	*Siddharāmēśvara Vacanagaḷu.* Karnatak University edition. In Kannaḍa.
ŚS Gū	*Śūnyasaṃpādane* [of Gūḷura Siddhavīraṇāryaru]. S.C. Nandimath et al. translation. Karnatak University edition. With Kannaḍa text.
ŚS Gum.	*Śūnyasaṃpādane* [of Gummulāpurada Siddhaliṅgadevaru]. Karnatak University edition. In Kannaḍa.
ŚS. Ha.	*Śūnyasaṃpādane* [of Halageya Dēvaru]. Mysore University Kannaḍa Institute MS no. KA 105. In Kannaḍa.
ŚS Śi.	*Śūnyasaṃpādane* [of Śivagaṇa Prasādi Mahādevayyanavaru]. Karnatak University edition. In Kannaḍa.
Vijayanagara 600*th.*	*Vijayanagara Sixcentenary Commemoration Volume.*
WZKSO.	*Wiener Zeitschrift fur die Kunde Sud- und Ostasiens.*

CHAPTER ONE

INTRODUCTION: THE VĪRAŚAIVAS AND THEIR CONTEXT

The South Indian Vīraśaivas, or Liṅgāyatas, have been often and uncritically called a "sect" and compared to Protestant Christian forms of religion. Insofar as they are distinct and to some extent separate from their Brahmanical Hindu neighbors, the appellation is acceptable; and insofar as they are a reformatory movement within a broader religious tradition, the comparison is apt. Under closer scrutiny and more accurate analysis, however, the Vīraśaivas exhibit many characteristics which are not at all "sect"-like, in the technical sense which that term has acquired within the comparative study of religious institutions through the work of Troeltsch, Weber, and numerous others.

The inaptitude of the sectarian characterization becomes clear when attention is given to focused study of a pivotal Vīraśaiva text, the fifteenth century *Śūnyasaṃpādane*. In that text, several competing ideals for what Vīraśaivism should be like emerge and compete, in a way which ultimately belies simplistic efforts to treat the movement simply as a "sect" and which reveals a much richer vision of the movement's nature as it develops into a regionally pervasive ecclesia. But, before such detailed analysis can bear fruit, it is helpful to make a broader investigation of Vīraśaivism based largely upon contemporary secondary literature and to note different major visions of the movement and its institutional organization which are implicit in that literature.

The Distinctness of Vīraśaivism

The Liṅgāyatas, or Vīraśaivas,[1] are a group of South Indian Śaivabhaktas common in Karnāṭaka State. There they comprise a pervasive community which constitutes roughly one-sixth the population of the state as a whole and over one-third the population in certain districts.[2] As the largest single caste or caste-community in the state, they play a prominent role in political and economic matters.[3]

Despite their considerable stature—both in numbers and in influence—the Liṅgāyatas, like many other Indian groups, have never been fully integrated into an homogeneous society. They have, rather, come to comprise a distinct and easily identifiable sub-cultural community within the pluralistic society of the southern Deccan. The numerical superiority of Brahmanical Hindus of various stripes is mitigated by innumerable divisions into caste and sub-caste based upon an intractable hierarchism,[4] and the Liṅgāyatas represent a potent political challenge to this group. Though the Liṅgāyatas themselves are sub-divided into numerous endogamous groups, an enduring egalitarianism and commonly faced pressures may have formed the base for a genuine class solidarity.

These *vīra*-, or "heroic", Śaivas are so called because of their ardent devotion towards Lord Śiva. On the basis of strongly felt experience of the Lord's power, the Liṅgāyatas have rejected many of the objective aids to faith commonly accepted by other Hindus. For example, they accord an, at best, equivocal authority to the "revealed scriptures" of the Hindu tradition (*śruti*) and prefer instead the accessible and more evocative Kannaḍa "sayings" (*vacanas*) of the early Vīraśaiva spiritual adepts (the *śaraṇas*). This Vīraśaiva antipathy toward the authority of the Sanskrit tradition is reflected in several of the *vacanas* attributed to Basava, the reputed twelfth-century founder of the movement. One such *vacana* reads:

> If one sings the Gītā, so what?
> If one hears the Śāstras and Purāṇas, so what?
> If one reads the Veda and Vedānta, so what?
> If one feels the highest experience, so what?
> Unless he knows whole-hearted devotion to *liṅga* and *jaṅgama*, so what?
> None but the true devotee is fit
> For our Lord of the Meeting Rivers.
>
> —Basava[5]

Whenever the Liṅgāyatas *have* turned to the Sanskrit tradition for scriptural guidance, they have preferred the sectarian Śaiva Āgamas over the Brahmanical *śruti* and *smṛti* literature. Though they have rejected outright many of the practices described therein and have modified others, their theological, cosmological, and metaphysical indebtedness to Āgamic tradition cannot be gainsaid.[6] Yet the process of selection and modification has brought the Liṅgāyatas into opposition with other Śaiva schools as well as with Brahmanical orthodoxy.[7]

The Liṅgāyatas have also aroused Brahmanical antipathies by their violation of certain norms of social behavior. They permit, in theory at least, the remarriage of a widow. They do not severely restrict the activities of a woman during her menses or immediately after childbirth, nor do they require a period of ritual purification for the family of a person recently deceased.[8] In fact, in violation of Brahmanical theory, they insist on burying rather than cremating their dead. These situations, which would be dangerously polluting for the Brahmin, are treated as mundane by Liṅgāyatas.[9]

Likewise, many occupations which would be considered polluting by Brahmins are fully acceptable to Liṅgāyatas. That this was the case in an earlier era is obvious from the number of *śaraṇas* who came from castes such as washermen, barbers, and scavengers.[10] That such egalitarianism holds true for the present is less clear since endogamous occupational groups do now exist among the Liṅgāyatas especially in areas where they constitute a large, diverse, and secure proportion of the population.[11] A thoroughgoing hierarchism, however, seems to have been avoided by general inter-caste commensality, at least among males.[12] Certainly the group's literary heritage calls for such commensality as, for example, in the following *vacana* by Basava:

> Of one who eats food blessed by you, wherever he be,
> What is the caste?
> Of one who is fit for your service, O Master,
> What is the caste?
> Of one who is drawn to your bosom, O God,
> What is the caste?
> O Lord of the Meeting Rivers.
>
> —Basava[13]

Besides their enmity with Brahmanical Hindus, the Liṅgāyatas have also experienced strained relations with other followers of Lord Śiva. The group's unique practice of wearing always about the body a small personal emblem of the Lord Śiva (the *iṣṭaliṅga*) provides a badge which readily sets them apart from other Śaivas. That mild distinction is, however, exacerbated by their vocal rejection of forms of worship common to other Śaivas.[14] The Liṅgāyatas go so far as to reject altogther the Śaiva worship of large, stone emblems (*sthāvaraliṅga*) fixed in permanent temple contexts. Instead, the puring of libations over a stone *liṅga* is ridiculed in favor of turning one's very self into a suitable emblem for the Lord:

> Soaking a stone for ever so long, can water soften it?
> Offering flowers for ever so long, can I come to know you?
> My mind is but a wandering ghost, unless it's clasp on you.
> O Lord of the Meeting Rivers.
>
> —Basava[15]

The group's own emphasis on its utter distinctness from its Brahmin neighborhood has been especially prominent during period of relative economic and political security. For example, under patronage from the Vijayanagara rulers, the Vīraśaivas of the fifteenth and sixteenth centuries produced exuberant, self-confident literature, such as the *Śūnyaṣampādane* and the *Prabhuliṅga-līle*.

The Śūnyaṣampādane,[16] for example, ends with the twelfth-century founding fathers of the movement dispersed from Kalyāṇa and in disarray, but it views that condition as ephemeral. The inevitable spiritual triumph of the movement is emphasized as all the principals attain union with the absolute, thereby verifying their divine missions.[17] The expectation that the worldly success of the movement will eventually verify this apparently purely spiritual success is reflected in the final chapters of the *Cennabasava Purāṇa*. There, the concluding "prophecy" tells of the dispersal of the *śaraṇas* from Kalyāṇa and of their separate fortunes thereafter. It also "predicts" the rise of Vijayanagara and the revitalization of Vīraśaiva tradition from the refugee community established by Cennabasava at Uḷuve.[18]

In these several ways, then, Vīraśaivism exhibits its distinctness from "orthodox" Brahmanical Hindu tradition.

Vīraśaivism's Relatedness to Brahmanical Orthodoxy

In the several ways mentioned above, Vīraśaivism appears rather distinct from the Brahmanical tradition within Hinduism. Often, however, Vīraśaivism, particularly during its later history, can be better understood when it is viewed in terms of its similarities to and close relation with the larger Hindu tradition. During significant portions of its history, Vīraśaiva literature has tended towards Sanskrit apologia. For example, in the fourteenth century, Śrīpati Paṇḍita wrote, in Sanskrit, the *Śrīkara Bhāṣya* in which he derived the principles of Vīraśaiva philosophy from the *Brahma Sūtras*.[19] Similarly, in the seventeenth century, Nandikeśvara defended the specifically Liṅgāyata practices of wearing the *liṅga* and of burial of the dead on the basis of orthodox *śruti* and *smṛti* literature in his *Liṅgadhāraṇa Candrikā*.[20] In these texts, and in others like them, the Vīraśaiva tradition turned from the language and literature of distinctness, the Kannaḍa *vacanaśāstra*, toward the Sanskrit language and *śruti* tradition—the language and literature of relatedness and unity in Brahmanical India.[21]

Another important way in which Vīraśaiva theory, if not practice, is closely allied with the Brahmanical is in the affirmation of *mokṣa* or release from the unpleasantness of worldly existence. While Liṅgāyatas may emphasize methods for reaching *mokṣa* which are absent from Brahmanical patterns or even directly opposed to Brahmanical norms, they nonetheless share that goal with Brahmanical Hindus. In this pursuit of release from *saṃsāra*, as in other matters, Liṅgāyata goals appear not so much as contradictions of Brahmanical values as they do as intensifications of certain central elements in the Brahmanical scheme. Note, for example, Siddharāmēśvara's plaint for extraction from the suffering of worldly rebirth:

> I have been trapped in *saṃsāra*, the demon's snout.
> Could I tell when he swallowed, when he spat out?
> Extract me! Protect me from that awful snout!
> O Lord of the Faultless Jasmines.
>
> —Siddharāmēśvara[22]

Indeed, many of their practices can be better understood when the behavior of the Liṅgāyatas is compared to that of those Hindus who are acknowledged as superior by all—the *saṃnyāsins*. Having progressed through the other three stages of life, the *saṃnyāsin* rejects not only the comforts of home when he begins his wandering mendicancy, but also the usual ritual observances and abstinences which protect him from pollution. The very sanctity of his state as an ascetic renouncer relieves him from the usual ceremonies and protects him from harmful pollution. In this respect, such Liṅgāyata practices as burial of the dead rather than cremation exactly parallel the pattern for Brahmanical Hindu ascetics.[23] Likewise, many of the pollution taboos which Liṅgāyatas ignore are also inapplicable to Brahmins who have renounced the worldly life.[24] Liṅgāyata practice, then, serves not to undermine Brahmanical values, but to highlight and emphasize them. It only insists that the pursuit of the highest goal, *mokṣa*, need not await the renunciation of worldly activity at the end of this or a later life but may be undertaken immediately by the sincere devotee.

In this, as in other ways, it is often helpful to view the Liṅgāyatas as merely one more caste, or caste complex, within the larger Brahmanical fold. One way in which the Liṅgāyatas reflect their Brahmanical affinities is their firm insistence on vegetarianism and on abstinence from alcoholic beverages. In fact, the Abbé Dubois attributes the undeniable animosity between Brahmins and Liṅgāyatas precisely to the latters' rigorism in these matters and the threat posed thereby to the Brahmins' hegemony.[25] Whatever the politics of the matter, certainly vegetarianism and abstinence are important values within the Vīraśaiva written heritage as asserted by Basava:

> From desires of the flesh, one takes meat and wine.
> From desires of the eyes, one cuckolds a friend.
> If one falters on the *liṅga* path,
> What use the *liṅga* he wears so well?
> If one incurs the *jaṅgama's* wrath,
> Then surely he plummets to Hell!
> O Lord of the Meeting Rivers.
>
> —Basava[26]

In the matter of occupational acceptability as well, the Liṅgāyatas followed certain Brahmanical patterns. As indicated above, many of the early Vīraśaiva saints (*śaraṇas*) had followed impure or immoral occupations. These were not denied entry into the Vīraśaiva fold, but they were required to renounce their old, polluting occupations. The Vīraśaiva challenge to Brahmanical standards was, therefore, not to the entire system of occupational purity but to the inevitability of one's lifelong vocation as a result of birth to a certain family. One could renounce a polluted past and become a new, unpolluted person; but, within the company of the *śaraṇas* only specific occupations could continue to be pursued. Basava again reflects his opposition to caste discrimination based on heredity, which is voiced throughout Vīraśaiva literature.

> The father of Vyāsa was a fisherman;
> Mārkendeya's mother, an outcaste;
> And Mȧṅdōdari was the daughter of a frog.
> O look not to caste! For who could say, anyway
> What he had been born in births past.
> Indeed, Agastya was a fowler;
> Durvāsa, a mason; Kaśyapa, a blacksmith;
> Kaundinya there, as everyone knows,
> Spent his lives cutting hair.
> 'So what if one had been a dog-eating outcaste?
> 'The devotee of Śiva is born into a good family.'
> So says our Lord of the Meeting Rivers.
>
> —Basava[27]

It should be noted here, however, that the *śaraṇas* did not condone just any occupation. Of whatever caste and to whatever occupation born, anyone was welcome among the *śaraṇas*; but, in their eyes, he must be "born again" through devotion to Lord Śiva into a new family and a new caste position. The former occupation and its attendant pollution must be set aside. In other words, the *śaraṇas* strove only to remove the unalterability of caste affiliation on the basis of birth; they did not undermine the basic purity gradient upon which caste itself was founded.

The tradition insisted that it was not by birth, but by behavior, that the saint could be known. Its view of the proper Brahmin was, similarly, that it is not by birth, but by behavior, that the true Brahmin should be known. Hence the characteristics which supposedly identified the true Brahmin were not rejected but were more broadly sought and more ardently affirmed. The esteem owed to the true Brahmin because of his moral and ritual purity was in no way lessened; its criteria were merely redefined. The basically hierarchical social patterning which provided honor and honorarium to those at the top was modified but not utterly rejected, and the bases upon which that hierarchy rested were altered but not destroyed. Siddharāmēśvara, for example, specifically describes those of correct knowledge and behavior as the true Brahmins.

> From merely reading and teaching the Veda,
> Can you become a Brahmin?
> Making the sacrifice, the six-fold ritual,
> Can you become a Brahmin?
> True Brahmin is he who knows the Truth,
> And understands Vedic writ, forsooth.
> Knowing Truth, in it he abides.
> That one is the true Brahmin, see!
> O Lord of the Faultless Jasmines.
>
> —Siddharāmēśvara[28]

The fact that many sincere Vīraśaivas, past and present, have struggled against the hierarchism of caste should not be overlooked. Neither, however, should it be overlooked that many sincere Vīraśaivas have accepted and do accept caste division, of some sort, as a natural and necessary component of their tradition.[29] Perhaps a bit of Kannaḍa folk humor best reflects the uneasy compromise of these two positions.

> Purity and bathing are easiest
> When the river is in flood.
> Caste distinctions are greatest
> When there is plenty of food.[30]

Without debating the details of the above accounts, it should be relatively clear that, within Vīraśaiva tradition itself, there has not been unanimity about the ideal relation of the movement to the broader context within which it originated and developed—namely that of Brahmanical Hinduism. Rather, there have been competing ideals of what that relation should be and ardent attempts to effect one or the other of those ideals.

Attempts to Understand the Vīraśaivas as a "Hindu" "Sect"

What is of interest to the present investigation is not, of course, whether Liṅgāyatas have castes or are teetotalers but what these characteristics indicate about the relation between Vīraśaivism and the "great tradition" of Sanskrit Brahmanical Hinduism. From the above comments it is clear that they may be viewed and have been viewed from two perspectives on this question.

Some have seen them as a group wholly independent of and vehemently opposed to the Brahmanical Hindu tradition.[31] Others have seen them as welcome rivals to Brahmin leadership in the effort to spread shared cultural and religious values throughout India's diverse geographical regions and distinct social strata. In any case, it becomes obvious that the rivalry between Liṅgāyatas and Brahmanical Hindus proceeds along dimensions of behaviour and social structure which are shared by both groups rather than along entirely divergent lines. In this respect, it may be inaccurate to draw too bold a dividing line between the two traditions. Rather than standing in intractable antipathy to Brahmanical Hinduism, the Liṅgāyatas may constitute a powerful and cohesive agency for spreading basic Brahmanical values.[32]

The problem of these two interpretations of Vīraśaivism has often been directly addressed under the question, "Are Liṅgāyatas Hindus?" From the above discussion it is clear that the answer to that question has been far from unanimous. Many have viewed them as Hindus, or, more accurately, as Brahmanical Hindus, while others have described them as an entirely separate religious tradition.[33] Without querying the utility of the question itself, many have attempted to provide an either-or answer.

It may be the case that the question itself is misdirected. More important than determining whether some particular label is appropriate to the group or not may be a determination of the nature of Vīraśaivism's relation to other religious movements within Indian society. In other words, the question becomes not whether the Liṅgāyatas are Hindus but "What is the relation of Liṅgāyata Indians to other Indians?"

This view is buttressed by a realization that the very word "Hinduism" is of recent and external origin. Traditionally, "Hindu" has meant not a member of any particular religious tradition but rather a resident of India. Thus one could once, without contradiction, refer to Hindu Muslims—meaning Indian Muslims.[34] In this sense, it is obvious that Liṅgāyatas are indeed Hindus—that is, Indians. Then little profits it to pose either-or questions. More useful is a determination of the place of Vīraśaivism within Indian society and Indian religious tradition. Focus falls then on the relation between Liṅgāyatas and other groups within the broad fold of Indian religious tradition.

One terminology which has been used to describe the relation of Vīraśaivism to the rest of Indian religious tradition has hinged upon the term "sect". In light of the group's distinctive practices and their concomitant differentiation from the community of Brahmanical Hindus at large, the use of this term is not surprising. Unfortunately, in describing the Liṅgāyatas as well as other Indian groups, the term has often been used in an entirely uncritical manner. Quite frequently it has provided nothing more than a general description of "a group of people who share a common set of religious beliefs".[35]

Examples of this uncritical usage begin, at least, with Bhandarkar who initiates his discussion of the Liṅgāyatas by attributing the "foundation of this *sect*...to Basava."[36] Similarly unreflective, Basham defines the Liṅgāyatas merely as a "Śaivite sect".[37] Even McCormack, in his enlightening article on the use of the term "sect" as applied to the Liṅgāyatas, proceeds no further than the second sentence before lapsing into an uncritical description of the group as "a large *sect*, which are to be found to-day residing in the towns and villages of the Kannaḍa-speaking region of south India".[38]

Other scholars have attempted a more careful definition of the term with special reference to the Indian context. Most noteworthy among these is Renou who prefaces his definition of the Indian sect with an insistence that there is little profit in attempting a radical distinction between "sectarians" and "Hindus". Rather, he insists, "the most active sects were themselves only isolated groups within the great body of believers".[39]

Having provided that caveat, Renou proceeds to construct a formal description of the Indian sect-type organization. He points to four essential characteristics: (1) adherence to a particular sacred writing and devotion to a particular deity, (2) adoption of a particular philosophical or doctrinal position which unavoidably involves some element of devotion to a personal Lord (*bhakti*), (3) recognition of an identifiable, individual founder and commitment to his teachings, and (4) an inherent reformist impetus which often actualizes itself in cultic purification, iconoclasm, antisacrificialism, broadened popular appeal, exotericization, egalitarian organization, and emphasis on the vernacular as a teaching medium.

Dumont has added two valuable amendments to Renou's formal definition. First, he has observed that (5) it is the personality of the individual founder and of his successors which provides the ineluctable element of renunciation to the Indian sect-type organization. In fact, he defines the sect in term of a group of religious virtuosi who have renounced the world and around whom a lay following forms a non-essential periphera.[40] Secondly, Dumont has pointed to (6) the crucial role which the ecstatic spirit-medium of Indian village worship plays in introducing the emotional *bhakti* element into popularized sect-type religiosity.[41]

The aptitude of this formal definition for describing Vīraśaivism is transparent. Early Vīraśaivism (1) rejected the *śruti* tradition and relied upon the vernacular Kannaḍa *vacana*, (2) subsumed its philosophizing under an intense devotion to Lord Śiva, (3) reverenced the memory and teachings of Basava,[42] (4) rejected the ritual, iconography, and priestly authority of the Brahmins, (5) called for frugality, renunciation, and self-sacrifice from its members,[43] and (6) adopted the ecstatic spiritism of such characters as Maruḷuśaṅkaradēva and Mahādēviyakka.[44]

It should be emphasized that both Renou and Dumont undertake their reflections on the nature of the Indian sect with their attention firmly focused on the Indian data.[45] It is most interesting, however, that the formal characteristics which they point out divide into two categories which have been found in the sect-type organization elsewhere. The first, second, third, and fifth characteristics they isolate—namely, (1) a particular scripture, (2) a personal deity, (3) an identifiable founder, and (5) a voluntary renunciation—reflect the general pattern of particularism which characterizes sectarian ecclesiology. The fourth and sixth characteristics—namely, (4) cultic purification and simplification and (6) an ecstatic and spiritual emotionalism—reflect common traits of subjectivism characteristic of sectarian soteriology worldwide.

The two major difficulties with this analysis of the Vīraśaivas' sectarian characteristics are that, by ignoring general structural characteristics of religious associations, it remains too Indo-specific and that it treats the matter in an absolutist fashion rather than asking, more wisely, "to what extent" the Vīraśaivas exhibit sectarian *and* non-sectarian (i.e. church-type) characteristics. Indeed, as the foregoing indicates, the Vīraśaivas have a complex and multiform organization which is by no means perfectly sectarian in nature. Some of the problems presented by these previous attempts to understand the Liṅgāyatas' relation to Brahmanical Hindus may be solved or circumvented by an analysis of the group utilizing a more general understanding of religious associations based upon their relative sect-type characteristics, as opposed to their relatively more "church"-like attributes.

Attempts to Understand the Vīvaśaivas as "Protestants"

Unfortunately much Western scholarship has failed to acknowledge these multiple dimensions of the Vīraśaiva movement—its distinctness and relatedness, its universalism and particularism, and its subjectivism and objectivism. Western attention has, rather, focused on the ways in which Vīraśaivism, like Protestant Christianity, zealously stood over and against its social and religious context as a distinct, particularist, and subjectivist reformatory movement. In fact, a persistently implicit and occasionally explicit evaluative comparison of Vīraśaivism to the norm of Protestant Christianity has permeated the literature.

Part of the blame for this partialism can be attributed, probably to his own chagrin, to the great sociologist of religion Max Weber. In his *Religion of India*, Weber offered a few brief but tantalizing observations on the Liṅgāyatas. First, he noted those characteristics of the group which distinguished it from the rest of Indian society. He explored those characteristics of its institutional associational patterns which marked it as a separate, identifiable "sect". Noting characteristics common, throughout the world, to the sectarian type of religious association, he observed that the Liṅgāyatas "...represented a type of particularly sharp and principled 'protestant' reaction to the Brahmans and the caste order."[46]

Next, Weber described those characteristics which linked the group to the more general patterns of Indian social structure. He noted the hierarchism and caste differentiation common to Liṅgāyata and Brahmin alike and explored these characteristics of its institutional patterns which mark it as a "church" or "ecclesia", inseparable from the societal context at large. Sensing characteristics common, throughout the world, to the church type of religious association, he observed, "For some time, the Liṅgāyat sect has undergone a characteristic process of status differentiation suggestive of the gentility claimed by the descendents of the Mayflower Pilgrims in New England."[47]

Thus, in his succinct manner, Weber indicated the two seemingly contradictory ideals of institutional association for which Vīraśaivas have often striven and by which students of Vīraśaiva ways have often been blinded and confused. And, as has often been the case with his observations, these words of Weber set the stage and suggested the script for most subsequent discussions of Vīraśaivism. Much of the sociological and anthropological discourse on the group has attempted to answer the questions which arise from these two opposed descriptions of the nature of Vīraśaivism. Is Vīraśaivism best characterised as a largely egalitarian "sect" consisting of a "principled 'protest...' " against the Indian social hierarchy, or does the movement's advanced "status differentiation" suggest some category other than "sect" to describe them? Are the Liṅgāyatas a sect within Hinduism, or do they constitute a group with pervasiveness and autonomy sufficient to warrant an appellation such as "church"?

Another set of questions is inherent in Weber's two cited statements. His insertion of the word "protestant" and his reference to the Pilgrims may or may not, within themselves, be "value-free" usages; but, following his lead, several other authors have found it profitable to discuss the Liṅgāyatas with reference to Protestant Christianity in general and the Calvinist Puritans in particular. Quite lyrically has R.E. Enthoven described them as "...a peaceable race of Hindu puritans."[48] Less carefully, has Will Durant allowed the upper case to betray an implicit comparison when he described the Liṅgāyatas as "...the most Puritanic sect in India."[49] H.M. Sadāsivaiah's spelling was less precise than his intention when he noted, "In both Vīraśaivism and Protestantism (*sic*) we find the spirit of 'wordly asceticism'..."[50] Though less explicit, similarly inclined was S.C. Nandimath who spoke of the Vīraśaiva's spiritual endeavors as "...the *pilgrim's progress* towards realization."[51]

Observing the canons of "value-free" science, it is certainly legitimate for the social scientist to make conscious comparisons between the institutional patterns of two religious traditions. Unfortunately, among many scholars subsequent to Weber and perhaps, to some extent, for Weber himself these comparisons between the institutional arrangements of the Liṅgāyatas and those of the Puritans became more evaluative than strictly descriptive and analytical. The propensity of European scholars to see Protestant Christian patterns as normative and to evaluate Oriental patterns against that norm has been matched only by the similar tendency among colonially trained apologists for the Oriental traditions themselves.

Certainly this evaluative tendency has characterized much of the investigation of Vīraśaivism. Studies conducted by Europeans have, by and large, expressed a fascination for this movement which in so many ways came so close to the patterns of "true" religion only to founder on the shoals of Brahmanical tradition. Vīraśaiva apologists have often noted the same similarities and have defended deviations from the preferred European pattern as legitimate and minor variations. Thus, the effort to understand the Vīraśaivas has often become rather an effort to establish the relative worth of the group in terms of its adherence to the criteria of the religion of conquest in the past several centuries—Protestant Christianity.[52]

Since the doctrinal and mythological complexes of the two traditions are seemingly worlds apart, the comparative and apologetic effort has often focused on similarities in religious practice —ethical, ritual, and institutional. Thus studies of membership patterns have emphasized the essential equality of all members. Likewise, much has been written about the simplification of existing ritual worship effected by the two traditions and the direct and individualized route to salvation which arose from those ritual reforms.

On the other hand, the ways in which Vīraśaiva religious patterns fell short not only of actual Protestant forms but also of the idealized Protestant norm have been prominently noted. The gradual shift from voluntary membership to automatic ascription of those born to Vīraśaiva parents has been explored. The concomitant shift from an egalitarian community to an hierarchical society has been often investigated and sometimes lamented.[53] The rise of an hierarchy of believers on the ladder to salvation and the assignment of salvific functions to certain specialists has also been noted, especially as these accompany the rise of a more elaborate system of ritual worship.[54]

What both these approaches have in common, of course, is

that they assign a normative, evaluative role to the associational characteristics and institutional patterns of Protestant Christianity. In fact, it is often not so much Protestant Christianity as practised by its adherents as that movement idealized by its own theorists, as well as by social scientists, to which Vīraśaiva practices have been compared. Whether by a sympathetic student who assiduously seeks points of comparison which will cast Vīraśaivism in a favorable light, or by an unsympathetic scholar who equally strives to cast aspersion on Vīraśaivism and to offer Christianity as a more attractive alternative—by one having either of these motives, a comparison which attempts to see Vīraśaivism against the norm of Protestant Christianity is doomed to failure in any effort at truly understanding what Vīraśaivism means to the persons who know the most about that movement—namely, Vīraśaiva individuals.

Prospectus for a Typological Analysis of Vīraśaiva Associational Patterns

Admittedly much of the pioneering work in the general understanding of religious institutions was undertaken by Protestant scholars and often involved a study of Christian institutions, and the interpretative scheme which most strongly informs the present study is one which emerged from just such an historical study of Christian institutions. The sect-type, church-type, and mystic-type of religious association which Ernst Troeltsch adduced in his famous study of Christianity[55] prove quite useful in categorizing the various Vīraśaiva institutional patterns.

In Troeltsch's view, a crucial dimension which underlay his typology was precisely the relative objectivity/subjectivity of the means of salvation. Whether the attainment of human salvation lay within the hands of objective human institutions, such as the priesthood and the sacraments, or whether such salvation was a private and individual matter for the subjective human being became a crucial typological distinction for Troeltsch. Others have suggested that a second essential dimension of this typology is the relative universality/particularity of a group's membership and recruitment.[56] Whether a group freely includes all who come within its geographical or social sphere or excludes all but those few who meet its rigorous membership standards is a critical question in determining its associational type. In other words, the relative objectivity/subjectivity of Vīraśaivism's means of salvation and the relative universality/particularity of its membership patterns, can become informative but non-evaluative dimensions for analysis of the group's relation to its Brahmanical context.

For analyzing the Vīraśaivas' religious hierarchy, sacramental system, and membership patterns, a wealth of data is presented in a fifteenth-century Kannaḍa text, the *Śūnyasaṃpādane*, wherein all the types of religious association suggested by Troeltsch are exhibited. The contents of that text provide both explicit and implicit evidence for understanding Vīraśaiva associational patterns as evidenced in the priestly hierarchy, the ritual system, and membership criteria. The competing ideals espoused within the text make it obvious that simplistic attempts to determine which type of religious association does or should characterize Vīraśaivism are misguided. In the text, each of the three principal characters consistently argue for and attempt to effect a different ideal pattern of Vīraśaiva organization. Simplicity of ritual practice, individual and subjective means to salvation and relatively egalitarian membership and organizational patterns are defended by Basava. Elaborate and sophisticated rituals, the objective availability of soteriological devices, and a primarily hierarchical organization of membership are promoted by Cennabasava. Allama Prabhu, on the other hand, exhibits a clear disdain for organized, communal rituals, a radical subjectivity with respect to attainment of mystic goals, and a fundamental anarchism in organizational matters.

In the *Śūnyasaṃpādane*, as in the entire history of the movement, no single institutional ideal predominates. From a careful study of the text, there emerge ample bases for arguing that several diverse types of religious association—sect, church, mystic, universalist, particularist, objectivist, subjectivist—all are legitimate institutional actualizations of Vīraśaivism's spiritual genius. Careful study of the *Śūnyasaṃpādane*, perforce, moves the analysis of the Vīraśaiva data beyond crude comparisons with Protestant Christianity toward a better understanding of Vīraśaiva institutional practices themselves and toward a more adequate understanding of religious institutional patterns in general.

Just as Troeltsch found all three associational types to be legitimate applications of the Gospel message to social conditions, so too do several patterns emerge as valuable ideals for Vīraśaiva practice. There arises no need to emphasize one aspect of Vīraśaiva religious association and to denigrate others simply along norms derived from an external source. A method which has borne fruit in the investigation of Christianity can be extended, again fruitfully, into the analysis of Vīraśaivism. Specifically, the tension with Vīraśaivism between unmediated direct spiritual experience and the use of certain aids to faith (the *aṣṭāvaraṇa*) administered solely by a class of religious specialists (the *guru* and the *jaṅgama*) provides primary data for coming to understand why certain Vīraśaivas have idealized the subjectivism and particularism of the sect-type organization while others have idealized the objectivism and universalism of the church-type.

The two dimensions of analysis chosen here—(1) objectivism/subjectivism as reflected in the nature of clerical hierarchy and patterns of ritual worship, and (2) universalism/particularism as reflected in criteria for membership in the group—have been often abused elsewhere. When evaluatively compared with a "normative" Protestant Christianity, other religious traditions have fared better if their religious hierarchy was not elaborate, their ritual system lacked complexity, and their membership criteria were voluntaristically rigid. With respect to Vīraśaivism, this factor has been obvious at least since Weber's somewhat piqued observation that "All in all, the rationalistic course which expressed itself in the purism of the sect was not able to shatter the massive hagiolatry and traditionalism of its predominantly peasant adherence."[57]

It is, however, possible to avoid both the overtly comparative style and the inherently evaluative nature of many previous studies. A set of concerns which grows out of one religious tradition, whether these be part of the spiritual or only of the intellectual background of an investigator, may be instructive for understanding issues and tensions within another religious tradition; and no comparative evaluation need be implied. It is possible and profitable to discern specific patterns within Vīraśaiva institutional organization which are common to religious movements around the world. That certain of these patterns have Protestant parallels while others are antithetical to Protestant theory is quite interesting, indeed informative, but that fact is itself neither laudable nor lamentable.

NOTES

1. In general, the term "Vīraśaivism" refers to a philosophical or theological system as well as to the historical, social and religious movement which originated from and expressed allegiance to that system. "Liṅgāyata" refers to the modern social group, sect, or caste which still professes this philosophy and lives in conscious continuity with the patterns established by the historical movement. In the following, an attempt will be made to use "Vīraśaiva" in this historical significance and "Liṅgāyata" in the anthropological one. The boundary between the usages is, however, far from clear, and consistency has not been reached.

2. These estimates are based on the *Censuses of India*, 1921 and 1931, which are the last in which caste affiliation information was specifically sought. See Appendix I.

3. See William McCormack, "On Liṅgāyat Culture", in *Speaking of Śiva*, trans. and introduced by A.K. Ramanujan (Baltimore: Penguin Books, Inc., 1973), pp. 177-78; Alan Beals, "Leadership in a Mysore Village", in *Leadership and Political Institutions in India*, ed. Richard L. Park and Irene Trinker (Princeton: Princeton University Press, 1959), pp. 433ff.; and, in their entirety, two works by C. Parvathamma, *Politics and Religion: A Study of Historical Interaction between Socio-Political Relationships in a Mysore Village* (New Delhi: Sterling Publishers (P) Ltd., 1971), and *Sociological Essays on Veerasaivism* (Bombay: Popular Prakashan, 1972).

4. The ineluctable hierarchism of Indian society and its effect on the Liṅgāyatas is explored most explicitly by Louis Dumont, *Homo Hierarchicus: An Essay on the Caste System*, trans. Mark Sainsbury (Chicago: University of Chicago Press, 1970), par. 93, pp. 187-91.

5. *BV* 188: (K) p. 81; (E) p. 61.

6. See S.C. Nandimath, "The Śaivāgamas: Their Literature and Theology", *JKU(H)* 6 (1962 June): 1-34 and *JKU(H)* 7 (1963): 1-48, and S.G. Sakharpekar, "Agamic Vīraśaivism", *PAIOC* 7 (1933): pp. 399-404. Unavailable to the present researcher but of doubtless interest would be S.D. Parvate, *Vīraśaiva Philosophy of the Śaivāgamas* (Hubli : [publisher unknown], 1927).

7. The distinctness of Vīraśaivas from other Śaivas forms the pre-eminent thesis of M.R. Sakhare, *History and Philosophy of Liṅgāyat Religion* (Belgaum: By the author, n.d. [1942]). Of particular interest is the chapter on the "Agamas", pt. I, pp. 237-303.

8. *Bhakti* groups, in general, have flaunted Brahmanical standards. For the Liṅgāyatas, see S.C. Nandimath, *A Handbook of Vīraśaivism* (Dharwar: L.E. Association, 1942), p. 88; and Abbé J.A. Dubois, *Hindu Manners, Customs and Ceremonies*, 3rd ed., trans. and ed. Henry K. Beauchamp (Oxford: Clarendon Press, 1906), p. 181. Liṅgāyata disdain for purificatory rituals is summarized in the folk aphorism, "There is no river for a Lingayat", meaning that the group does not recognize nor enjoy the benefits of ablutions. See Dubois, *Hindu*, p. 116. The impurity for Brahmanical Hindus arising from the conditions mentioned by Nandimath find scriptural sanction at *Manu* V. 58-63 and 71-77 for birth and death and at *Manu* III. 45-46 and IV. 40-41 for men-

struation. In English, see *SBE*, vol. 25: *The Laws of Manu*, trans G. Bühler [subsequently issued separately at New York: Dover Publications, Inc., 1969, pp. 83-84, 135, and 177-81.]

9. The critical relation between ritual purity/impurity and the religious experience of transcendent power, or "The Holy", was explored generally by Nathan Söderblom, *ERE*, s. v. "Holiness (General and Primitive)"; and with reference to India by Mary Douglas, *Purity* and *Danger: An Analysis of Concepts of Pollution and Taboo* (New York: Praeger Publishers, 1966), pp. 8-10 and 123-27.

10. For example, in the *Śūnyasaṃpādane* as well as in other texts portraying events in twelfth-century Kalyāṇa, Maḍivāḷa Mācayya is depicted as a washerman; Haḍapada Apaṇṇa, as a barber; and Maruḷu Śaṅkaradēva, as a simpleton and a scavenger.

11. The caste structure of the Liṅgāyatas is discussed briefly by McCormack, "Liṅgayat Culture", pp. 178-79; C.P. Brown, "Essay on the Creed, Customs and Literature of Jangamas", *Journal of Literature and Science* (Madras) 11 (1840): pp. 143-77; R.C. Artal, "A Short Account of the Reformed Shaiva or Veerashaiva Faith", *Journal of the Anthropological Society of Bombay* 8.3 (1909): pp. 250-55; R.E. Enthoven, *ERE*, s.v. "Lingayats", pp. 72-73; and K. Chandrasekhariah, "A Sociological Analysis of Vīraśaivism" (Ph.D. dissertation, Johann Wolfgang Goethe University, Frankfurt am Main, 1955), pp. 45-68.

12. At least, so avers this researcher's informant who also attests to fairly general exogamy among Liṅgāyata occupation groups in southern Karnāṭaka, where their minority status tends to minimize intra-movement factionalism and to maximize group solidarity vis-à-vis Brahmanical groups. Clement Marro notes the quasi-caste nature of Liṅgāyata *jaṅgamas* who freely interdine but do not intermarry with non-*jaṅgamas*. See his "Role and Position of the Guru and of the Jangama in Lingayatism", *Bangalore Theological Forum* 6.2 (1974 July-December): 47.

13. *BV* 731: (K) p. 292; (E) p. 241.

14. The fixed versus the mobile modes of worship in Vīraśaivism have been revealingly discussed by A.K. Ramanujan, Introduction to *Speaking of Śiva*, ed. and trans. A.K. Ramanujan (Baltimore: Penguin Books, Inc., 1973), pp. 20ff. Ramanujan has tended, however, to place emphasis on the textual ideal of the mobile and dynamic elements of Vīraśaiva tradition with less attention to the static ideal. While the fixed stone *liṅga* plays little part in Vīraśaiva worship, that static, centered function is served by another focus of veneration. In many of the larger *maṭhas*, one of the most important chambers is one in which the tomb or image of a deceased *svāmiji* is venerated to the accompaniment of circumambulation, gongs, *ārati*, flowers, etc. In other words, most of the important components of Brahmanical temple worship are also present in this context. The present researcher has observed and participated in such worship at the Murugha Maṭha in Dharwar and at the Mūru Sāvira Maṭha in Hubli. The practice is attested beyond those locations by informants. Similarly, on the veneration of a static *liṅga*, see Herbert C. Wolf's recent account in his "The *Liṅga* as Center: A Study in Religious Phenomenology", *Journal of the American Academy of Religion* 46.3K.2 Supplement (1978 September): 365.

See also R. Blake Michael, "*Linga* as Lord Supreme in the *Vacanas* of Basava", *Numen* 29.2 (1982 December).

15. *BV* 99: (K) pp. 47-48; (E) pp. 32-33.

16. The text exists in several versions and editions. The most accessible is *Śūnyasaṃpādane* [of Gūḷūra Siddhavīranāryaru]; 5 vols.; edited with Introduction, Text, Transliteration, Translation, Notes and Comments by S.C. Nandimath et al.; with Forewords by D.C. Pavate *et al.* (Dharwar: Karnatak University, 1965-72), [*ŚS.* Gū.]. The recent appearance of this translation has already spawned considerable interest in the Vīraśaivas in general and the text in particular. See, for example, Raymond Allchin, "The Attaining of the Void—A Review of Some Recent Contributions in English to the Study of Vīraśaivism", *Religious Studies* 7.4 (1971 December): pp. 339-59, which is a shallow, but serviceable, review summary of readily available materials.

17. The final chapter of the *Śūnyasaṃpādane* begins with Allama Prabhu's victory in yogic competition over a Gōrakṣī and concludes with the spiritual victory of union with the Lord which is attained by Allama Prabhu at Śrīśaila, by Basava at Kappaḍi Saṅgama, and by Cennabasava at Uḷuve. See *ŚS* Gū., vol. V, pp. 376-81 and 383-463. Note that all four versions of the *Śūnyasaṃpādane* have been assigned to dates well within the period of Vijayanagara's exuberance, C.E. 1420-1520. See R.C. Hiremath, Introduction to *ŚS* Gum., pp. 7-10.

18. Actually, the *Cennabasava Purāṇa* was compiled shortly after the fall of Vijayanagara and the passage of the dynasty's influence to its vicegerents at Śrīraṅgapatna, where the Wodeyars of Mysore eventually assumed control of the remnants of Vijayanagara suzerainty. The parallelism between the fall of Kalyāṇa and its eventual resurrection and that of Vijayanagara is transparent in the *Cennabasava Purāṇa.* This text is available in English paraphrase as "Channa-Basava Purāṇa of the Lingaits", trans. G. Würth, *Journal of the Bombay Branch of the Royal Asiatic Society* 8.24 (1865-66): especially chaps. 62-63, pp. 219-21. On the basis of internal evidence, Würth (p. 221) has assigned this text to the year C.E. 1585.

19. This text, together with a massive introduction and analysis, but no translation, has been published as *The Śrīkara Bhāshya*; Being the *Vīraśaiva Commentary on the Vedānta-Sūtras,* 2 vols., ed. C. Hayavadana Rao (Bangalore City: n.p., 1936). In his Introduction, Hayavadana Rao (vol. 1, p. 31) argues that the traditional twelfth-century dates for the text are impossible and places it rather tentatively between C.E. 1300 and 1400 and definitely post-Madhvācārya. Thus ruled out is the suggestion that this commentary may be late-twelfth century by J.N. Farquhar, *An Outline of the Religious Literature of India* (London: Humphrey Milford, Oxford University Press, 1920), p. 264. Farquhar's later implication that the text may belong between the sixteenth and eighteenth centuries is partially vitiated, but not definitively disproven, by Hayavadana Rao's argument from lithic and literary evidence. See Farquhar (p. 287) as discussed by Hayavadana Rao in *Śrīkara*, vol. 1, p. 30.

20. The complete Sanskrit text containing both the *pūrva bhāga* which deals specifically with the wearing of the *liṅga* and the *uttara bhāga* which defends the practice of burial was published at Benares in C.E. 1905 [as *LDC*]. The text, a translation, notes, and an Introduction have, for the *pūrva bhāga* only,

been published more recently by Sakhare in his *Liṅgāyat Religion*. Sakhare's edition also contains the commentary of Śivakumāra, but he clearly considers that commentary erroneous, misleading, and the work of a "hack writer" (pp. 658-60). On the basis of quotations from Śivayōgī, Paṇḍitārādhya, and Appayyadīkṣita and other internal evidence, Sakhare (p. 657) assigns the text to the seventeenth century. His failure, however, to provide a *terminus ad quem* for the text lends credence to the claims of certain scholars that the work is a later production. In fact, the possibility that it is a late nineteenth-century fraud has been intimated in person communication by the late Professor G. Maruḷusiddhaiah of Mysore University. For present purposes, the resolution of that issue, however interesting, seems ill-advised.

21. That Sanskrit has often served this unifying function or, at least, has reflected unified conditions is evidenced by its vogue during several of the great empires of India—notably the Guptas in the north and the Pallavas in the south.

22. *SRV* (K) 25, p. 11.

23. See *LDC* for the Vīraśaiva defence of burial, and note R. Blake Michael, "To Burn or To Bury", paper presented at the Association of Asian Studies annual meeting, Chicago, Illinois, 1982 April.

24. The duties as well as the licenses applicable to the *saṃnyāsin* are discussed briefly at Mrs. Sinclair Stevenson, *The Rites of the Twice-Born*, 2nd ed. (New Delhi: Oriental Books Reprint Corporation, 1971; originally published at London: Oxford University Press, 1920), pp. 418-27. Principal sanction for his practice is found at *Manu* VI.33-97, where renunciation of house and family, silent wandering, and living without the fire of sacrifice are commended alongside the particulars of personal hygiene, begging accroutements, etc. See *SBE*, vol. 25, pp. 204-16.

25. Dubois (*Hindu*, pp. 114 and 560) specifically indicates how the Liṅgāyatas rival, if not surpass, the Brahmins in fastidious abstinence from alcohol and meat. It must be remembered that vegetarianism and teetotalism were not ideals of the Brāhmaṇa texts; they found their earliest and most ardent proclamation among the Buddhists and Jainas; and they may be reassertions of indigenous values against Aryan hegemony. Nonetheless, throughout the late medieval and early modern periods, which witness the rise and development of the Liṅgāyatas, these were important values of the Brahmins. The broader residence and stricter observation of these basically ascetical values within Vīraśaivism again represents a sect-type characteristic—egalitarian intensification of religious observances.

26. *BV* 106: (K) p. 50; (E) p. 35

27. *BV* 588: (K) p. 236; (E) pp. 192-93.

28. *SRV* (K) 453, p. 137.

29. Beyond this covert affirmation of basic Brahmanical standards, the Liṅgāyatas actually practice a division into hereditary caste groupings based largely on occupation. At the simplest level, this system merely reflects a division into priest-specialists and laypersons, but beyond that it elaborates into numerous castes and sub-castes enjoying various degrees of entitlement to Vīraśaiva ritual benefits and social intercourse. The matter is discussed in more detail later in this chapter.

30. My translation. Another translation and the verse itself appear at Artal, "Veerashaiva Faith", pp. 253-54: *koḷu heccadāre kulācāra heccu. nīru heccādare nēmaniṣthe heccu.*

31. Of particular interest in this respect are those who have seen the Vīraśaivas as defenders and preservers of Dravidian culture in its struggle against the ever assertive Aryan culture. An example of this approach is that taken by Sakhare who tries to establish definite links between Liṅgāyata practices and those of the Indus Valley Civilization. See especially Chapters I-IV of his *Liṅgāyat Religion*, pp. 1-176.

32. It may well be that Vīraśaivism's distinctness from Brahmanical Hinduism is characteristic of an earlier, more strident period in the group's history and that its accommodations to Brahmanical Hinduism are characteristic of a later, mellower period. The chronology of those supposed periods is a matter of some difficulty, but suggestions towards its constructions appear in the present work, specifically in the conclusion.

33. The group's self-understanding has usually affirmed an integral relation to Brahmanical Hinduism, but it has generally emphasized the distinctness and indeed superiority of Liṅgāyatas vis-à-vis their "fellow" Hindus. For example, in a recent popular work, the Jagadguru Māte Mahādēvi has asserted unequivocally that Liṅgāyatas are Hindus because they recognize the power of the mystical word (*Oṃ*). She insists, however, that equally Hindu are Buddhists, Jainas, Sikhs, and Vaidics. She compares Vaidic Hindus to unmarried women whose true glory emerges only when they wed. Like the married woman, Liṅgāyatas wear the emblem of their relationship to their Lord on their bodies always. See Jagadguru Māte Mahādēvi, *A Guide to Lingayatism* (Dharwar: Suyidhana Sugarantha Maale, Jaganmatta Akkamahadevi Ashrama, 1973), pp. 5-7. More critically has the same conclusion been reached by McCormack, "Lingayat Culture", p. 175. On the other hand, one who is ardent in answering this question negatively is Sakhare, *Liṅgayat Religion*, pp. ix-xii, where the argues that Liṅgāyata rejection of *varṇāśramadharma* is itself sufficient evidence for considering them a separate group, not within the Hindu fold.

34. Wilfred Cantwell Smith, *Religious Diversity: Essays by Wilfred Cantwell Smith*, ed. Willard G. Oxtoby (New York: Harper & Row, Publishers, 1976), p. 65.

35. The loose definition is Webster's. An example of this type usage of the term is available at R.G. Bhandarkar, *Vaiṣṇavism, Śaivism and Minor Religious Systems* (Strassburg: Karl J. Trübner, 1913), pp. 131ff. In his article, "Lingayats as a Sect", William McCormack wrongly indicates Bhandarkar's as one of the first uses of the term in reference to the Liṅgāyatas. In fact, it had been used much earlier to describe the Liṅgāyatas by the Abbé J.A. Dubois, *Description of the Character, Manners, and Customs of the People of India; . and of their Institutions, Religious and Civil*, trans. from the French manuscript (London: Longman, Hurst, Rees, Orme, and Brown, 1817), p. 5.

36. Bhandarkar, *Vaiṣṇavism*, p 131. Emphasis added.

37. A.L. Basham, *The Wonder That Was India: A Survey of the Culture of the Indian Sub-Continent before the Coming of the Muslims* (New York; Grove Press, Inc., 1959), p. 554.

38. William McCormack, "Lingayats as a Sect", *The Journal of the Royal Anthropological Institute of Great Britain and Ireland* 93 (1963 January to June): 59. Emphasis added. But note R. Blake Michael, "Foundation Myths of the Two Denominations of Vīraśaivism: *Viraktas* and *Gurusthalins*", *Journal of Asian Studies* XLII.2 (1983 February).

39. Louis Renou, *Religions of Ancient India* (New York: Schocken Books, 1968) p. 89.

40. Dumont, *Hierarchicus*, pp. 187ff. The same point is made more clearly by the same author, "Le renoncement dans les religions de l'inde", *Archives de sociologie des religions* 7 (1959 January-June): 66ff.

41. Dumont, "Renoncement", pp. 65-66.

42. Though the identifiable, individual founder is a functional requisite, he/she need not be an actual historical person. So long as the group in question testifies to the reality of the founder, critical investigation does not sway the matter. The critical investigation of Basava's historical reality, however, has been creditably begun by P.B. Desai, *Basavesvara and His Times* (Dharwar: Kannada Research Institute, Karnatak University, 1968).

43. For example, note the story of Āydakki Mārayya and his wife Lakkamma at *ŚS* Gū., vol. IV, pp. 1-9 for English summary; pp. 11-57 for Kannaḍa text and translation. Also, see the story of Mōḷigeya Mārayya at *ŚS* Gū., vol. IV, pp. 58-68 for English summary; pp. 69-126 for Kannaḍa text and translation.

44. See Maruḷuśaṅkara's story at *ŚS* Gū., vol. II, pp. 216-28 for English summary; pp. 229-95 for Kannaḍa text and translation. Mahādēviyakka's tale is exposed at *ŚS* Gū, vol. IV, pp. 261-75 for English summary; pp. 277-372 for Kannaḍa text and translation.

45. Dumont, *Hierarchicus*, p. 187.

46. Max Weber, *The Religion of India: The Sociology of Hinduism and Buddhism*, trans. and ed. Hans H. Gerth and Don Martindate (New York: The Free Press, 1958), pp. 19-20.

47. Ibid.

48. *ERE*, s.v. "Lingayats", p. 69. Actually the phrase is an improperly acknowledged quotation from C.P. Brown, "Jangamas", p. 176.

49. Will Durant, *The Story of Civilization*, vol. 1: *Our Oriental Heritage* (New York: Simon and Schuster, 1935), p. 519.

50. H.M. Sadasivaiah, *A Comparative Study of Two Vīraśaiva Monasteries: A Study in Sociology of Religion* (Mysore: Prasaranga, Manasa Gangotri, 1967), p. 68.

51. Nandimath, *Handbook*, p. 181. Emphasis added.

52. One who views Vīraśaivism as a preparation for the gospel is. N.C. Sargant, *The Lingayats: The Vira-saiva Religion* (Bangalore, Christian Institute for the Study of Religion and Society, 1963). Most of the scholars who contributed to the Śrī Basavēśvara octo-centennial volume (*Basava 800th*) are apologists of the latter type.

53. Such lamentation shadows Clement Marro's observation. "Basavaṇṇa wanted a Vīraśaiva Community without differences among its members; we have seen that through the centuries this Community has taken another direction." See his "Role of the Guru", p. 51.

54. Following Weber, *India*, pp. 19, 23, and 298-305, Louis Dumont and

David Mandelbaum have referred to the Liṅgāyatas in the course of their studies, but the most explicit investigation has been undertaken by McCormack, "Sect", pp. 59-71.

55. Ernst Troeltsch, *The Social Teaching of the Christian Churches*, 2 vols., trans. Olive Wyon (New York: Harper & Row, Publishers; Harper Torchbooks, 1960), pp. 331-43. See also Appendix II.

56. The primary locus for this discussion is Paul Gustafson, "UO-US-PS-PO: A Restatement of Troeltsch's Church-Sect Typology", *Journal for the Scientific Study of Religion* 6.1 (1967 Spring): 64-68.

57. Weber, *India*, p. 305.

CHAPTER TWO

THE ŚŪNYASAMPĀDANE: Its Context, Composition and Content

A rapid review of the contents of the *Śūnyasaṃpādane* illustrates the nature of the text as a record of debates and arguments about matters of practice and of theory for Vīraśaivas. Those debates range over such topics as the nature of mystical attainment, the devices for achieving spiritual perfection, the role of human assistants in the quest for that perfection, the requirements for membership in the company of Vīraśaivas, and the proper rituals for a member of that company.

One striking characteristic of the debates is their resolution along diverse and often contradictory lines. No consistent theoretical pattern for Vīraśaiva organization and practice emerges from the debates. Sometimes highly individualized and subjective solutions are adopted; at other times, complex institutionalized and objective solutions prevail. Sometimes the community's boundaries seem flexible and inclusive; at other times, admission to the group is seen to be contingent upon fulfilment of rather stringent doctrinal and ritual requirements.

After a glimpse at the context in which the *Śūnyasaṃpādane* was compiled and a glance at the process by which its four versions were edited, an overall review of the plot narrative of that text will provide a useful background for detailed analysis of associational ideals as taken up in a more detailed manner in later portions of the present research.

The Context: Vijayanagara

The fourteenth, fifteenth and sixteenth centuries witnessed, in South India, as assertion of indigenous political control and a resurgence of domestic cultural forms in reaction to increasing pressures from Muslim kingdoms in the northern Dekkhan. These Muslim kingdoms themselves often exercised only partial or short-lived control over portions of the South and were forced to rely upon Hindu feudatories in order to maintain that control.[1]

As a result, periods of iconoclastic destruction, though notable, were often of shorter duration than periods of tolerence and even of appreciation for elements of the indigenous culture.[2] These Muslim kingdoms were, nonetheless, primarily founded upon alien cultural traditions which they firmly and consistently propagated. It was, at least partially, in reaction to such pressures that there arose that most celebrated of the resurgent Hindu principalities,[3] the empire ruled from the famous "City of Victory", Vijayanagara.

Insofar as legendary, historical, and epigraphical evidence converge, it seems that Vijayanagara was founded by the two brothers Harihara and Bukka, sons of Sangama.[4] While in the service of the Kampili king, they were defeated and captured by the Delhi sultan who carried them back to his capital. There they enjoyed relatively favorable circumstances due to conversion to Islam, and eventually the two were entrusted with administering Kampili for their sultan. After earning confidence and building a power base among the people, the two renounced their allegiance to their erstwhile suzerian and established themselves as independent monarchs ruling the area just south of the Tuṅgabhadrā and vying for control of the Kṛṣṇā and Tuṅgabhadrā doab.[5]

In establishing their rule, in ruling, in constructing their beautiful capital, and in reconverting from Islam, Harihara and Bukka were assisted, according to tradition, by Vidyāraṇya, the sagely "Forest of Wisdom" to whom are attributed several important Sanskrit texts.[6] Probably the prestige of some such respected Hindu saint was necessary in legitimizing to the Hindu populace their reconversion, and they generously acknowledged his assistance by endowing and protecting works of philosophical, religious, and aesthetic merit.[7]

The confident atmosphere of a self-consciously Hindu society and the direct patronage of the imperial court, nurtured an exuberant literary blossoming in Sanskrit, Telugu, and Kannaḍa.[8] Reflecting the values, ideals, and tastes of non-Muslim India, these literatures provided further support to the political rationale of the Vijayanagara dynasties. Both in honor of its founding sage and in recognition of this cultural awakening, Vijayanagara enjoys another, nearly homonymous title, Vidyānagara—the City of Knowledge.[9]

Among the beneficiaries of and contributors to the salubrious cultural atmosphere of Vijayanagara were the Vīraśaivas.[10] Many of their most polished works owe their creation to the imperial patronage of that era. Following the imperial precedent of the Guptas, Pallavas, and others, literary composition in Sanskrit rather than in colloquial Kannaḍa began to appear from Vīraśaiva and others' pens; but the outpouring was not limited to Sanskrit.[11] A more polished style of Kannaḍa also emerged as Vīraśaiva ideas and practices found a place at the royal court.[12] The pre-eminent Vīraśaiva Kannaḍa work from that period, the *Śūnyasaṃpādane*, provides a rich lode for assaying the mettle of Vīraśaiva ideals, values, and organizational forms.

The Composition: *The Four Editions*

The editorial format: In format, the *Śūnyasaṃpādane* is not the original work of a single author but a collection of prose-poems or free verses, called *vacanas*,[13] attributed to several original authors—notably Allama Prabhu, Basava, Cennabasava, Siddharāma, and others—who were reputedly original twelfth century adherents to the movement. *Vacanas* attributed to these individuals, which may appear elsewhere as collections under the name of each person, have been, in the *Śūnyasaṃpādane*, organized and compiled into a coherent whole by a single editor.[14] The *vacanas* themselves are discrete units both semantically and aesthetically. Any single *vacana* can be and probably has been detached from the whole text without harm to that *vacana's* beauty and meaning and usually with only minimal damage to the overall text.

What the editor has done is to give these discrete units a cohesive structure by means of a loosely narrative plot account. Relying upon usually brief prose inserts and the supplementary general knowledge and imagination of the reader or hearer, the editor has constructed a single work which exceeds, both didactically and artistically, the sum of its individual parts. Within this narrative structure, the essentially discrete *vacanas* take on a dialectical character in presenting argument, counter-argument, and tolerant synthesis. In this dialectic, they lead the reader from one quite partial spiritual insight to a higher, more comprehensive one. In fact, it is precisely this dialectical character of spiritual progression which lends the text its name *Śūnyasaṃpādane*, The Graduated Attainment of the Void (or of the Absolute).[15]

It should not be imagined, however, that the structure given to the debate is entirely a creation of the editor's mind. Hagiographic material from an earlier era provides an account of events at Kalyāṇa which is, by and large, followed by the *Śūnyasampādane*'s editor. The establishment of the Anubhāva Maṇṭapa as a place for spiritual learning and debate; the debates within that society by Basava, Allama Prabhu, and others; and the gradual ascendency of the latter to spiritual leadership within that society are all events chronicled in works as early as the first part of the thirteenth century.[16] Other contemporaneous texts, such as the *Prabhuliṅgalīle*,[17] develop a narrative quite similar to that in the *Śūnyasampādane*.

The real genius of the text's editor was in telling that story utilizing the most powerful expressions of the Vīraśaiva spirit—the *vacanas*. Assembling them into a polished, cohesive structure, he gave form and function to those materials which they had not previously enjoyed. His sophisticated presentation of Vīraśaiva teachings based upon independent *vacana* collections and organized into a coherent developmental dialectic became the summary textbook of *śaraṇa* teachings, at least insofar as those were expressed in the Kannaḍa language.

The Four Versions and Their Editors

While the above discussion has spoken of *the Śūnyasampādane* and of *the* editor, there are, in fact, at least four clearly distinguishable versions of the text compiled by four separate editors over the course of the fifteenth and early sixteenth centuries.

The idea for such a work appears to have occurred first to Śivagaṇaprasādi Mahādēvayya during the early fifteenth century revival of Vīraśaivism at Vijayanagara under the rule of Prauḍha Dēvarāya.[18] Sometime around C.E. 1420, Śivagaṇaprasādi Mahādēvayya selected[19] a number of *vacanas* from each of the major founding figures of Vīraśaivism and, in accordance with available hagiographic materials, edited those into a narrative of events and debates as they may have occurred in twelfth-century Kalyāṇa. Utilizing a minimum of prose introductory and connective passages, he allowed the Kannaḍa prose-poems to tell their own story, subject only to the ordering which he had given them.

Sometime later, probably around C.E. 1495, either Keñcavīraṇṇodeyaru or his teacher Halageya Dēvaru undertook to improve upon Śivagaṇaprasādi Mahādēvayya's work.[20] Noting that that early work omitted entirely a well-known event from the time of the *śaraṇas*, namely the initiation of Siddharāma at the hands of Cennabasava, one of these gentlemen undertook a new version of the *Śūnyasaṃpādane* which would include that important event.[21] Other slight improvements were made primarily by way of adding extra *vacanas* to round out each episode already presented by Śivagaṇaprasādi Mahādēvayya.[22]

Gummaḷāpurada Siddhaliṅgadēvaru, in about C.E. 1500,[23] again undertook a revision of Śivagaṇaprasādi Mahādēvayya's work. Unlike the previous revision which had consisted largely of additional *vacanas* with little embellishment of the original's prose, Gummaḷāpurada Siddhaliṅgadēvaru's relied heavily on additional prose narrative and also on entirely new episodes introduced into the narrative.[24] Furthermore, Gummaḷāpurada Siddhaliṅgadēvaru seems to have had a different view of the divine nature of Allama Prabhu for his introductory account attributes a heavenly origin to Prabhudēvaru which is quite unlike Śivagaṇaprasādi Mahādēvayya's.[25] Most prominently, however, his version differs from the original largely in its presentation of additional episodes about the *saraṇas* which find no mention at all in the original.

Within a decade,[26] yet a fourth version of the *Śūnyasaṃpādane* appeared from the pen of Gūḷūra Siddhavīraṇāryaru. Following most closely the recent version by Gummaḷāpurada Siddhaliṅgadēvaru, Gūḷūra Siddhavīraṇāryaru greatly expanded the introductory and connective prose passages and, in the process, introduced many previously unstated interpretations of events portrayed. Retaining virtually all the *vacanas* from Śivagaṇaprasādi Mahādēvayya's original but omitting many from the second and third versions, he added several episodes of his own.[27]

The net result is that, after nearly ninety years of evolution, the *Śūnyasaṃpādane* attained a greatly amplified and non-insignificantly-altered form. Clearly these four versions are not merely textual variants but are quite distinct editorial efforts. While they follow similar outlines and utilize much of the same *vacana* material, they exhibit significant differences both in the selection of certain of those materials for inclusion and in the overall conception of the work.[28]

Gūlūru Siddhavīraṇāryaru's Version

A detailed analysis of the differences among these versions, while promising, will have to await further research.[29] For the present, however, attention to one of the versions—that by Gūḷūra Siddhavīraṇāryaru—provides a basis for analysing elements common to all four, particularly as these shed light on the types of religious associations idealized by Vīraśaivas.

Gūḷūra Siddhavīraṇāryaru's *Śūnyasampādane* recommends itself for this task for two basic reasons. First, it is more readily accessible than the other versions. Several editions of the work have been published in the present century. The last of these editions provides, besides the Kannaḍa text and useful notes, an English translation—the only translation of any version into a Western language to date.[30]

Secondly, Gūḷūra Siddhavīraṇāryaru's method of organization provides a clarity to the narrative which is missing from the other versions. Though sharing many characteristics with the other three versions, his *Śūnyasampādane* is distinct in its execution of narrative detail. While the events and debates it depicts are often identical and always at least similar to those of the other versions, it exhibits a peculiar perspicuity due, in large part, to its organization into twenty-one separate *upadēśas*, or Lessons, or Chapters. Whereas the other versions flow rather indistinctly from one event or character to another, Gūḷūra Siddhavīraṇāryaru's clearly delineates episodic boundaries by these chapter divisions.[31] In this manner, the personal progression of Allama Prabhu from humble seeker, through accomplished *yōgi*, to spiritual leader of the mystic fellowship is highlighted. Upon this progressive narrative are woven his encounters with numerous other spiritual seekers who both learn from his example and assist him in attaining ever-higher mystic insights.

The contents of this narrative bear brief but interesting review.

The Content: *Twenty Tales of the Saints*

Though the social, political, and cultural context reflected in the *Śūnyasampādane* resembles and was probably modelled upon conditions at fifteenth century Vijayanagara,[32] the explicit setting of the text is three hundred years earlier and three hundred kilometers north at twelfth-century Kalyāṇa. The splendors of the court, the wealth of the kingdom, the militant religiosity of important ministers, and other conditions which are known to have obtained at Vijayanagara are portrayed by the text as having been present at Kalyāṇa.[33] The images in the minds of the several editors may have been inspired more by the conditions of their own day than by any accurate historical knowledge of the events and conditions at Kalyāṇa, but it is these twelfth century events which are purportedly described and narrated by the text.

Explicitly, the events surrounding the establishment and functioning of a society for spiritual intensification and theological debate in that Kālachurya capital provide the plot outline for the text.[34] Around that outline are woven the intricate and intimate spiritual experiences of the main character, Allama Prabhu, and of other important *śaraṇas*, including Basava, Cennabasava, Siddharāmeśvara and others. Allama Prabhu's progress from spiritual seeker, through accomplished *yōgi*, through elder spokesman for and to the *śaraṇas*, to identical union with his Lord provides a framework within which matters of yogic practice, mystical accomplishment, ritual behavior, and organizational debate are presented and discussed. Basava's role as political patron to the movement; Cennabasava's, as theological and institutional systematizer for the movement; and Siddharāma's, as accomplished outsider but reluctant member of the group are explored and explicated in terms of their relation to Allama Prabhu's spiritual journey.

A chapter-by-chapter summary of these events as protrayed in the *Śūnyasampādane* by its editor, Gūḷūra Siddhavīraṇāryaru,[35] reveals the overall structure of the work and the step-by-step nature of the Attainment of the Void.

Lesson One: *ALLAMA'S INITIATION*

After acknowledging his indebtedness to others who had compiled editions of the *vacana* materials into the *Śūnyasampādane* format[36] and paying homage to the line of teachers through whom he received his spiritual instruction (*gurupāramparya*),[37] Gūḷūra Siddhavīraṇāryaru stated the purpose of his work—to record the enlightened discourses of Allama Prabhu with the other devotees of Lord Śiva.

Wandering about, ruminating upon source and substance, form and formlessness, and being and non-being,[38] Allama intimated the greatness of his true nature in a triumphal *vacana* which celebrated his victory over the forces of ignorance and delusion[39] and explained that he had become incarnate on earth now, as in ages past, in order to protect and promote *bhakti*.[40] In concrete illustration of his prowess and his purpose, Allama taught a wayside farmer, Goggayya, that the true garden is the earthly body and the true seed is the power of self-realization.[41]

Yet, despite his spiritual greatness, Allama himself was ever questing for higher and fuller insight and understanding. It was this quest which lead him to the cave of Animiṣa, the unblinking and unspeaking saint who became Allama's silent instructor and initiator into the ultimate knowledge of Śiva's reality. Standing with bated breath before the immobile image of the perfect *yōgi*,[42] Allama discerned that at last he had found the *guru* whom he had sought, and that in finding him he had also found the ineffable ultimate incarnate. In surrender to the perfect master, he exclaimed:

Not grasping the seen, I reach for the unseen.
Not catching that one, I'm utterly undone.
But when I grasp the *guru*'s feet, which I can see,
Then do I see the thing unseen, there before me.
O Lord of the Hidden Caverns.

—Allama Prabhu[43]

Anxious, expectant Allama sought initiation from Animiṣa, but the *guru* maintained his undisturbed meditative silence. Entreating then imploring, hoping then despairing, Allama sought initiation at the hands of the perfect master who would not respond. Finally, however, Allama's earnest quest was rewarded, not by the action of Animiṣa, but by Allama's own realization of the essential identity of disciple and master.[44]

If I say one, there then are two.
If I say two, there then is one.
On single-dual, now I see
No need at all to ask of thee.
In union free of inner break,
Hair splitting one jot will not make.
For teacher-student, can there be
A bond except identity?
O Lord of the Hidden Caverns.

—Allama Prabhu[45]

Bearing the knowledge, perfected by experience, that student and teacher—partial and complete, individual and cosmic—are all essentially one reality, Allama continued his pilgrimage. Now, however, instead of seeking the perfect *guru*, he had himself become the *guru*. The remainder of the *Śūnyasampādane* is largely an account of those whom Allama encountered and instructed during the course of this earthly journey.

Lesson Two: *SISTER MUKTĀYI AND BROTHER AJAGAṆṆA*[46]

It is of interest that among the first people encountered and enlightened by the wandering Allama was the woman Muktāyi,[47] who was grieving over the death of her beloved brother, Ajagaṇṇa. Ajagaṇṇa had practised a particularly severe yogic vow which consisted of holding always suspended half-way down his throat a *liṅga*. Chanting the sacred *mantra* mentally,[48] Ajagaṇṇa was bound to perpetual silence.[49] Unfortunately, after years of conscientiously observing that vow of silence while contemplating the *mantra*, on one occasion Ajagaṇṇa lost his control and recited the *mantra* aloud. Stricken by horror at the violation of his purpose and perhaps choking on the *liṅga* suspended in his throat, Ajagaṇṇa immediately fell dead.

Having always focused her devotion to the Lord upon her brother as an exemplar of yogic accomplishment, Muktāyi was plunged into doubt and despair by the loss of that human assistant, that *guru*. Into the valley of her doubt and disillusionment wandered Allama, fresh from his initiation in the presence of Animiṣa; but she was dubious about the quality of his yogic attainment. Surely the constant discussion and advice of this brash newcomer was no match for her departed brother's self-imposed silence. Pointing out the unavoidable duality of any speech, even speech about non-duality, she challenged him.

> Saying 'I speak not', do you not speak?
> Saying 'I act not', do you not act?
> Saying 'I think not', do you not think?
> Saying 'I purge my mind', is that not a knowledge of purges?
> Saying 'I merge my body', is that not a body which merges?
> Saying 'I am free of senses', is that not a sense of pleasures?
> Saying 'I am just myself', is that not an ego which measures?

Can we forget that we have known? On just that point, I
must be shown.
If there be anyone of knowledge devoid of ignorance free,
It's my dear Ajagaṇṇa—brother, *guru*. Who else could it be?
—Muktāyyaka[50]

Meeting Muktāyi's challenge with patience and wisdom, Allama demonstrated to her that the true *guru* is not the one who performs the most difficult feats of yogic practice, but the one who has overcome the self-imagined boundaries of disciple and teacher, or relative and absolute.

Without the duality—mind and mere bone,
For him who has merged his own Self with the Lord,
All actions are actions of *liṅga* alone.
With mind given rest from its usual toil,
For him who has merged his own Self with the Lord,
All thoughts of attainment his knowledge be spoil.
Himself into Self having joined with great yoke,
For him there's no dual, no unity broke.
O Lord of the Hidden Caverns.
—Allama Prabhu[51]

Thus having defended the capability of full enlightenment for those who continue to dwell in the world and to participate in mundane discourse[52] and having assisted Muktāyi to maintain her spiritual progress despite her grief, Allama continued his journey.

Lesson Three: *SIDDHARĀMAYYA*

Travelling to Sonnalige,[53] Allama encountered Siddharāma who was noted for the power of his yogic accomplishment and the magnitude of his philanthropic work in building temples, canals, tanks, etc.[54] Recognizing the greatness of this person's spirituality and wishing to direct it away from involvement in karmic pursuits towards pure, unattached knowledge of the Lord, Allama spoke to Siddharāma disparaging purposive action and praising detached devotion.[55] Insulted and angered, Siddharāma revealed the scorching power of his yogic third eye.[56] Allama, however, was unaffected by the attack and responded with the full force of the *śaraṇa*'s power—an even more resplendent light located in his feet.[57] After an extended debate over matters philosophical and matters ritual, Siddharāma realized the erroneous dualism inherent in his previous pursuits and resolved to follow thenceforth Allama's pure path of knowledge. Graciously acknowledging the error of his previous activities, he gratefully rejoiced in the new-found grace of Allama's path.

Because I aimed at tanks, canals, and temples,
I found your honor.
Like tripping on a stone, then looking, finding
A brilliant treasure.
My nescience like the very pit of darkness
Reborn the brighter.
The grace of Prabhudēva rent my error;
I thought that God could be contained in sculpture.
O Lord of the Faultless Jasmines.
—Siddharāmayya[58]

Lesson Four: *BASAVA INITIATES CENNABASAVA*

While Allama and Siddharāma journey from Sonnalige, the scene shifts ahead to simultaneous events at their point of destination. There Basava, the great devotee and patron of those who followed Lord Śiva, was being importuned by his learned nephew, Cennabasava, to initiate the latter into the *śaraṇa* fold.[59] Basava's reluctance to perform the initiation stemmed both from his own bashful humility and from his considered opinion that it was better of old when

The men who were saved of old
Themselves did save themselves.
—Basava [60]

In face of increasingly sophisticated arguments from his nephew, however, Basava relented and performed a curious initiation ceremony for Cennabasava. Taking Cennabasava's *iṣṭqliṅga* into his own palm, noting the absence of characteristics on this symbol of ultimate reality, turning that insight into a lesson about Cennabasava's own role in the objectification of cultic worship, and returning the object to the latter's palm,[61] Basava gave a veiled blessing.

O Cennabasava,
It's you who created *guru*; it's you who created *liṅga*;
It's you who created *jaṅgama*; it's you who created *prasāda*;
It's you who created initiation;
It's you who set me up (as judge).
I cannot assent; I cannot dissent.
For that my witness is
Our Lord of the Meeting Rivers.
—Basava[62]

Apparently satisfied by this cryptic blessing, Cennabasava rejoiced in his good fortune, elaborated the meaning of Basava's actions to a bewildered Basava himself,[63] and predicted the coming to Kalyāṇa of the great mystic Allama,[64] who, at that very moment, was standing outside the city praising the glories and devotion of its inhabitants.[65]

Lesson Five: *ALLAMA'S COMING TO KALYĀṆA*
When Allama and Siddharāma finally called at the door of Basava's palace, however, that devotee sat in rapt contemplation of his *iṣṭaliṅga*, worshipping the Lord. Not wishing to interrupt his worship, he sent his servant to welcome the strangers within the compound;[66] but the illustrious guests were angered by this affront to propriety—Basava's failure to receive them in person—and indicated their displeasure by refusing to enter.[67] Finally, persuaded of the impropriety of his actions by Cennabasava and belatedly recognizing the eminence of his guests, Basava interrupted his *liṅga* worship and came forth to receive his guests. In the process, he received a lesson in appropriate behaviour toward the unannounced guest whether that one be an eminent personage or not.[68] Disturbed at his own weakness and inability perfectly to display concern for all the Lord's creatures, Basava lamented his attention to the lifeless Lord of *liṅga* when outside his door stood the living Lord of *jaṅgama*.

So that *jaṅgama* may come to my hut, I worship *liṅga*.
If then *jaṅgama* should come to my hut, I'd leave off *liṅga*;
I'd worship *jaṅgama*.
When asked, 'Why?' then I reply:
Just rank, reward, rebirth with *liṅga* do go.

No rank, reward, rebirth does *jaṅgama* know.
Not to *liṅga* but to *jaṅgama* worship you should raise.
Between *liṅga* and *jaṅgama*, the latter I'd praise.
For in this birth, in that birth of *jaṅgama* I'll go.
O Lord of the Meeting Rivers.
—Basava[69]

Allama, however, was not wholly appeased by Basava's confession and utilized the opportunity to teach Basava and the assembled *śaraṇas* much about mystic lore. It was only after repeated attempts at intellectual solutions to Basava's plight had been rejected that Allama's anger was assuaged by Basava's contrite surrender to the *guru* before him.

Only Thou, Lord, art my thought, the goal I've sought.
Only Thou, Lord, art my *guru*, my highest teacher.
Only Thou, Lord, art the light in my inner reaches.
You are the teacher for me; I am your pupil, you see.
Your saintly Siddharāma there can bear witness to that.
Have mercy on me, O Prabhu,
O Lord of the Meeting Rivers.
—Basava[70]

Lesson Six: *MARULUŚAṄKARADĒVA*

After a reconciliation between Basava and Allama, the latter continued teaching about mystic spirituality. Specifically he attempted to demonstrate the many and unexpected forms in which intimations of the divine reach human beings. He took as a case in point Maruḷuśaṅkara,[71] a simpleton who dwelt in the refuse heap outside the city gate of Kalyāṇa. Looking beneath the tattered clothing, soiled countenance, and abhorrant behavior of Maruḷuśaṅkara, he discerned a spiritual presence which he pointed out to Basava and the other *śaraṇas*.

O Basavaṇṇa,
Can't you see the *liṅga* standing there?
Waiting, serving, near beside your sill,
Dressed though like a man of doubtful will,
Pure man, good friend, Brahman beyond compare.
See, he's made his one and true home,

Right where gifts by us are often thrown,
To our Lord of the Hidden Caverns.
—Allama Prabhu[72]

After a lengthy discussion with Allama, in which Basava again discerned ever-widening implications of the spiritual quest, the latter was led to recognize not only the greatness of Maruḷuśaṅkara's soul, but also that of others of the Lord's seemingly lowly creatures.

The majesty of Śiva's band,
In heaven, earth, and hell,
No one can rightly tell.
They have done the undone.
Their fame's a glorious one.
In truth, they are folk untainted.
Dare praise I ones so sainted
By our Lord of the Meeting Rivers?
—Basava[73]

Lesson Seven: *BASAVA*

In their first encounter and again in the episode of Maruḷuśaṅkara, it had been Allama who was the teacher and Basava, the pupil. Allama indeed had much to teach Basava about spiritual practice, mystical experience, and non-dualist philosophy. Reciprocally, however, Basava's whole-hearted devotion to the service of the Lord and to the service of the Lord's followers provided an exemplary lesson for the more esoteric Allama. In the Seventh Lesson, the dialogue between these two eminent figures serves to communicate both Allama's complex mysticism and Basava's simpler pietism.

Attempting to help Basava to understand fully the implications of a non-dualist philosophical interpretation of spiritual practice, Allama posed the familiar dilemma: "If all reality is indeed one, who or what is it that observes that unity?" His *vacana* asked.

If you say that Śiva is both truth and error,
Does that please those who know the True?
If you say that you too are both Lord and power,
Does that please those who've touched His shoe?

If you say that Brahman and all else are the same,
But would ever deny your own limited frame,
Do you please with your karmic word
Our Lord of the Hidden Caverns?

—Allama Prabhu[74]

Now it was Basava's turn to dispel philosophical doubt not by giving a coherent, conceptual answer but by pointing to the overwhelming reality of an experience which, though based upon a dualist notion of Lord and devotee, overcame that dualism in a blinding, stupefying experience of unified reality.

Greater than the Great am I
While deep in the Great I lie,
Where whatever I should say
Meaningless my word would lay.
I see the wonderous sight
Inside the perfect light
Of our Lord of the Meeting Rivers.

—Basava[75]

From that point onward, Basava and Allama tried to outdo each other in praise for the other. While Basava was being lead from one level of understanding to another by Allama's probing questions, Allama was discerning the genuineness and intensity of wholly direct devotion to the Lord. Out of that dialogue, the reader or hearer receives an education into the depth of Vīraśaiva experience as well as the complexities of the movement's language about that experience.

Lesson Eight: *CENNABASAVA*[76]

After having listened to numerous interchanges between Basava and Allama and having noted the basic philosophical differences in each *śaraṇa*'s interpretation of mystical experience, Cennabasava discerned a problem. Reflecting his characteristic concern to construct a coherent philosophical system based firmly upon genuine spirituality,[77] he directly challenged those two to cease their verbal obfuscation and give witness to their spiritual attainment.

Basava accepts form. Allama reject form.
Whom should I affirm? Whom should I deny?
Though both are good at trickiness,
I see here no *liṅga* richness.
O Lord of the Lovely Waters.
—Cennabasava[78]

Thus challenging their glib disputation, Cennabasava urged Allama and Basava to bear true witness to their spiritual attainment of essential unity as *jaṅgama* and *bhakta* respectively.[79] In fact, in rather harsh words, Cennabasava accused Allama of a heinous crime. Referring to Animiṣa's immediate demise after the initiatory experience of Allama, Cennabasava chided that *śaraṇa.*

Whence did you get
Your *liṅga* without a *guru*?
You killed your *guru* to capture it!
—Cennabasava[80]

To Cennabasava's heated challenge, Allama responded in his usual patient manner and utilized the opportunity to teach Basava's nephew many things about the nature of being a *śaraṇa*: (1) the relation of the accomplished *śaraṇa* to the body; (2) the gradations of knowledge about deepest reality; (3) the importance and nature of discipline; (4) what true service (*dāsāhaṃbhāva* or *dāsōha*) means for the *bhakta*; (5) the characteristics of the *śaraṇa* who has achieved full realization; and (6) the relation between the *iṣṭaliṅga* image and the inner reality of *prāṇaliṅga.*[81]

At the end of this discourse, after Allama had taught Cennabasava the esoteric details of Vīraśaiva lore and after Cennabasava had shared his own more systematic erudition with Allama, the younger *śaraṇa* capitulated to the spiritual mastery of Allama.

Before one is accomplished, *guru*, *liṅga*, *jaṅgama*, and *prasāda* are there;
After one is accomplished, *guru*, *liṅga*, *jaṅgama*, and *prasāda* are air.
O blessed Prabhu, we have seen in you
None other than Self
As our Lord of the Lovely Waters.
—Cennabasava[82]

Lesson Nine : ***MAḌIVĀLA MĀCAYYA***[83]

Indicative of Vīraśaivism's radical challenge to established social patterns was its disregard for traditional caste boundaries. Setting its own members apart from the society at large, it evolved its own internal patterns of essentially egalitarian social interaction. A prime illustration of this characteristic was Maḍivāḷa Mācayya, a washerman, whose dedication and service to the *śaraṇa* band was matched only by the quickness of his temper and the intensity of his anger—redeeming characteristics only insofar as they were directed to the defence and promotion of Lord Śiva's domain. For example, on one occasion, Maḍivāḷa Mācayya was returning to the city with a load of newly laundered clothes for the *śaraṇas* when a non-believer happened to touch the purified bundle. Incensed that the clothing of the Lord's saints should be thus defiled, Maḍivāḷa Mācayya, by means of his spiritual power, struck the *bhavi* dead.[84] After supplications by King Bijjaḷa, Maḍivāḷa Mācayya's anger abated and he restored the unfortunate sinner to life.[85]

The Ninth Lesson of the *Śūnyasampādane* represents an attempt by Allama to fathom the depths of Maḍivāḷa Mācayya's intense devotion and, hopefully, to redirect some of its intensity into more benign expressions. To that end, Allama directly, almost rudely, addressed the nature of Maḍivāḷa Mācayya's spiritual accomplishment as evidenced by his possession of the yogic third eye[86] but without other hope for fruits of the spirit.

How can this be, O Maḍivāḷa Mācayya?
You have the yogic third eye on your crown,
But there is hateful envy in your frown.
Your words gush the syrup of sweet devotion,
But is this knowledge or an egoic notion?
Of leaving learning and *liṅga* you speak,
But where's the wisdom and *bhakti* we seek?
If you destroy the outward sign,
But do not purge the inner mind,
There is no grace given you here
Unless you cast away your fear
Upon our Lord of the Hidden Caverns.

—Allama Prabhu[87]

Maḍivāḷa Mācayya's response was to cast himself upon the wisdom and compassion of his *guru*, Basava, and thereby he demonstrated that he had indeed overcome dualistic illusions born of egoity. In full submission to his *guru*'s will, he attained a perfected understanding of unitive spiritual experience. Accordingly, he directed Allama's complex philosophical questions to Basava, his *sadguru*.

> After dissolving, how to come back home?
> After perceiving, how to escape the *ōṃ*?
> How to abide in the place untainted?
> Ask thou thy Basava, devotee sainted!
> O Lord of the End of Time.
>
> —Maḍivāḷa Mācayya[88]

Thus demonstrating his total conquest of dualistic egoity by his utter reliance on his *guru*, Maḍivāḷa Mācayya attained the favor of Allama and the other *śaraṇas* and became an important leader of the movement in his own right.

Lesson Ten: *THE INITIATION OF SIDDHARĀMA*

The debate over Siddharāma's initiation is subjected to detailed discussion in later chapters of the present work. Presently, it is useful only to trace the barest outline of that debate as it appears in the Tenth Lesson of the *Śūnyasaṃpādane*.

The primary issue was whether an accomplished *yōgi* like Siddharāma needed to undergo initiation in order to be admitted to the inner company of the *śaraṇas*. Since, by his good deeds, by his yogic prowess, by his general wisdom, and by his debates with Allama, he had already demonstrated his physical, mental, and spiritual perfection, the ceremony of initiation appeared superfluous.[89] Worse than that, it appeared a denial of the ultimate importance of inner attainment in favor of external signs.[90] For these reasons, Siddharāma presented his objections to the initiatory process and investiture with the *iṣṭaliṅga*.

> O Cennabasava,
> In my mind, there's no idea of body.
> In my ken, there's no idea of knowledge.
> Knowledge, mind, and body—

When these three have become as one,
What should I hang the *liṅga* on?
Prabhu is my breath, and Basava is my body.
See, there is no inside, and there is no outside,
For our Lord of the Faultless Jasmines!
—Siddharāma[91]

The debate was long and complex, involving important contributions by many of the *śaraṇa* band, including Allama, Basava, Cennabasava, Maruḷuśaṅkara, Maḍivāḷa Mācayya, and *śaraṇas* of lesser fame.[92] Finally, Siddharāma discerned that his resistance to the outward sign of initiation involved resistance to a true inner identity between himself and his *guru*. Yielding to that complete identity he received initation from Cennabasava.

Of physics and metaphysics you may speak,
But for me this is metaphysical prattle.
Making small the *śivaliṅga* which had been great,
After putting it on the palm's small saddle,
What more distant metaphysics should we seek?

Discerning the heavenly sacred *ōṃ*,
Bringing it down to rest upon my palm,
Exclaiming, 'This indeed is the highest prize',
Guru Cenna made me equal in his eyes.

Cennabasava's grace has made me fit
With your illustrous coterie to sit.
Note that, O Lord of the Faultless Jasmines!
—Siddharāma[93]

Lesson Eleven: *THE GLORIFICATION OF PRABHUDĒVA*
After the initiation of Siddharāma, he and his holy companion, Allama, entered into the inner chambers of Basava's house where the most celebrated of the *śaraṇas* were meeting.[94] Though Allama had been in Kalyāṇa for sometime, this was the occasion of his official reception as a spiritual leader of the saintly assembly there. At that reception, the *śaraṇas* engaged in effusive praise of the illustrious Allama Prabhu[95] who, in turn, complimented each of them on his or her spiritual merit.

The central event of this reception, however, was a ceremony of *guru* veneration with Allama Prabhudēva[96] as the focus. It is unclear whether the worship offered to Prabhudēva involved actual performance of physical rituals or only mental contemplation of his greatness,[97] but in either case the effect of the ceremony was to offer praise and worship to Prabhudēva—the *guru* as Lord incarnate. Cennabasava was one of those who most eloquently expressed the benefit which he received from reliance upon the *guru*'s grace and from veneration of the *guru*'s feet.

> Whenever the *jaṅgama* called Supreme Consciousness comes
> And the devotee called Eternal Vigilance is home,
> Washing his feet in water which is not real,
> That is the greatest joy that ever you'll feel.
> With water made from joyous soul,
> Having bathed his lotus sole,
> Having drunk that pure water out,
> Then you are free of this, no doubt.
> Like that my worship, I performed;
> Now totally, I am transformed.
> O Lord of the Lovely Waters.
>
> —Cennabasava[98]

Mutual praise among all the *śaraṇas* completed the evening, but the event left little room for doubt that Prabhudēva was indeed the first among equals in the company of saints. The events of later Lessons in the *Śūnyasaṃpādane*, when Prabhudēva is consecrated upon the Throne of the Void (*śūnyasiṃhāsana*) are presaged in this Lesson.

Lesson Twelve: *ĀYDAKKI MĀRAYYA AND LAKKAMMA*[99]

Lessons Twelve, Thirteen and Fourteen provide valuable insights into the economic ethic of Vīraśaivism. Although many have attempted to claim for the Vīraśaivas something identical to Weber's notion of the "Protestant ethic" of hard work, frugality, and capital investment, the economic ethic which appears in the present Vīraśaiva text, at least, is somewhat different from that notion.[100]

It is true, of course, that the value of diligent work in a worldly vocation was not overlooked by Vīraśaiva theorists and adherents alike. The famous, "Work is heaven itself,"[101] was indeed adopted and applied by generations of Vīraśaivas. On the whole, it was quite comparable to the Lutheran understanding of calling (*Beruf*). It evoked an almost ascetical commitment to live within the world of social and economic concern without becoming enslaved by those concerns. The movement's emphasis on honest labor (*kāyaka*) and selfless service (*dāsōha*) did not, however, for whatever socio-political reasons, result in the systematic maximization of production and profit comparable to rational capitalism as described by Weber. It was, rather, a call away from worldly lethargy and pettiness and also away from idle dreams of otherworldly reward toward activity and altruism within the world of imperfect everyday reality. Response to this call is pre-eminently evidenced by Āydakki Mārayya, the rice gleaner, and Lakkamma, his wife.

The hallmark of Āydakki Mārayya's devotion to the Lord was his persistent but unspectacular steadfastness in his work. Without complaint or ambition, he followed his calling as a gleaner of rice fields. Everyday he went to the fields and threshing floors of Kalyāṇa to glean the left-over rice. His occupation, however, did not lead him away from an intense interest in religious matters. Occasionally, in fact, he was remiss in the performance of his duties while he sat in rapt attention listening to the debates of those gathered at Basava's house.

On one such occasion, having neglected to perform his daily work, Āydakki Mārayya sat at court engaged in a debate over the adequacy of dedicated labor as a devotional path.[102] The participants were praising the glories of dedicated labor and Āydakki Mārayya's exemplification of that ideal when, into the assembly, strode his wife Lakkamma. Barring no holds, there in front of his spiritual companions, she soundly berated her husband for his neglect of his duty.[103]

Shamed into action, Āyadakki Mārayya sped from the assembly and began his daily gleaning. In his haste to correct his neglect, however, he erred on the side of excess and gathered twice his usual measure of grains. Bringing this bounty home, he again faced rebuke from his wife who was disturbed by the lack of trust which this abundant provender implied.[104] In order to teach her devout but simple husband a lesson, she ordered him to return to the assembly of *śaraṇas* and to invite them all to be guests at his humble table. Fretting over what he should serve to so many illustrious guests from his meager supplies, Āydakki Mārayya, nonetheless, obeyed his spouse and invited the *śaraṇas*.[105]

To the surprise not only of Āydakki Mārayya but also of the entire saintly band, Lakkamma turned the day's double, but nonetheless small, gleanings into a sumptuous feast which was more than adequate for all the assembled *śaraṇas*.[106] The simplicity of her faith and the firmness of her devotion led to a manifold multiplication of the fruits of her dedicated labor. Her husband's efforts to understand the nature of his vocation and to glory in the praises of the *śaraṇas* as he engaged them in spiritual discussions paled by the glow of her dedicated labor.

Though it was left to his wife to exemplify and explicate the full meaning of his words, the entire teaching of the Twelfth Lesson was concisely stated by Āydakki Mārayya in its first *vacana* which had initiated the debate in the assembly.

> For one who is steadfast in his own calling,
> The sight of the *guru* must be forgotten;
> The worship of *liṅga* must be forgotten;
> The fetters to *jaṅgama* must be set falling.
> Doing one's labor is heaven on earth;
> Even the Lord must perform his day's worth.
> O Lord of the Living Liṅga.
> —Āydakki Mārayya[107]

Lesson Thirteen: MŌLIGEYA MĀRAYYA AND MAHĀDĒVIYAMMA[108]

Though he had once been a great king in Kaśmir.[109] Mōḷigeya Mārayya had renounced that life of luxury in order to enter the service of the Lord. His present occupation as wood cutter provided little beyond the bare essentials for the lives of himself and his spouse. That lady, Mahādēviyamma, nonetheless, was famous for a rich, nourishing, and delicious porridge which she prepared. Many of the *śaraṇas* who had tasted that delicious stew raved about its qualities in the assembly. Basava himself decided to go to the house of Mōḷigeya Mārayya and there to sample the celebrated concoction. Coming in the guise of an ordinary *bhakta*, he presented himself at Mahādēviyamma's door.[110] She immediately took him in, made him comfortable, and fed him her best porridge. Basava was beside himself with enjoyment of the dish and while taking his leave committed an act inappropriate for an accomplished *śaraṇa.* He left two bags of gold hidden behind the household altar as payment to the poor wood cutter and his wife.[111]

Upon returning home, Mōḷigeya Mārayya sensed the hidden treasure and, being told of the *bhakta's* visit and meal, immediately guessed that it was Basava who had come and dishonored him by attempting to pay for a meal freely given to a saint of the Lord.[112] Confronting Basava with the deed, he obtained an admission and apology from Basava who had merely been carried away by the delightful food and the poverty of Mōḷigeya Mārayya's external life.[113] Mōḷigeya Mārayya forgave Basava, but, of course, he used the occasion to teach that illustrious one a lesson about true dedication to one's vocation, however humble. In fact, he used the occasion to teach an important lesson on the value of disinterested activity even when that activity is worship of the Lord. His sentiments as well as hers are summarized in Mahādēviyamma's *vacana.*

'I shall get to heaven for the *bhakti* which I've shown,'
Having said that, you're less truthful than a coolie.
Dissembling and disclaiming your desire that's well known,
When true welfare is explained you and your folly you've been shown,
There's no use in all your scheming with no sense of true *bhakti.*

Both this world and that world are wholly intertwined;
To that meeting surely your clear focus should be lined.
Here, there, and everywhere
My heart takes joy in your image,
O Lord of the Stainless Jasmines.

—Mahādēviyamma[114]

Lesson Fourteen: NULIYA CANDAYYA[115]

The story of Nuliya Candayya is instructive of Vīraśaiva teachings not only about the necessity of labor in service of the Lord's company but also about the role of such visible foci of worship as the *iṣṭaliṅga*—a symbol of the absolute in concrete form—and the *jaṅgama*—a symbol of the absolute in human form.

Nuliya Candayya was an accomplished *śaraṇa* who expressed

his devotion, through dedication to his calling as a rope maker. One day, while cutting reeds to be woven into ropes, Nuliya Candayya suffered an unfortunate accident. His *iṣṭaliṅga*, which he wore always about his neck and from which he should never have been separate, slipped from his neck and fell into the water. Arguing that to stop and search for the *liṅga* would interfere with his selfless service (*dāsōha*) of the Lord's followers and that anyway the absolute was all pervasively present and not confined to a small stone, he refused to search for it and continued about his business.

Though the *liṅga* rose to the top of the water and called out for Nuliya Candayya to remember his duty always to wear *iṣṭaliṅga*, the rope maker continued about his business. Then, in a delightful image, the *liṅga* sprouted arms, legs, and head and chased after Nuliya Candayya; and, since the duty to maintain relation between *liṅga* and *aṅga* (the human body) was reciprocal, implored that *śaraṇa* to take it with him.

Nuliya Candayya, heedless, continued walking until the pair came to the house of Maḍivāḷa Mācayya, the washerman, whose mediation the *liṅga* sought for their dispute.[116] Nuliya Candayya stated his position forcefully when he submitted to Maḍivāḷa Mācayya that veneration of *guru*, *liṅga*, and *jaṅgama* were, in fact, only one identical worship, which was itself a non-dualist inner purification rather than external rite.

> O Maḍivāḷayya,
> True worship of *guru* is the purification of the heart.
> True worship of *liṅga* is the purification of knowledge.
> True worship of *jaṅgama* is the cleansing of the three-fold taint
> From the senses three-fold.
> Doing the threefold worship in these three ways,
> Is but a single worship which goes always
> To our Lord of the Lovely Liṅga.
>
> —Nuliya Candayya[117]

After hearing their arguments, Maḍivāḷa Mācayya persuaded Nuliya Candayya to receive back his *liṅga*,[118] but that *śaraṇa* agreed to do so only on the condition that the *liṅga* itself agree thenceforth to perform service to *jaṅgamas*—symbols of the Absolute incarnate in human bodies.[119] The *liṅga* agreed, and thus was established the principle that even the Absolute itself, as embodied in *liṅga*, was bound to perform service to the Absolute, as incarnate in the *jaṅgama*.[120]

Lesson Fifteen: *GHAṬṬIVĀLAYYA*[121]

Another *śaraṇa* who practised his calling diligently in service of the Lord and without thought of earthly gain was Ghaṭṭivāḷayya, an entertainer who acted, danced, and played the drum. Despite his joyous occupation, he practised his devotion in an austere solitude which contributed to his disgust with the easy life and luxurious surroundings of the *śaraṇas* who frequented Basava's home. This disgust provoked his most instructive encounter with the assembly of saints.

Appalled at the luxury and laxity of the *śaraṇas*' life style, Ghaṭṭivāḷayya berated them for allowing worldly comforts to interfere with their spiritual practice.

> Why should I lose inner peace for outer cares,
> Like a dog who, for a scrap, is caught in the trap,
> If I am able to become all aware,
> Of our Lord of the Simple Pleasures?
>
> —Ghaṭṭivāḷayya[120]

Angered by the rigor of Ghaṭṭivāḷayya's ascetic challenge, the *śaraṇa* assembly reacted *en masse* and, tearing the dancer's *iṣṭaliṅga* from around his neck, they taunted him for his obvious poverty and his solitary pursuit of spiritual perfection.[123] The ardor of Ghaṭṭivāḷayya's devotion, however, was undiminished. In comment upon the apparent glow on his breast where the *liṅga* should have hung, Cennabasava praised his spiritual depth.

> Knowledge having diminished and *liṅga* disappeared,
> Why is there still the glow of a *liṅga*
> On the body of Ghaṭṭivāḷayya?
> Here, who is the knower, here who the known?
> Mark ye well the void which here's full blown!
> Except your Ghaṭṭivāḷayya,
> Who else could fully know of you,
> O Lord of the Lovely Waters?
>
> —Cennabasava[124]

Summoning a large boulder to come and rest about his neck as his new *iṣṭaliṅga*, the dancer demonstrated the power of his *bhakti* to all the assembly.[125] They, accordingly, returned his small *iṣṭaliṅga* to him, and he immediately merged the large stone into that small one.[126]

Despite well-earned praise from the *śaraṇa* band, Gaṭṭivāḷayya did not join them but continued his solitary path. Eventually, achieving a highly perfected spirituality, he left his earthly body and merged his spirit into the Absolute. Coming to retrieve his body from the street where it had fallen, the *śaraṇas* were amazed to find that even the physical remains had lost all substantial existence and disappeared before their eyes. Basava's *vacana* echoes their astonishment.

> He is beyond death or birth;
> He is beyond doubt and stain;
> Look you, he is not form,
> Nor formless he!
>
> O Lord of the Meeting Rivers.
>
> —Basava[127]

Lesson Sixteen: ***MAHĀDĒVIYAKKA***[128]

Vīraśaivism's egalitarian acceptance of people from widely varying status positions is illustrated again by the story of the woman saint Mahādēviyakka. The same story, however, illustrates the rigors and ridicule taken on by the *śaraṇa* as well as the rigid exclusion of the movement towards all who did not surrender to Lord Śiva's call.

Born to dedicated devotees of Lord Śiva, Mahādēviyakka matured both in physical beauty and in devotion to the Lord. Unfortunately, these two excellences led her into a crisis when the Jaina king of her realm saw her and desired her in marriage. Mahādēviyakka agreed to marry the king only on the condition that he convert from the Jaina to the Śaiva path. Furiously he refused and threatened execution of her beloved parents unless she acceded to his desires.

Forced to a rash but courageous course of action, Mahādēviyakka renounced her parents, her suitor, her home, and even her clothes and left her village clad only in her long tresses. Asserting that she could never wed any man, much less a Jaina, she revealed that she was already married to none other than the Lord himself and that she would keep herself only unto him.[129] She described the miraculous allegory of the wedding.

> *Guru* was the kinsman,
> *Liṅga* was the bridegroom,
> And I the happy bride.
> All the host of heaven,
> My mother and father.
> That no one can hide.
> See here, in the worldly station,
> I've no other Lord.
> Like Prabhu's own mansion,
> Is my one beloved,
> The Lord of the Lovely Jasmines.
>
> —Mahādēviyakka[130]

Wandering about naked and seeking ever-greater understanding of her spiritual experiences, the maiden eventually came to the assembly of *śaraṇas* at Kalyāṇa. Before being admitted into the assembly, however, she had to face rather severe questioning.[130] Some merely wanted to know her spiritual credentials; others felt that no unmarried woman could possibly be fit for their company; and still others were simply appalled by her nudity.

Prabhudēva, however, felt that her nudity did not go far enough. He wondered why she persisted in wearing her long braids so that they strategically covered her private parts. Did this residual modesty not suggest some lingering sense of duality rather than complete surrender to the Lord?

> God is pleased; you are pleased. Why is that?
> Purifying the mind, abandoning the dress,
> Why cover up yourself with your lovely tresses?
> Thus the shame of your inner heart
> Shows itself on your outer parts.
> Can this be pleasing
> To our Lord of the Hidden Caverns?
>
> —Allama Prabhu[132]

Adequate to the ordeal, Mahādēviyakka, through her words and her actions, convinced the *śaraṇas* that she was indeed utterly dedicated to the Lord as is a good wife (*satī*) to her husband.

> Having offered the body to *liṅga*, the body becomes bodiless.
> Having offered the mind to knowledge, the mind becomes free.
> Having offered the passions to true joy, the passions become empty.
> Having destroyed body, mind, and will, the body becomes bodiless.
> Having foisted upon the *liṅga* all the pleasures of embodiment,
> I have become a devotee, a good wife, to my Lord the *liṅga*.
> I have touched and merged into
> My Lord of the Lovely Jasmines.
>
> —Mahādēviyakka[133]

Within the society of saints, Mahādēviyakka continued to grow in spiritual knowledge and to help others attain their full potential. Eventually tiring of the mundane life, she once again set off wandering. Her journey ended in the holy plaintain grove at the Śrī Śaila mountain where she attained final unity with the universe.[134]

Lesson Seventeen: *PRABHUDĒVA'S TOUR AND RETURN*

After having taught his wisdom to the *śaraṇa* assembly in Kalyāṇa and having himself learned much about the breadth and depth of spiritual experience which was available to followers of the Lord Śiva. Allama Prabhu set out on a tour of the rest of India in order to expand the boundaries of ardent devotion to the Lord.[135] Having visited the East, the South, and the West, he came finally to the northern Himālayas where he spent several years sitting in a cave locked in trance.[136] His tour is described in the miraculous images reserved for the gods, such as the fact that he did not actually walk upon the earth but floated slightly above it.[137] As the apotheosis of the spirit of Śaiva wisdom spreading over and engulfing the land, he received praise from converts wherever he went.

> Like a stratospheric wind,
> The perfect *yōgi* stands.
> Swallowing the elements down,

He does not spit them out. Why not?
Slipping the equatorial band around the world,
The great teacher, Prabhu, disappears into the void,
Calling, 'O Gūhēśvara, O Lord of the Hidden Caverns."
—an anonymous *saraṇa*[138]

Meanwhile, back in Kalyāṇa, Basava and the others were hoping and praying for Prabhu to return and assume active leadership of their spiritual society. In anticipation of his return, they officially organized themselves into a Society for Spiritual Progress and established at Basava's court residence a place for discussion of religious experience, the celebrated Anubhava Maṇṭapa. Furthermore, they actually constructed, in that meeting place, a seat or throne which they hoped would eventually be occupied by Prabhu as the fully invested leader of their society.[139]

In poignant words, reminiscent of *bhakti* poetry throughout India which dwells upon the agony of separation as separation from spiritual perfection, Basava reflected his longing for the return of Prabhu as the authoritative spiritual leader for the movement at Kalyāṇa.

Like an infant, having lost its way, longing for its mother,
Like a calf, having gone astray, longing for the udder,
So is my longing for the coming of Your Eminence.
Like the blooming of the lotus at the rising of the sun,
Is my longing for Your Eminence, to Kalyāṇa, to come,
O Lord of the Meeting Rivers.
—Basava[140]

Unknown to Basava, however, Prabhu was, at that very moment, waiting outside the gates of Kalyāṇa disguised as a vagabond.[141]

Lesson Eighteen: ***PRABHUDĒVA'S INVESTITURE***

After his years of travel and rigorous meditation, Allama Prabhu returned to a Kalyāṇa, the sight of which made him quite sad. Basava's court had ceased to be the simple meeting place of earnest spiritual seekers and had become a palace clad in opulence. In scenes reminiscent of the Pāṇḍava court, the once simple *śaraṇas* lounged about ridiculing folk who could not distinguish the emerald pavement from shining pools of water.[142]

No greater was Prabhu's displeasure at this decadent scene than was that of the *śaraṇas* at the coming of this uncouth and unrecognized vagabond into their opulent surroundings. Basava, however, immediately discerned Prabhu's identity and rejoiced that, at last, true leadership had returned to a society for which the prime minister's simple generosity was as much bane as boon.[143] Basava joyfully received his teacher.

> You be on my tongue in the nectar of your name.
> You be in my eye in the beauty of your frame.
> You be in my mind, in my memory always.
> You be in my ear as your everlasting praise.
> A bee I'll become in your lotus-blossom feet,
> O Lord of the Meeting Rivers.
>
> —Basava[144]

The rest of the *śaraṇas*, unfortunately, were less than joyful and continued to ridicule Prabhu's poor and filthy outward appearance. Seeing Basava's insistence on retaining this unseemly individual in their company, many of the society's members stormed out in anger and embarrassment.[145] Prabhu dismissed them as imperfectly divorced from worldly involvements and unlikely candidates for spiritual perfection.

> They are just a mass of bodies
> Come together for their pleasure.
> How could they know the *liṅga's* measure?
> They are merely selves in bodies
> Enduring all anxiety.
> How could they know God's propriety?
> Like besotted *sādhus*, they mumble;
> How could they help but stumble
> From the realm of our Lord of the Hidden Caverns?
>
> —Allama Prabhu[146]

After supplication by Basava and the others who had remained in the assembly,[147] Prabhu agreed to assume the duties of leadership of the remaining *śaraṇas*. Many who had left were reconciled to the movement and under Prabhu's leadership it experienced a resurgence of intense spiritual quest and ascetic rigor.

Lesson Ninteen: ***PRABHUDĒVA'S STRANGE FEAST***

Though he had denied any necessity for worldly food,[148] Allama Prabhu, in order to test the spiritual insight of the devotees, requested that Basava prepare a coronation feast for him.[149] Basava cheerfully did so and offered enormous quantities of the succulent dishes to his *guru.*[150] Prabhu, however, almost instantaneously gobbled down the foodstuffs and requested more. Foolishly, Basava attempted to comply by ordering ever-increasing quantities of food prepared. Prabhu, of course, was no more satiated by this portion than by the first.[151]

Basava continued trying to fulfil Prabhu's voracity with material food until his nephew stepped forward to explain what Prabhu really wanted. Cennabasava discerned that something more than food must be given in order to satisfy Prabhu. Nothing short of total surrender of their entire selves would appease the master. He advised Basava.

> This whole earth, of nine parts and five hundred crores broad,
> Is hidden in the one universe.
> Madness befalls this Master, who hopes to offer food
> To this great sage, swallowing up fourteen universes.
> What shall I say?
> 'Look here, Basava!' I cry.
> 'There's no greater advice.
> 'I must be the curry,
> 'And you must be the rice!'
> If we wish to satisfy
> Our Lord of the Lovely Waters.
>
> —Cennabasava[152]

In a lengthy triadic debate, Allama Prabhu, Cennabasava, and Basava discussed the nature and implications of total surrender to the will of the Lord as incarnate in the *guru.*[153] Quite compelling in this context is Basava's abject surrender to Prabhu as the Lord incarnate.

> Kick me with your left foot,
> I will hold your right foot.
> Stamp me with your right foot,
> I will grasp your left foot.
> Save me! Protect me!

I am a disgrace;
You're the saving grace.
I'm but a tiny baby
In the arms of your mercy,
O Lord of the Meeting Rivers.
—Basava[154]

Lesson Twenty: *PRABHUDĒVA ON THE FINAL DAYS*

In this penultimate Lesson, Allama Prabhu predicted the coming of the end of the Vīraśaivas' privileged position at Kalyāṇa. Sensing that the earthly mission of himself, Basava, and the others was nearing its completion, he intimated the coming dispersal of the *śaraṇas* and their departure from phenomenal life as they would merge into one cosmic reality.[155] While Basava and the others engaged in mutual adoration and praise, Prabhu prohibited any further praise of himself and refused to join in their panegyric.[156] Interestingly, beginning to sound like an echo of Muktāyakka's defence of Ajjagaṇṇa and finally perceiving the full import of Animiśa's unblinking silence, Prabhu argued that perfected spiritual experience transcends the need for wordy explanation. He argued that full and perfect religious experience leads to absolute silence (*niḥśabda*) in which even the necessity of calling upon the name of the Lord has been surpassed.[157]

Describing this final state of perfected experience and absolute silence, Cennabasava reflected Prabhu's exhortation in his *vacana*.

What is the fruit of non-phenomenality—
Just to be rid of sentimentality?
What is the fruit of non-ideality—
Just to be rid of subject-objectivity?
What is the fruit of no I-it duality?—
No longer to call from inner deficiency
Upon our Lord of the Lovely Waters!
—Cennabasava[158]

Lesson Twentyone: *GŌRAKṢA'S CHALLENGE AND THE END OF THE ŚARAṆAS*

As the final chapter, this Lesson must serve more than one purpose. First it relates the story of Allama Prabhu's encounter with the great *siddha*, Gōrakṣa.[159]

Gōrakṣa had been an accomplished yogic practitioner who had

perfected many miraculous powers. Once, however, in yogic contest with the great Vīraśaiva *ācārya*, Rēvaṇasiddha, Gōrakṣa was tested and humiliated. In response to that experience, he undertook even greater austerities and penances until he had made his entire body perfectly adamantine.[160] Coming again to challenge the Vīraśaiva way, he met and challenged Prabhu. When hit with a sword, Gōrakṣa's body repelled the weapon as though it had struck a stone.[161]

Prabhu, of course, was not to be outdone by this yogic trickery. Wishing to teach something about the value of attaining a complete emptiness of one's self, he asked to have the sword swung at him. Neither clanging against a rock-hard worldly body nor injuring Prabhu in any way, the sword merely passed through him as thought it were cutting the wind.[162] Prabhu's feat was accompanied by a lesson on the foolishness of yogic tricks.

> The tricks of a crooked rogue,
> In roots and vines entwined,
> Is no true *yōga*.
> The trance of the inner soul,
> Of body, and of mind
> Is no true *yōga*.
> The consubstantial bind
> Is the true *yōga*!
> O Lord of the Hidden Caverns.
>
> —Allama Prabhu[163]

In the second part of the Twenty-first Lesson, a new character, Basava's wife Nīlamma,[164] emerges. She demonstrates that, though she had been a quiet helpmate in the background of Basava's life, she had simultaneously grown great in spiritual wisdom.

After Prabhu had left Kalyāṇa for Śrī Śaila and the *śaraṇa* band had incurred royal displeasure, that group dispersed to several places throughout Karnāṭaka.[165] Having returned to his spiritual birthplace at Kappaḍi Kūḍala Saṅgama, Basava meditated upon the *liṅga* and sought union with the Lord. Sensing that that accomplishment was near, he sent a messenger back to Kalyāṇa to fetch his wife, Nīlamma. She, however, demonstrated the depth of her spiritual insight by refusing to comply.[166] Her *vacanas* argued that she had Basava were already one in spirit and therefore physical proximity was of little purpose.

What if I be there; what if I be here
In the union of me and you,
Form and figure are matchless.
When we have become limbless,
Then do we possess pleasure true!
Between Basava and me, there's no interval,
O Appaṇṇa.
I'm totally devoid of all inner will,
O Saṅgayya.

—Nīlamma[167]

The final portions of this Lesson describe the last moments of the *śaraṇas* as each attains ultimate unity with the divine.[168] Most potently was the event portrayed in Prabhu's last words as he used the metaphor of a plaintain thicket to symbolize the problems which must be overcome in earthly life if the highest beatitude is to be attained.

The great bramble called the body cannot be bound.
The great ocean called *saṃsāra* encircles it round.
The great forest called the will is most nearly drowned
By a great poison called the senses.

Entering the bramble and beating it down,
Not touching the throns,
Unscathed, untorn,
Standing entranced under *liṅga's* control,
I am more tranquil than tranquillity whole.
O Lord of the Hidden Caverns.

—Allama Prabhu[169]

Patterns of Diversity in the Śūnyasaṃpādane

Besides serving as introduction to the content of that text, the foregoing account makes one thing quite clear: the *Śūnyasaṃpādane*, as a record of debates about concerns crucial to the corporate life of the Vīraśaiva community, offered no single ideal form for Vīraśaivism which would best resolve all these disputes. Its proffered solutions to theological and institutional problems of the community were various and often simply contradictory.

In one place, it could argue for the necessity of physical initiation and in another could insist that the initiation of the spirit was more important than the initiation of the body. In one place, it could argue that one needed no help in attaining spiritual perfection save the help of the Lord Himself and in another could insist that highest beatitude was to be obtained only in prostration at the feet of the *guru*. Sometimes highly individualized and subjective solutions were adopted; at other times complex institutionalized and objective solutions prevailed. Sometimes the community's boundaries seemed flexible and inclusive of all who professed the Lord's love; at other times admission to the group was contingent upon fulfilment of rather stringent doctrinal and ritual requirements. In one place, Basava could accept, as a saintly presence, Maruḷuśaṅkara despite his unclean scavenging and his unseemly madness, and in another Cennabasava could endorse Ghaṭṭivālayya's rigorist purge of the insincere among those assembled under Basava's patronage. In one place, Allama Prabhu could seek inner enlightenment so ardently that he could seize the *liṅga* from Animiṣa's palm and initiate himself, and in another Cennabasava could reject Siddharāma's admission to the assembly due to the latter's lack of a properly bestowed *iṣṭaliṅga*.

In sum, several types of religious associations—objectivist, subjectivist, universalist, and particularist—all appear and find prominent proponents within the *Śūnyasaṃpādane*.

NOTES

1. An overview of these kingdoms and their methods of acquiring and maintaining political control is given by S. Krishnaswami Aiyangar, *South India and Her Muhammadan Invaders* (New Delhi: S. Chand & Co. Pvt. Ltd., [1921]). That the Muslim sultans found it necessary to rely upon "native" rulers is illustrated by the appointment of Harihara and Bukka as vicegerents in Kampili though these two were only recent and, as it turned out, nominal converts to Islam.

2. This point should not, of course, be overstated; however, it does little good to draw too bold a line between Hindu and Muslim monarchs when the relations among Hindu monarchs or among Muslim monarchs were often little better than those between Hindu and Muslim. Competition for political

control and economic benefit was not confined to intercommunal strife. An attempt to discern the amicable nature of certain Hindu-Muslim relations has been undertaken briefly by B.A. Saletore, *Social and Political Life in the Vijayanagara Empire* 1346 1646-*A.D.*), 2 vols., (Madras: B.G. Paul & Co., Publishers, 1934), vol. I, pp. 395-413. Perhaps more striking is the simple personal testimony of the Muslim traveller Ibn Batuta who relates: "It is the custom throughout India, for nobody to enter the presence of the Sovereign bare-footed. Now, I had no boots, but an idolater gave me a pair, though there were a certain number of Mussalmans in this place. I was surprised that idolaters showed greater generosity than they (Mussalmans)." Cited in Krishnaswami Aiyangar, *South India*, p. 235.

3. That Vijayanagara enjoys this image as defender of the Hindu faith, at least among modern Hindus, is amply attested by the content as well as the title of an article by C.C. Srinivasachari, "A Great Contribution of Vijayanagara to the Tamil Country: The Conquest of the Madura Sultanate and the Restoration of Hindu Orthodoxy", *KHR* 4.1-2 (1937 January-June): 6-14.

4. A determination of the origin of the Vijayanagara Empire has, in itself, warranted more than one book. The legendary accounts of its origins generally rely upon two seemingly separate traditions. In the first, a king who was out hunting came across a hare which, rather than fleeing, turned upon the pursuing dogs and defeated them in tooth-to-tooth combat. Taking this sign to be an omen of a seemingly weaker kingdom which would arise against its oppressors, the king took upon himself the role of the hare, founded a capital city upon the spot, and launched the fortunes of a great Hindu empire. This account is given by, among others, a fifteenth-century Portuguese visitor to Vijayanagara, Fernão Nuniz as translated and published by Robert Sewell, *A Forgotten Empire* (*Vijayanagara*): *A Contribution to the History of India* (London: Swan Sonnenschein & Co., Lt., 1900), pp. 299-300. This story is similar in detail to the Tamil legend of one great king, Kaṭṭa-bomman. In the second account, the great *advaita* sage Mādhava Vidyāraṇya prevailed upon two sons of Saṅgama to establish a Hindu dynasty in defence against the Muslim threat. This event is mentioned, for example, in an inscription from Cannagiri at *EC*, vol. VII, pt. I: *Inscriptions in the Shimoga District*, ed. B. Lewis Rice (Bangalore: Mysore Government Central Press, 1902), inscription no. Cannagiri 62, p. 458 for text, p. 334 for transliteration and p. 189 for translation, which reads: "...Lord of the throne of Vidyānagarī which Harihara-mahārāya built and consecrated in the name of Vidyāraṇya-śrīpāda..." Another account conflates the two motifs and has the king encounter the hare while en route to Vidyāraṇya's hermitage, where the omens are interpreted for him and he decides upon the construction of the city. *EC*, vol. X: *Inscriptions in the Kolar District*, ed. B. Lewis Rice (Mangalore: Basel Mission Press, '05), inscription no. Bg. 70, p. 291 for text, p. 241 for translation. A recent attempt to distinguish such legendary materials from historical facts has been made by P.B. Desai, "The Foundation of Vijayangara", *JKU* (*SS*) 6 (1970): 175-94; and "The Legendary Origin of Vijayanagara", *JKU* (*SS*) 8 (1972): 61-69. The Telingana, as opposed to Kannaḍiga, origins of the empire have been explored and dismissed by B.A. Saletcre, "Theories Concerning the Origin of Vijayanagara", in *Vijayanagara 600th*, pp. 139-59.

Though somewhat dated, the best in-depth exploration of epigraphical, legendary, and documentary materials remains H. Heras, *Beginnings of Vijayanagara History* (Bombay: Indian Historical Research Institute, 1929). After a detailed comparison of all the available material with respect to the several theories of the empire's origin, Father Heras argues, rather convincingly, that its foundation lies in the decaying remnants of Hoysaḷa power and that many of the documentary accounts by Muslim court historians are generally reliable but often fail to discriminate between the Hoysaḷa and Saṅgama dynasties—between Dvārasamudra and Vijayanagara. Though relying heavily upon Heras' work, N. Venkata Ramanayya advances several original ideas and alternative interpretations of the data—particularly with reference to the original name of the city as either Vijayangara or Vidyānagara. His monograph appears as *Vijayanagara: Origin of the City and the Empire*, ed. K.A. Nilakanta Sastri (Madras: University of Madras, 1933).

5. For a summary account, such as the present one, complex issues concerning the origin of the empire must be laid aside in favor of a brief and coherent account. Such is given in the present paragraphs and follows, for the most part, the concise and highly readable version given by K.A. Nilakanta Sastri, *A History of South India from Prehistoric Times to the Fall of Vijayanagara*, 3rd ed. (London: Oxford University Press, 1966), pp. 237-39.

6. These works include a paraphrase commentary on several of the Upaniṣads, *Sarvopaniṣadarthānubhūtiprakāśa*; works on ritual and ethical practice, *Parāśarasmṛtibhāṣya* and *Kālanirṇaya*; descriptive and analytic works on the schools of Indian philosophy, *Sarvadarśanasaṃgraha* and *Vivaraṇaprameyasaṃgraha*; a work on soteriological doctrine, *Jīvanmuktiviveka*; and a work dealing with theistic practice and *advaita* ideas, *Pañcadaśī*. Perhaps more to the point is his work in establishing a vital and flourishing institutional basis for Hinduism as head of the Śṛṅgiri *maṭha*, supposedly founded by Śaṅkara. His work, *Śaṅkaradigvijaya*, provides a rationale for a cohesive Hindu monastic organization among the *advaita* monasteries. In fact, Paul Hacker has argued that Śaṅkara owes his pre-eminence as a religious figure and reputed founder of the *advaita* monasteries to the fourteenth century efforts of Vidyāraṇya to provide a legitimizing legend for that monastic structure and, at the same time, to bolster the spirits of Hindu Vijayanagara against the Muslims. See his "Zur Geschichte und Beurteilung des Hinduismus: Kritik einiger verbreiteter Ansichten", [A review of J. Gonda's *Die Religionen Indiens*, vol. II], *Orientalische Literaturzeitung* 59.5-6 (1964): pp. 231-45. Vidyāraṇya's role in the foundation and maintenance of the empire has been explored, at least briefly, by most of the secondary sources on Vijayanagara. Specifically, but rather uncritically, has this role been chronicled by S. Shrikantaya, "Vijayanagara and Vidyaranya", in *Vijayanagara 600th*, pp. 161-68. More critically has Father Heras attacked the issue and concluded that, whatever role Vidyāraṇya may have played at Vijayanagara, it must have come some time after the founding of the city and the empire Heras, *Beginnings*, pp. 14-8 Heras, pp. 19-35, goes to great lengths to chart the development of the Vidyāraṇya legend. It should be noted, however, that his work in no way mitigates the importance of Vidyāraṇya for Vijayanagara's history, only for its actual founding. Secondly, it should be noted, that Father

Heras merely substitutes another pontiff of the *Śṛṅgiri maṭha*, Bhāratī Tīrtha Śrīpāda, the immediate predecessor of Vidyāraṇya. The role of that monastery and its head is not thereby diminished in the founding of the empire.

7. The role of Vijayanagara in synthesizing and preserving Indian culture has been highlighted by H. Heras and V. K. Bhandarkar, "Vijayanagara Empire: A Synthesis of South Indian Culture", in *Vijayanagara 600th*, pp. 29-38. Support of Hinduism, especially of the Śṛṅgiri *maṭha*, by the emperors of Vijayanagara is evidenced by an inscription from Kadūr District commemorating a grant of several villages on C.E. 1346 March 9. See *EC*, vol. VI: *Inscriptions in the Kadūr District*, ed. B. Lewis Rice (Bangalore Mysore Government Central Press, 1901), inscription no. Śriṅgeri Jāgīr 1, p. 347 for text, p. 190 for transliteration, and p. 92 for translation.

8. Besides Mādhava Vidyāraṇya, several other Sanskrit authors require mention: Vedānta Deśika, Sāyaṇa, Nemicandra, and the gifted emperor Kṛṣṇadēva Rāya, who compiled a *Brahma Sūtra* commentary and other works. A detailed accounting is made by S. Srikantha Sastri, "Development of Sanskrit Literature under Vijayanagara", in *Vijayanagara 600th*, pp. 295-328; and by T.V. Mahalingam, *Administration and Social Life under Vijayanagara* (Madras: University of Madras, 1940), pp. 354-372. Telugu literature saw the names of such authors as Nācana Sōmanātha, Śrīnātha, the emperor Kṛṣṇadēva Rāya and his eight court poets, Rāmabhadraiah, Rāma Rāja Bhūṣaṇa, and others. The Telugu literary flourishing is discussed by K. Iswara Dutt, "Telugu Literature under the Vijayanagara Empire", in *Vijayanagara 600th*, pp. 53-68; and by Mahalingam, op. cit., pp. 354-380. Kannaḍa authors who demand mention include Bhīmakavi, Lakṣmaṇa Daṇḍanātha, Kumāra Vyāsa, Cāmarasa, Śantikīrti, and Virūpākṣa Paṇḍita. Detailed discussions are given by D.L. Narasimha Char, "Kannada Literature under Vijayanagara", in *Vijayanagara 600th*, pp. 347-366; and by Mahalingam, op. cit., pp. 380-383.

9. Venkata Ramanayya, *Vijayanagara: Origin*, pp. 181-184 & 52f, is of the opinion that the names Vidyānagara and Vijayanagara were co-original. His view is shared by the traditional accounts. Farther Heras, *Beginnings*, pp. 19-35, indicates that all the early inscriptions refer to Vijayanagara whereas, during the later third and fourth dynasties, the name Vidyānagara appears. He attributed this fact, as well as the growth of the Vidyāraṇya legend to selfish motives by the Śṛṅgiri pontiffs who wished to enhance their prestige and power positions (p. 34). In fact, Heras, pp. 44-45, argues that the city must have first been named *vijaya* for it was founded by the Hoysaḷa emperor Vīra Ballāḷa III and named after his son, not simply Vijayanagara but Śrī Vīra Vijaya Vīrūpākshapura, which was later shortened to the more simple form. Venkata Ramanayya, op. cit., pp. 129-47, explicitly rejects this view largely on the basis of Vīra Ballāḷa's and Harihara's reputed enmity for one another. In his "Ballāḷa III and Vijayanagara", *JKU* (*SS*)7 (1971): 119-130, P.B. Desai takes an intermediate position as he maintains the traditional account of Harihara as founder of the city and empire. He rejects, however, the notion that there was ill feeling between Vīra Ballāḷa III and Harihara and portrays them, instead, as allies.

10. The early Vijayanagara rulers seem to have been staunchly Śaiva and often explicitly Vīraśaiva. The early fifteenth century ruler, Dēva Rāya II, even bore the title Vīra Śaivāgama Saṃpanna. See Srikantha Sastri, "Sanskrit",

in *Vijayanagara 600th*, p. 309. Later rulers leaned toward Vaiṣṇavism and *viśiṣṭādvaita* philosophy. The trends in religious preference at Vijayanagara are explored by R. Rama Rao, "Hinduism under Vijayanagara Kings", in *Vijayanagara 600th*, pp. 39-52. The specifically Vīraśaiva contributions to that overall religious complex are discussed briefly by T.V. Mahalingam, *Administration*, p. 308; and in somewhat greater detail by B.A. Saletore, "The Vira Śaivas and their Contribution to Vijayanagara", *KHR* 4.1-2 (1937 January-June): 57-60.

11. For example, Śrīpati Paṇḍita's *Śrīkara Bhāṣya* on the *Brahma Sūtras* from approximately C.E. 1350 and Śivayōgi's *Siddhānta Śikhāmaṇi* of the same era.

12. For example, Bhīmakavi's Kannaḍa *Basava Purāṇa* from about C.E. 1369 and Cāmarasa's elegant *Prabhuliṅgalīle* from a century later. See *BP* (K) and *PLL* (sam) respectively.

13. The *vacanas* do not follow the rules of classical Sanskrit or Kannaḍa metre nor do they adhere closely to any of the poetical formulae of classical poetical devices (*alaṃkāras*). In fact, they explicitly reject much of what is contrived in classical poetry in favor or freedom and spontaneity. They are not, however, totally lacking in poetical nature. Many of the simpler devices of classical poetry do occur from time to time, and metrical patterns are sometimes discernible. The thrust of the *vacana* style is not the total rejection of all established form; it is rather the insistence that substance takes precedence over form. In line with that thrust, relatively simpler but nonetheless quite beautiful poetic forms are employed in the *vacana* medium. The rules of classical Kannaḍa poetry have been discussed by J.S.F. MacKenzie, "On the Rules which Govern Kanarese Poetry", *Indian Antiquary* 2 (1873): 109-112; and the specific use of the popular *tripadi* metre in the *vacanas* has been demonstrated by M. Cidānanda Mūrti whose work is brought to light by A.K. Ramanujan's Introduction to *Speaking of Śiva* (Baltimore: Penguin Books, Inc., 1973), pp. 38-39. Ramanujan has also explored other devices of folk poetry present in the *vacanas*, such as grammatical parallelism, opposition, and code switching (pp. 42-47). The lucidity of his discussion is surpassed only by the success he has had in finding marvelous equivalents to the *vacanas*' beauties in the language he chose for translation, English.

14. Actually, of course, there are at least four editors—one for each of the versions of the *Śūnyasaṃpādane*. These will be discussed below.

15. A third alternative translation of the title, which would be less literal but perhaps no less accurate might be The Path to Perfection.

16. For example, in the Telugu *Basava Purāṇamu* of Pālkurike Sōmanātha, and also more explicitly, in the *Prabhudēvara Ragaḷe* in Harihara's *Hariharana Ragaḷegaḷu: Samagrasamputa*, ed. P.G. Haḷakaṭṭi (Dharwar: Samāj Pustakālaya, 1968).

17. See either the full text of Cāmarasa's *Prabhuliṅgalīle* or the condensation edited by M.S. Basavaliṅgayya and M.R. Śrīnivāsamūrti as *PLL* (sam).

18. L. Basavarāju has shown that the kernel for Śivagaṇaprasādi Mahādēvayya's idea probably dates back to Harihara in the thirteenth century and finds further impetus from Siṅgirāja in the late fourteenth century. It is then Śivagaṇaprasādi Mahādēvayya who, in the early fifteenth, brings the idea to

fruition in his *Śūnyasaṃpādane*. Basavarāju's ideas appear in the Preface to his edition of that work, *Prabhudēvara Śūnyasaṃpādane* [Śivagaṇaprasādi Mahādēvayyana], ed. L. Basavarāju (Citradurga: Śrī Bṛhanmaṭha Saṇsthāna, 1969), pp. 41-49. H. Thipperudraswamy, *Śūnyasaṃpādane Vivaraṇātmake Paricaya* (Mysore: D.V.K. Murthy, 1973), pp. 29-30, takes up these suggestions. Note that according to R.C. Hiremath in his Introduction to *ŚS Śi.*, p. 9, Prauḍha Dēva Rāya's reign was from about C.E. 1419-1446 though he may have been merely a minister in his father's administration during the first several of those years. See Nilakanta Sastri, *History*, p. 269.

19. The word "selected" is used advisedly. The process as the various *Śūnyasaṃpādane* editors describe it was one of arranging collected *vacanas* into a narrative. It is not known whether they used all the available *vacanas* in that process or only selected those which seemed most appropriate. The fact that no two of the four used exactly the same *vacanas* would argue for the later alternative. All *vacana* collections as they exist at present, however, are probably much later than the fifteenth century and may contain materials not available to the *Śūnyasaṃpādane* editors. Much critical labor needs be spent in determining the authenticity of portions of these collections. Bhoosnurmath and other have taken tentative steps in this direction by placing a number of Basava's *vacanas*, which are of identifiable provenance, in an appendix rather than in the *ṣaṭsthala* sequence where they appear in the vulgate text. Compare, for example, *BV* (K) with *Basavaṇṇanavara Vacanagalu* (*Bhāvārtha Sahita*), (Hubli: City Book Stall, n.d.).

20. The date is Hiremath's in his Introduction to *ŚS* Śi., p. 10. The confusion about whether there are four or five versions could be resolved by a close textual comparison of manuscripts which has, as yet, not been done. Hiremath takes Keñcavīraṇṇadeyaru's version to be earlier and separate from that of his teacher Halageya Dēvaru which did not appear until about C.E. 1520. Thipperudraswamy, *Śūnyasaṃpādane*, pp. 30-31, however, argues that, while these two are separate individuals, the texts attributed to them are, in fact, identical and both date from C.E. 1495. As such, this single text, attributed to separate editors, comes second in the sequence of composition—after *ŚS* Śi. and before both *ŚS* Gum. and *ŚS* Gū.

21. Gummaḷāpurada Siddhaliṅgadēvaru specifically states Śivagaṇaprasādi Mahādēvayya's omission of Siddharāma's *dīkṣā* as the necessitating reason for his own effort, *ŚS* Gum., Introductory Prose; p. 1: *siddharāmayyadevaṅguṛe dīkṣākramavilladaḍe*. Gūḷūra Siddhavīraṇāryaru states the same reason and also acknowledges Gummaḷāpurada Siddhaliṅgadēvaru's work, but proceeds to give his own arrangement nonetheless. See *ŚS* Gū., Introductory Prose; I. 50 and 55.

22. Thipperudraswamy, *Śūnyasaṃpādane*, p. 43.

23. Dating from Gummaḷāpurada Siddhaliṅgadēvaru's *gurupāramparya*, Hiremath places that editor about C.E. 1500. See *ŚS* Gum., p. 8.

24. Among the episodes added by Gummaḷāpurada Siddhaliṅgadēvaru are those of Āydakki Mārayya and Gōrakṣa. See Thipperudraswamy, *Śūnyasaṃpādane*, p. 44.

25. Thipperudraswamy, *Śūnyasaṃpādane*, p. 35.

26. Around C.E. 1510 according to Hiremath's Introduction to *ŚS* Gum., pp. 8-9.

27. Specifically, Gūḷūra Siddhaliṅgadēvaru adds the stories of Mōḷigeya Mārayya and Ghaṭṭivāḷayya. See Thipperudraswamy, *Śūnyasaṃpādane*, p. 44.

28. Most obviously, this independence is evidenced by the number of *vacanas* which are not shared by all four versions. The following chart, suggested by Hiremath's Introduction to *ŚS* Gum., p. 95, highlights the vast differences in *vacana* selection.

Items Unique to Each Śūnyasaṃpādane Edition

Editor	*Vacanas*	*Songs*
Sivagaṇaprasādi Mahādēvayyaru	4	0
Halageya Dēvaru	384	19
Gummaḷāpurada Siddhaliṅgadēvaru	162	1
Gūḷūra Siddhavīraṇāryaru	243	3
	793	23

29. The preliminary steps in a detailed comparison of two of these versions have been taken by the present researcher in an as-yet- unpublished article "Comparative Tables for *Śūnyasaṃpādane* Studies".

30. The first modern edition of Gūḷūra Siddhavīraṇāryaru's work was undertaken by P. C. Haḷakaṭṭi (Bijapur: n.p., 1930). A revised edition was issued by S. S. Bhoosnurmath (n.p.: Ravur Kalmathadhisvara, 1958). The edition used for the present research and the one for which a translation has been made appeared in 5 vols. ed. S. C. Nandimath et. al. (Dharwar: Karnatak University, 1965-72).

31. The episodic boundaries are also enhanced by Gūḷūra Siddhavīranārya-ru's penchant for expanded prose introductions and explanatory materials for each episode.

32. Ready for comparison, of course, are the figure of Basava in the court of Bijjaḷa and that of Vidyāraṇya at Vijayanagara. The legends make of Basava a slightly more practical, political, and economic influence and of Vidāraṇya a philosophical and religious legitimizer of the politics of his monarch. Each, however, exhibits a strong presence in assisting, both directly and indirectly, the hegemony of his respective ruler. Surprisingly, no one to date has undertaken such a functional comparison of these two giants of Karnāṭak history.

33. The chronicles of Paes and Nuniz give ample testimony to the splendour of Vijayanagara, but the attempt to reconstruct conditions at Kalyāṇa has had to rely heavily upon relatively untrustworthy literature from a later era. For examples of this contrast, compare Sewell, *Forgotten Empire* with P. B. Desai, *Basavesvara and His Times* (Dharwar: Kannaḍa Research Institute, Karnatak University, 1968).

34. The similar openness to debate and desire to acquire knowledge and wisdom which characterized the court at Vijayanagara under Prauḍha Dēva Rāya and under Kṛṣṇa Dēva Rāya should not be overlooked. The involvement of the emperors in cultural matters has been explored especially for Kṛṣṇa Dēva Rāya. See, for example, K. Raghavacharlu, "Krishna Raya, The Man", in *Vijayanagara* 600*th*, pp. 181-90; and Nidhathavolu Venkat Rao, "Krishna-

devaraya and his Literary Circle", in *Vijayanagara* 600*th*, pp. 231-40. The parallel to contemporaneous events at the court of Akbar is also instructive.

35. The following account utilizes the order and chapter divisions of Gūḷūra Siddhavīraṇāryaru, but it provides, whenever possible, the location of the same or similar material in the other versions of the *Śūnyasaṃpādane*. Comparative work is thus facilitated. This comparative location of *vacanas* is based on a Kannaḍa index which appears in Hiremath's Introduction to *ŚS* Śi. and to *ŚS* Gum. A recapitulation of the abbreviations used in this process and the order in which citations are given follows:

ŚS Śi. —*Śūnyasaṃpādane* [Śivagaṇa Prasādi Mahādēvayyanavara], ed. R. C. Hiremath, with a Foreword by A. S. Adke (Dharwar: Karnatak University, 1971).

ŚS Ha. —*Śūnyasaṃpādane* [Halageya Dēvara]. Unpublished manuscript in the Kannaḍa Institute, University of Mysore, Mysore, India. Catalogue no. KA 105.

ŚS Gum. —*Śūnyasaṃpādane* [Gummaḷāpurada Siddhaliṅgadēvara], ed. R.C. Hiremath, with a Foreword by A. S. Adke (Dharwar: Karnatak University, 1972).

ŚS Gū. —*Śūnyasaṃpādane* [Gūḷūra Siddhavīraṇāryara]; 5 vols.; edited with Introduction, Text, Transliteration, Translation, Notes and Comments by S. C. Nandimath, L. M. A. Menezes, R. C. Hiremath, S. S. Bhoosnurmath, and M. S. Sunkapur; with Forewords by D. C. Pavate and A. S. Adke (Dharwar: Karnatak University, 1965-72).

36. Namely Śivagaṇaprasādi Mahādēvayya and Gummaḷāpurada Siddhaliṅgadēvaru. See *ŚS* Gū., Introductory Prose; I, 50 and 55.

37. Namely Bōḷabasavēśvara and Tōṇṭada Siddhaliṅgēśvara. See *ŚS* Gū., Introductory Prose; I, 48 and 52. Gūḷūra Siddhavīraṇāryaru's spiritual lineage as well as the epigraphical evidence for it appear in Hiremath's Introduction to *ŚS* Gum., pp. 17-18.

38. *ŚS* Śi., 3/ Ha., 238/Gum., 3/Gū., 1:3; I, 57f.

39. *ŚS* Śi., 5/ Ha., 5/ Gum., 5/ Gū., 1:5; I, 59f. The story of Allama's triumph over Māyā is given in English from oral tradition by Würth at *BP* (K-E), pp. 71-72. The details of Śiva and Parvatī's heavenly argument, earthly incarnation as Allama Prabhu and Princess Māyā, flirtatious combat, and eventual affirmation of the power of asceticism to dispel desire and delusion are told at *PLL* (sam), pp. 1-49.

40. *ŚS* Śi., 6/ Ha., 6/ Gum., 6/ Gū., 1:6; I, 60f. Compare the periodic incarnations of the Lord in order to uphold the Right and defeat the Wrong in *Bhagavad Gītā* 4:7.

41. *ŚS* —/ —/ —/ Gū., 1:29; I, 76f. Note that the story of Goggayya is one of those added by Gūḷūra Siddhavīraṇārya and does not occur in the other versions of the text. The tale does, however, occur at *PLL* (sam), pp. 64-70 and Goggayya receives brief mention in *BP* (K) 36:6 and 57:6.

42. The paradigm for such perfected *yōga* is, of course, the Lord Śiva himself as He sat in ascetic trance while Kāma attempted to arouse His earthly passions. The tale occurs, among other places, at *Śiva Mahāpurāṇa*, Rudrēśvara Saṃhitā, III.18-19. The image of the unblinking *yōgi* is compared in that same

purāṇa (Vāyavīya Saṃhitā II.37:66) to a lamp in a windless spot which never flickers.

43. *ŚS* Śi., 34/ Ha., 34/ Gum., 33/ Gū., 1:32; I, 81f.

44. Marro, Clement, "Role and Position of the Guru and of the Jangama in Lingayatism", *Bangalore Theological Forum* 6.2 (1974 July-December): pp. 33-34, has discussed the process of self-initiation by identification with the *guru*. He reports an interesting conversation with a Vīraśaiva religious leader: "A Swamiji told me that if the Guru at the time of the initiation thought that he was superior to the initiate, then the whole process would be spoiled. In that case, there could not be a deep communion between the two and such a communion is necessary to make the initiation possible."

45. *ŚS* Śi., 38/ Ha., 38/ Gum., 37/ Gū., 1;36; I, 85f.

46. Outside the *Śūnyasaṃpādane*, the principal reference for the story of Muktāyi is the contemporaneous *Prabhuliṅgalīle* of Cāmarasa. See *PLL* (sam), pp. 71-74.

47. Muktāyi's premier position in the tale is reflective of the position of women in Vīraśaivism where, though without full equality, they were not subject to many of the restrictions placed upon them in Brahmanical Hinduism. It is interesting to note that, in contrast to Mahādēviyakka, Āṇḍāḷ, and Mīrābāi, Muktāyi did not break from societal expectations about the woman's role by entering into a "marriage" with the Lord Himself. Her break was somewhat less radical in that she pursued her life of devotion under the protection of her brother Ajagaṇṇa. Other of the female *śaraṇas* managed to reconcile a life of devotion to the married state as the stories of Mahādēviyamma, Lakkamma, and others will amply attest. The possibility of such a reconcilation with worldly demands may, for the Vīraśaivas, be more significant than the lives of such stunning world-rejectors as Mahādēviyakka. More on this point follows below and is further detailed at R. Blake Michael, "Women of the *Śūnyasaṃpādane*: Housewives and Saints in Vīraśaivism", *Journal of the American Oriental Society* 103.2 (1983 April-June): 361-368.

48. Presumably this *mantra* was either *oṃ namaḥ śivāya* or simply *namaḥ śivāya*. One of the *aṣṭāvaraṇas* or eight coverings which are aids to faith for every Liṅgāyata, this is the only *mantra* which the observant Liṅgāyata should use. Part of the movement's exclusivistic rigorism was its denial of efficacy to other *mantras* and to other gods. In English, see S. C. Nandimaṭh, *A Handbook of Vīraśaivism* (Dharwar: L. E. Association, 1942), pp. 63-64; or, in Kannaḍa, *Aṣṭāvaraṇagaḷa Mahatva* [Mailāraśaraṇara], (Dharwar: Murugha Math, 1971), pp. 32-38.

49. The efficacious power of the spoken word has been an important element of belief and practice in many societies and occurs in folklore and literature from around the world. The power of the solemn word to produce results underlies the power of such women as Damayantī (at *Mahābhārata* 3.53.16-20) to evoke salvific responses from the gods in the face of difficulty. Undertaking a particular vow in order to perfect oneself or to achieve spiritual merit is commonly attested among ascetics in many cultures. The similarity of such a pattern among the ancient Greeks and Indians has been explored by Daniel H. H. Ingalls, "Cynics and Pāśupatas: The Seeking of Dishonor", *Harvard Theological Review* 55 (1962): pp. 281-98. A more specific exploration of the

practice among medieval Śaiva groups which may have had mutual influence with Vīraśaivism is provided by David N. Lorenzen, *The Kāpālikas and Kālāmukhas: Two Lost Śaivite Sects* (Berkeley: University of California Press, 1972), particularly pp. 73-82. The vow of silence itself, or at least the benefits of such silence, is attested by the law code of Vaśiṣṭha 29:5, "By (a vow of) silence (he obtains) happiness". See *SBE*, vol. 14: *The Sacred Laws of the Āryas (as taught in the schools of) Āpastamba, Gautama, Vāsiṣṭha, and Baudhāyana*, pt. 2: "Vasiṣṭha and Baudhāyana", trans. Georg Bühler (Oxford: Clarendon Press, 1882), p. 136. The force of the vow is evidenced by the horrible consequences from breaking it. The more general characteristics of the vow receive extended and detailed treatment by Pandurang Vaman Kane, *History of Dharmaśāstra (Ancient and Mediaeval Religious and Civil Law in India)*, Government Oriental Series, class B, no. 6, Vol. V, pt. I: *Vratas, Utsavas and Kāla etc.* (Poona: Bhandarkar Oriental Research Institute, 1958).

50. *ŚS* Śi., 110/ Ha., 91/ Gum., 109/ Gū., 2:35; I, 190f.

51. *ŚS* Śi., 11/ Ha., 92/ Gum., 110/ Gū., 2:36; I, 191f.

52. The idea of the perfected seeker who continues living out his earthly days without the further accumulation of merit and demerit—the idea of the *jīvanmukta*—is well-known. It bears mention, however, that the foremost text elucidating and elaborating this doctrine is attributed to Vidyāraṇya of Vijayanagara. His text is readily available in several editions both Sanskrit and English. *Jīvanmuktivivēka* by Vidyāraṇya, Ānandāśrama Sanskrit Series, no. 20, ed. Wāsudeva Śāstri Paṇaśīkara (Poona: Mahādeva Chimanājī Āptē, 1890); *Jivanmuktiviveka* by Vidyaranya, Kashi Sanskrit Series, no. 39, ed. with Hindi commentary by Thakur Udaya Narayan Sinha (Benares: Jai Krishna Das Hari Das Gupta for the Chowkhamba Sanskrit Series Office, 1913); *The Jivanmukti-Viveka or the Path to Liberation-in-this-Life* by Vidyāraṇya, ed. and trans. S. Subrahmaṇya Śāstri and T. R. Śrīnivāsa Ayyangār (Madras: The Theosophical Publishing House, 1935); and *The Jivanmukti-Viveka or the Path to Liberation in This Life* by Vidyāraṇya, trans. Manilal N. Dvivedi (Bombay: Tookaram Tatya for the Theosophical Publication Fund, 1897). The nature and place of the doctrine throughout Sanskrit literature has been ably described in four articles by J. F. Sprockhoff, "Die Vorbereitung der Vorstellung von der Erlōsung bei Lebzeiten in den Upaniṣads", *Wiener Zeitschrift für die Kunde Süd- und Ostasiens* 6 (1962): 151-78; "Die Idee der Jīvanmukti in den späten Upaniṣads", *WZKSO* 7 (1963): 190-208; "Der Weg zur Erlösung bei Lebzeiten, ihr Wesen und ihr Wert, nach dem Jīvanmuktiviveka des Vidyāraṇya", *WZKSO* 8 (1964): 224-62; and that article concluded at *WZKSO* 14 (1970): 131-60.

53. Sonnalige is the modern Sholapur in Mahārāṣṭra.

54. Siddharāma's activities are portrayed also in the *Basava Purāṇa* at *BP* (K) 9:11, 33, 38; 46:38; 52:27; and 54:53. In *BP* (K-E) some of these events appear on pp. 76-77. *Cennabasava Purāṇa* also narrates several episodes from Siddharāma's life at *CBP* (K-E), pp. 102, 133-34, 200, 209-10, & 219-20. The *vacanas* attributed to this figure are numerous. Some 1297 of them are assembled in a recent edition by R. C. Hiremath [*SRV*]. Of primary interest among epigraphical mentions of this figure is a late thirteenth-century inscription from North Kanara which mentions Siddharāma of Sonnalige and gives

two *vacanas* said to have been composed by that saint. *EI*, 23.5 (1936 January): 189-96, inscription no. 30.

55. *ŚS* Śi., 122-3/ Ha., 103-4/ Gum., 121-2/ Gū., 3:6-7; I, 222ff. The intent of these *vacanas*—that detached devotion is more important than attached and entrapping work—as well as the image they use—the uselessness of tanks and dams amidst the flood force of true devotion—begs comparison to *Bhagavad Gītā* 2:46-47.

56. *ŚS* Śi., 131-2/ Ha., 112-3/ Gum., 130-1/ Gū., 3:15-6; I, 232f. The most famous owner of three eyes is none other than Śiva Himself. He is so identified (as *tryambaka*) at least as early as Ṛg Veda 7.59.12.

57. *ŚS*. Śi., 136-9/ Ha., 117-20/ Gum., 135-8/Gū., 3:20-3; I, 237ff.

58. *ŚS*. —/ —/ —/ Gū., 3:131; I, 348.

59. *ŚS* Śi., 240 and 242/ Ha., 302 and 304/ Gum., 235 and 237/ Gū., 4:1 and 4:3; II, 26f and 29f.

60. *ŚS* Śi., 241/ Ha., 303/Gum., 648/Gū., 4:2; II, 28f. Translation by Bhoosnurmath and Menezes.

61. *ŚS* Śi., 246/ Ha., 312 /Gum., 241/ Gū., 4:7; II, 36f.

62. *ŚS* Śi., 245/ Ha., 307/ Gum., 240/ Gū., 4:6; II, 35.

63. *ŚS* Śi., 246-258/ Ha., 312-319/ Gum., 241-253/ Gū., 4:7-20; II, 36-51. It is relatively clear that Basava's basic response was to refuse to perform any formal initiation for Cennabasava. Having had the *liṅga* forced upon him, he returned it to his nephew forthwith, but Cennabasava interpreted even this action as a valid initiation. Part of *vacana* *ŚS* Gū., 4:7 reads (in Bhoosnurmath and Menezes' translation): "If I should place the Liṅga in your hand,/ That you may mark its features, and if you, / Thinking it impermissible say: 'Take, take it back, take back your god!' / I've nonetheless received it as your grace!"

64. *ŚS* Śi., 269/ —/ Gum., 264/ Gū., 4:31; II, 66ff.

65. *ŚS* Śi., 271 & 281/ Ha., 333 & 342/ Gum., 266 & 276/ Gū., 4:33 & 4:43; II, 71f & 95f. It is, perhaps, noteworthy that, unlike the description of great, beautiful, and wealthy cities which abound in Sanskrit literature, Allama's description of Kalyāṇa dwells upon the spiritual excellence of the people who live there and of the activities which transpire within the city. He insists (*ŚS* Gū., 4:33) that wherever the true devotee of Śiva dwells is a holy place which is not to be abandoned (*avimukti*). Comparison may be made to praises of other holy places in India such as Benares (near which, coincidentally, exists a holy *tīrtha* called Avimukti). A delightful description of that city as holy place, both in the present and in the traditional *māhātmya* literature is provided by Diana Louise Eck, *Banaras, City of Light* (New York: Alfred A. Knopf, 1982).

66. *ŚS* Śi., 289/ Ha., 351/Gum., 284/ Gū., 5:2; II, 118. Basava's actions were actually quite well-intentioned. He discerned that the Lord was one whether on the palm as *iṣṭaliṅga* or outside the door as *jaṅgama*. Given that identity, why interrupt concentration upon the *iṣṭaliṅga*?

67. *ŚS* Śi., 295/ Ha., 357/ Gum., 290/ Gū., 5:8; II, 125ff.

68. Proper behaviour toward the guest who has arrived unannounced (*atithi*) is prescribed in the law codes of Āpastamba, Gautama, and Vasiṣṭha. Rules requiring the sacrifice of an animal as an offering to the guest occur in

the *Śāṅkhāyana Gṛhya Sūtra.* The specific injunction to go forth and meet the guest and make him comfortable, in the words of Āpastamba, reads: "He shall go to meet such (a guest), honour him according to his age (by the formulas of salutation prescribed), and cause a seat to be given to him." See *SBE*, vol. 2: *The Sacred Laws of the Āryas (as taught in the schools of) Āpastamba, Gautama, Vāsiṣṭha, and Baudhāyana*, pt. 1: "Āpastamba and Gautama", trans. Georg Bühler (Oxford: Clarendon Press, 1879), pp. 114-22 and 204-7; *SBE*, vol 14, pp. 43-45 and 49-51; and *SBE*, vol. 29: *The Gṛhya-Sūtras: Rules of Vedic Domestic Ceremonies*, trans. Hermann Oldenberg (Oxford: Clarendon Press, 1886), pp. 87-90.

69. *ŚS* Śi., 307/ Ha., 383/ Gum., 302/ Gū., 5:20; II, 143f.

70. *ŚS* Śi., 364/ Ha., 473/ Gum., 360/ Gū., 5:77; II, 194f.

71. Maruḷuśaṅkara also finds mention in the *Cennabasava Purāṇa* 57:55 and in *PLL* (sam), p. 92. The editors have provided informative data about him at *ŚS* Gū., vol. II, p. 215 n. 2; and at vol. II, p. 216 nn. 1 and 3. Note that Basava compares himself to a madman or a village idiot—a fool for the Lord—in *vacanas* at *BV* 460, 471, and 519: (K) pp. 180, 184, and 204; (E) pp. 149, 152, and 167. The intentional pursuit of scorn as a means of acquiring religious merit has been explored by Ingalls, "Cynics and Pāśupatas".

72. *ŚS* —/ —/ —/ Gū., 6:8; II, 241.

73. *ŚS* Śi., 391/ Ha., 856/ Gum., 682/ Gū., 6:49 (6:44); II, 292. [Due to different systems for the enumeration of *padas* (songs), the versification can vary slightly in different editions of the same version. The first number given is from the Karnatak University, Dharwar edition. The number in parentheses (called by some 'brackets') may be found in other editions or in indices keyed to other editions.]

74. *ŚS* Śi., 413/ Ha., 883/ Gum., 705/ Gū., 7:12; II, 321f.

75. *ŚS* Śi., 416/ Ha., 886/ Gum., 708/ Gū., 7.15; II, 325f. The same *vacana* recurs in all four texts at *ŚS* Śi., 893/ Ha., 1353/ Gum., 1263/ Gū., 20:39 (20:27); V, 331.

76. The small number of early references to Cennabasava in *BP* (K) and in Harihara's *Ragalegalu* as well as the relative lateness of the *CBP* itself have been discussed in the previous chapter. The epigraphical evidence for Cennabasava is, similarly, rather late. Dating from as late as the seventeenth century, inscriptions refer to Cennabasava both by the mere mention of his name and in an elaborate presentation of his philosophical system. For the former, see *EC*, vol. V: inscription no. Ak 94; pt. i, pp. 345-46 for transliteration; pt. I, pp. 149-50 for translation; and pt. ii, pp. 461-64 for text. For the latter, see *EC*, vol. XII: *Inscriptions in the Tumkur District*, ed. B. Lewis Rice (Bangalore: Mysore Government Central Press, 1904), inscription no. Mi. 8, p. 368 for text, p. 176 for transliteration, and p. 104 for translation.

77. *ŚS* Śi., 438/ Ha., 503 and again at 581/ Gum., 730/ Gū , 8:1; III, 18f.

78. *ŚS* —/ —/ —/ Gū., 8:2; III, 19.

79. *ŚS* Śi., 440-441/ Ha., 505-506/ Gum., 732-733/ Gū., 8:4-5; III, 21ff.

80. *ŚS* Śi., 497/ Ha., 522/ Gum , 791/ Gū., 8:65 (8:60); III, 88f. Translation by Bhoosnurmath and Menezes occurs at *ŚS* Gū , III, 89.

81. The primary locus for each of these topics is as follows:

(1) *ŚS* Śi., 467/ Ha., 549/ Gum., 761/ Gū , 8:35 (8:30); III, 59.

(2) *ŚS* Śi., 496/ Ha., 521/ Gum., 790 (789)/ Gū., 8:64 (8:59); III, 87f.
(3) *ŚS* Śi., 449/ Ha., 538/ Gum., 741/ Gū., 8:13-18: III, 41-48.
(4) *ŚS* Śi., 475/ Ha., 586/ Gum., 769/ Gū., 8:43 (8:38); III, 66f.
(5) *ŚS* Śi., 476-483/ Ha., 587-594/ Gum., 770-777/ Gū., 8:44-51 (8:39-46); III, 67-74.
(6) *ŚS* Śi., 500/ Ha., 524/ Gum., 794/ Gū., 8:68 (8:63); III, 91f.

82. *ŚS* Śi., 502/ Ha., 527/ Gum., 796/ Gū., 8:75 (8:70); III, 96.

83. Maḍivāḷa Mācayya finds mention throughout the *Basava Purāṇa*. Some of his more important contributions are told at *BP* (K), chaps. 20, 21, 35, 36, and 60, *BP* (K-E), pp. 82-83. Several texts reputedly dealing with Maḍivāḷa Mācayya but unavailable for the present research are mentioned at *ŚS* Gū., vol. III, p. 109 n. 6: (1) Caluva's C.E. 1725 *Maḍivāḷayyanacarite*, (2) the C.E. 1650 *Maḍivālayyana Tārāvali*, and (3) Ānanda Basavaliṅga Śivayōgi's C.E. 1500 *Mācidēvana Manōvilāsa*. Epigraphical references include a grant record from the twelfth century at Kalyāṇa and a Telugu copper plate from uselessly recent dates. The former appears in full at Desai, *Basavesvara*, pp. 362-64; the latter, at *EC*, vol. IX: *Inscriptions in the Bangalore District*, vol. ed. B. Lewis Rice (Bangalore: Mysore Government Central Press, 1905), inscription no. Kn. 89, p. 287 for text, p. 164 for transliteration, and p. 132 for translation.

84. In Vīraśaiva parlance, *bhavi* is a technical antonym for *bhakta*. From its primary meaning as "living, being, having life and sensation; a living being", it acquires the restricted meaning of "a person that is subject to transmigration, a worldling, a miserable wretch". See F. Kittel, *A Kannaḍa-English Dictionary* (Mangalore: Basel Mission Book and Tract Depository, 1894), s.v. "*bhavi*".

85. This incident forms the basis for Allama Prabhu's present encounter with Maḍivāḷa Mācayya but does not itself occur in the *Śūnyasaṃpādane*. It does occur in the *Basava Purāṇa* at *BP* (K-E), pp. 82-83.

86. The incident of the yogic third eye should be compared to Allama's initial encounter with Siddharāma in *ŚS* Gū., chap. III.

87. *ŚS* Śi., 515/ Ha., 626/ Gum., 375 (374)/ Gū., 9:5; III, 133f.

88. *ŚS* Śi., 531/ Ha., 642/ Gum., 825 (826)/ Gū., 9:21; III, 151.

89. See the "*Saṃpādane* of Siddharāma", *ŚS* Gū., chap. III.

90. *ŚS* Śi., 568/Ha., 736/ Gum., 480/ Gū., 10:1; III, 206f.

91. *ŚS* Śi., 563/ Ha., 487 and 674/ Gum., 394/ Gū., 10:7; III, 212f.

92. Among these lesser lights are the following:
(1) Amugidēvayya—*ŚS* —/ Ha., 727/ Gum., 425/ Gū., 10:26; III, 230.
(2) Uriliṅgapeddapaṇṇa—*ŚS* —/ Ha., 712/ Gum., 409/ Gū., 10:23; III, 227f. His collected *vacanas* appear at *SPV*, pp. 411-22.
(3) Dakkeya Bommaṇṇa—*ŚS* —/ —/ Gum., 423-424/ Gū., —, 10:25; III, 229. Collected *vacanas* are at *SPV*, pp. 217-41.
(4) Telugu Jommaṇṇa—*ŚS* —/ Ha., 726/ Gum., 429/ Gū., 10:28; III, 231f. The *Telugu Bommayyana Ragaḷe* occurs at Harihara, *Ragaḷegaḷu*, pp. 330-347. See *BP* (K) 3:82; 14:17, 23, 25; 29:31, 72; 33:1, 3; 36:38; 46:36; 53:73; and 57:6. This character seems to be the Bommidēva of *BP* (K-E), pp. 83-84, who robs from the rich to give to the *śaranas* and of *CBP* (K-E), p. 194, who stabs an impious Brahmin.
(5) Dāsimayya—*ŚS* —/ —/ Gum., 403/ Gū., 10:21; III, 226. *BP* (K) 8:38 and 57:4 mention him. His role as a pre-Basava intensifier of

Śaivism has been discussed and several of his *vacanas* translated by Ramanujan, *Speaking of Śiva*, pp. 91-110. His works found publication under the edition of P. G. Haḷakaṭṭi (Bijapur, n. p., 1955).

(6) Mēṟēmiṇḍadēva—*ŚS* —/ —/ —/ Gū., 10:22; III, 227. *Vacanas* given at *SPV*, pp. 77-102. See *BP* (K) 25:1, 15, 21; 26: 75; and 36:44.

(7) Mōḷigeya Mārayya—*ŚS* —/ —/ Gum., 404-408/ Gū., 10:18-20; II, 224ff. *ŚS* Gū., chap. XIII treats this saint in detail.

(8) Rāyasada Mañcaṇṇa—*ŚS* —/ Ha., 689/ Gum., 421/ Gū., 10:24; III, 228. Perhaps the Mañcidēva of *BP* (K) 8:39 is the same.

(9) Śivanāgamayyagaḷa—*ŚS* —/ —/ Gum., 426-427/ Gū., —, 10:27; III, 231. See *BP* (K) 37:46; 54:2; and 56:80-82, 86-89.

Despite minor differences Ha., Gum., and Gū., generally agree on the above characters and events. Śivagaṇa, of course, omits the entire episode of Siddharāma's initiation and those in attendance. In addition, Gum. alone tells of several other minor *śaraṇas*.

(10) Ambigara Cavuḍayya—*ŚS* —/ —/ Gum., 417-418/ —/. Collected *vacanas* appear at *SPV*, pp. 379-410.

(11) Aṟivina Māritande—*ŚS* —/ —/ Gum., 411-412/ —/. His collected *vacanas* are at *SPV*, pp. 103-82.

(12) Ekānta Rāmayya—*ŚS* —/ —/ Gum., 420/ —/. Though his role is small in the present context, Ekānta is, of course, important in the overall history and legendary self-understanding of Vīraśaivism. See the discussion in S. C. Nandimath, *Handbook*, pp. 15-16, which treats his role as one of the five great *ācāryas*. See also Harihara, *Ragaḷegaḷu*, pp. 449-64; *BP* (K) 8:47; chap. 48; chap. 51; and 57:6; and *EI* 5 (1898-99): 242. Also see *CBP* (K-E), pp. 198-99.

(13) Kōla Śantayya—*ŚS* —/ —/ Gum., 413-414/ —/. He is mentioned at *BP* (K) 57:10; and his collected *vacanas* are at *SPV*, pp. 1-30.

(14) Prasāda Bhōgaṇṇa—*ŚS* —/ —/ Gum., 410/ —/.

(15) Bibba Bācayya—*ŚS* —/ —/ Gum., 422/ —/. *Vacanas* collected at *SPV*, pp. 53-76. See *BP* (K) 8:45; 55:1, 10, 14, 25, 30, 40 & 47.

(16) Manasanda Mārayya—*ŚS* —/ —/ Gum., 419/ —/. *Vacanas* are at *SPV*, pp. 355-78.

(17) Śivaleṅka Mañcaṇṇa—*ŚS* —/ —/ Gum., 415-416/ —/. *Vacanas* collected at *SPV*, pp. 183-216. *BP* (K) 1:10 & 52:55-66.

93. *ŚS* —/ Ha., 785/ Gum., 502/ Gū., 10:50 (10:47); III, 260ff.

94. Allama Prabhu's entry into the glorious court, which compared favorably to the Pāṇḍava's or to Rāma's is, told at *ŚS* Śi., 394-395/ Ha., 861-862/ Gum., 685-686/ Gū., 11:1-2; III, 330-333.

95. Basava's two hymns in praise of Prabhu occur at *ŚS* Śi., 395/ Ha., 862/ Gum., 686 and 646/ Gū., 11:3-7 (11:2) and 11:19-23 (11:13); III, 333f and III, 345f. Cennabasava's two are at *ŚS* Śi., 395/ Ha., 864/ Gum., 688 and 646/ Gū., 11:10-14 (11:9) and 11:24-28 (11:13); III, 337ff and III, 346-350. Siddharāma's is at *ŚS* —/ —/ Gum., 684/ Gū., 11:29-35 (11:13); III, 350-354. Other hymns are sung by Maḍivāḷa Mācayya at *ŚS* Śi., 398/ Ha., 865/ Gum., 690/ Gū., 11:15; III, 339f. By Soddala Bācārasa at *ŚS* Śi., 399-400/ Ha., 866-867/ Gum., 691-692/ Gū., ii 16-17; III, 341ff. By Haḍapada Appaṇṇa at *ŚS* Śi., 401/ Ha., 868/ Gum., 693/ Gū., 11:18; III, 344. Of these, Maḍivāḷa Mācayya was discussed

above and Soḍḍala Bācarasa appears at *BP* (K) 8:42; 46-38; chap. 52; 53:1; and 57:1; and also at *BP* (K-E), pp. 86-87.

96. Prabhu's reciprocal praise occurs at *ŚS* Śi., 573-575/ Ha., 799-801/ Gum., 934-936/ Gū., 11:36-38 (11:14-16); III, 354ff, for Cennabasava. For Basava, at *ŚS* Śi., 576-577/ Ha., 802-803/ Gum., 937-938/ Gū., 11:39-40 (11:17); III, 357f. Cennabasava, Basava, and Maḍivāḷa Mācayya in company find praise at *ŚS* Śi., 583, —/ Ha., 809, —/ Gum., 944, —/ Gū., 11:49-50 (11:27-28); III, 367f.

97. For example, the water of the libation is referred to as *jalajalavilla*, "water-no-water" (i.e. "water which is not real water"). Probably the entire ceremony is to be understood in a figurative sense rather than literally and physically, but this is only a probability, not a certainty.

98. *ŚS* Śi., 396/ Ha., 863/ Gum., 687/ Gū., 11:8; III, 335.

99. These two are mentioned at *BP* (K) 57:3. Supposedly they also appear in the *Cennabasava Purāṇa* at 57:30 though their story is missing from Würth's paraphrase *CBP* (K-E).

100. The apparent similarities between the Protestant Christian and Vīraśaiva ethics of work as well as the theoretical differences vis-à-vis the Weberian thesis have been explored in some detail in two papers by R. Blake Michael: "Ascetic Protestantism and Vīraśaivism: A Comparison with Respect to the Spirit of Capitalism" (Course paper, Harvard University, 1973) and "Work as Worship in Vīraśaiva Tradition," *Journal of the American Academy of Religion* L.4 (1982 December): 101-15. The latter explored the materials of these three chapters within the *Śūnyasampādane* in a detailed analysis of the movement's specific teachings on the importance of work and on the limits to legitimate remuneration. The former looked at such materials in somewhat less detail but carried the analysis beyond explicit teachings to the role of ritual and priesthood in establishing acceptable channels for soteriological anxieties which mitigated systematic economic acquisition and investment. Both papers essentially supported Weber's conclusion that a certain "traditionalism" within Vīraśaivism blocked development along the "rationalistic course which expressed itself in the purism of the sect". See Max Weber, *Religion of India: The Sociology of Hinduism and Buddhism*, trans. and ed. Hans H. Gerth and Don Martindale (New York: The Free Press, 1958), p. 305. It may be, however, that the arrest of that development arose less from the ideal factors of doctrine and ritual soteriology, as Weber contended, than from material factors in the realm of politics, economic self-interest, and social organization. Whatever the causes, it is relatively clear that, in the final analysis, the Vīraśaiva work ethic could perhaps best be compared not to the Calvinist Puritan one but to the Lutheran "concept of the calling [which] remained traditionalistic". See Max Weber, *The Protestant Ethic and the Spirit of Capitalism*, trans. Talcott Parsons (New York: Charles Scribner's Sons, 1958), p. 85.

101. The popular phrase is *kāyakave kailāsa* and is usually attributed to Basava, whose actual words seem to have been the nearly equivalent *kāyave kailāsa* (i.e. "the body is heaven" or "the body is the abode of Śiva"), at ***BV*** 139: (K) p. 63; (E) p. 46; and at *BV* 872: (K) p. 358; (E) p. 293. Less critical editions, however, often interchange the phrases. See, for example, ***Basavaṇṇavara** Vacanagaḷu* (*Bhāvārtha Sahita*), (Hubli: City Book Stall, n.d.), p. 53.

Within the *Śūnyasaṃpādane,* the phrase is attributed to Āydakki Mārayya in its fuller form, which appears at *ŚS* —/ —/ Gum., 838/ Gū., 12:1; IV, 14f., as *kāyakave kailāsavāda kāraṇa.* An example of the ubiquity and importance of this phrase may be its appearance in large letters on the facade of the Sanskrit school at Siddhagaṅgā Maṭha near Tumkur. The motto dominates that building which itself dominates the monastery complex. The monastic complex itself, though not the bemottoed facade, is diagrammed by H. M. Sadasivaiah, *A Comparative Study of Two Vīraśaiva Monasteries: A Study in Sociology of Religion* (Mysore: Prasaranga, Manasa Gangotri, 1967), pp. 188f.

102. *ŚS* —/ —/ Gum., 838-847/ Gū., 12:1-10; IV, 14-21.

103. *ŚS* —/ —/ Gum., 848-849/ Gū., 12:11-12; IV, 22f.

104. Her tirade occurs at *ŚS* —/ —/ Gum., 850-859/ Gū., 12:13-22; IV, 24-38.

105. These events appear at *ŚS* —/ —/ Gum., 871-875/ Gū., 12:34-38; IV, 39-44.

106. *ŚS* —/ —/ Gum., 880-881/ Gū., 12:43-44; IV, 47f.

107. *ŚS* —/ —/ Gum., 838/ Gū., 12:1; IV, 14f. The form of the phrase here is *kāyakave kailāsavāda kāraṇa.*

108. The editors of *ŚS* Gū., vol. IV, p. xvii, mention a *Mōḷigayyana Purāṇa* (Dharwar: n.p., 1951), His *vacanas* are collected at *SPV*, pp. 481-654. He finds mention at *BP* (K) 29:1 and 4 and 57:7; and at *BP* (K-E), p. 84.

109. See the prose to *ŚS* Gū., 13:1; IV, 73.

110. *ŚS* —/—/ —/ Gū., 13:2; IV, 74.

111. See the prose to *ŚS* Gū., 13:3; IV, 75f.

112. See the prose to *ŚS* Gū., 13:5; IV, 77.

113. *ŚS* —/ —/ —/ Gū., 13:7-8; IV, 79f.

114. *ŚS* —/ —/ —/ Gū., 13:44; IV, 119f.

115. Apparently Nuliya Candayya finds mention at *Śaraṇalīlāmṛta* X, for so say the editors at *ŚS* Gū., vol. IV, p. 127. His story does appear at *BP* (K) 35:58 and 57:7.

116. Actually this entire narrative only provides the background for the context in which the *vacanas* of Lesson Fourteen are recited. The narrative occurs in the prose introduction to *ŚS* Gū., chap. 14; IV, 142-143. *ŚS* Śi. omits the incident entirely. The narrative occurs prior to *ŚS* Gum., 885 which is the *vacana* found at *ŚS*. Ha., 930.

117. *ŚS* —/ Ha., 936/ Gum., 891/ Gū., 14:7; IV, 148.

118. *ŚS* —/ Ha., 937-941/ Gum., 892-896/ Gū., 14:8-12; IV, 148-152.

119. *ŚS* —/ Ha., 942/ Gum., 897/ Gū., 14:13; IV, 153.

120. Actually, Nuliya Candayya's troubles with his *liṅga* did not end there. Ordered to go sell ropes in the market, the *liṅga* returned with much gold (*ŚS* Gū., 14:14 prose). Distraught that his work had brought more than its fair price, Nuliya Candayya admonished the *liṅga* (*ŚS* Gū., 14:16 prose) and taught it the value of honest labor (*ŚS* Gū., 14:34-36). Maḍivāḷa Mācayya again intervened on behalf of the well-intentioned *liṅga* (*ŚS* Gū., 14:17) and ultimately Nuliya Candayya and his peripatetic *liṅga* were reunited (*ŚS* Gū., 14:49 and the prose thereto). See *ŚS* —/ Ha., 943-946, 963-965, and 978/ Gum., 898-901, 918-920, & 933 and the prose thereto/ Gū., 14:14-17 and prose, 14:34-36, and 14:49 and prose; IV, 154-159, 172ff., and 191f.

121. Ghaṭṭivāḷayya finds a place in *CBP* (K-E), p. 127. Another account of a dancer-musician who was a *śaraṇa*, though not identified by name, occurs at *BP* (K-E), p. 85.

122. *ŚS* —/ —/ —/ Gū., 15:4; IV, 209.

123. *ŚS* —/ —/ —/ Gū., 15:11-15; IV, 214-217.

124. *ŚS* —/ —/ —/ Gū., 15:25: IV, 227.

125. *ŚS* —/ —/ —/ Gū., 15:33; IV, 231f.

126. *ŚS* —/ —/ —/ Gū., 15:49-50; IV, 245ff.

127. *ŚS* —/ —/ —/ Gū., 15-36 and prose; IV, 252f. The translation is by Bhoosnurmath and Menezes.

128. Sister Mahādēvi's story appears in *PLL* (sam), pp. 58-63. Ramanujan, *Speaking of Śiva*, pp. 111-142, gives a brief sketch of her life and translates selected *vacanas*. A fine edition of her collected *vacanas* was published by the erstwhile Vice-Chancellor of Karnatak University, Dharwar. Containing *vacanas*, notes, translation, and an Introduction, the work appeared as *Vacanas of Akkamahādēvi*, trans. Armando Menezes and S. M. Angadi (Dharwar: Shri Manohar Appasaheb Adke, 1973).

129. See Michael, "Women of the *Śūnyasaṃpādane*", and note also that previously A. K. Ramanujan, in a lecture, "Men, Women, and Saints", given at Harvard Divinity School, Cambridge, 1977 April, had drawn attention to the common nature of women mystics' experience vis-à-vis their social context. The patterns of a sudden break with a former life which characterizes male converts is often obscured for females. For them there seems to be necessitated a legitimising event in early childhood which explains their aberrant social attitudes. That event is often a spiritual marriage to the Lord himself. The pattern is not limited to the Indian context, but it does find powerful expression there in the persons of Mīrābāi and Āṇḍāḷ as well as Mahādēviyakka. Mahādēviyakka and Mīrābāi have been specifically compared by S. S. Kabbina, *Akkamahādēvi mattu Mīrābāyi* (Dharwar: Karnatak University, 1971).

130. *ŚS* Śi., 596/ Ha., 1001/ Gum., 961/ Gū., 16:14; IV, 286f. See *MAV* 53, pp. 57 and pt. ii, 17.

131. The actual Lesson begins here with Mahādēviyakka's arrival in Kalyāṇa and interrogation by the *śaraṇas* at *ŚS* Śi., 589/ Ha., 993/ Gum., 950/ Gū., 16:4; IV, 286f. The previous narrative can only be inferred from the following debate or known from other sources, such as *PLL* (sam), pp. 58-63 and a reputed *Mahādēviyakkana Purāṇa*, ed. B. N. Chandrayya (Mysore: Sharath Prakashana, 1968).

132. *ŚS* —/ —/ —/ Gū., 16:17; IV, 298. The same idea was present in *ŚS* Gū., 16:15.

133. *ŚS* —/ Ha., 1005/ —/ Gū., 16:33; IV, 310f. See *MAV* 231, pp. 111-12 and pt. ii, 85.

134. Mahādēviyakka's departure from Kalyāṇa, her lonely journey, the awesome plantain grove at the holy Śrī Śaila mountain, and her final attainment of unity with the universe are described at *ŚS* —/ Ha., 1051-1073/ Gum., 988-1002/ Gū., 16:75-90; IV, 354-369.

135. Prabhu's departure is described in the prose introductions to *ŚS* Śi.,

621/ Ha., 1057/ Gum., 1005/ Gū., 17:1, V, 10f. The tour itself is described and praised by Maḍivāḷa Mācayya at *ŚS* —/ —/ —/ Gū., 17:10; V, 18f.

136. Prabhu's coming to the cave retreat and his meditation is narrated in the prose to *ŚS* Śi., 633/ Ha., 1089/ Gum., 1017/ Gū., 17:15; V, 24f. His sublime trance receives copious description at *ŚS* Śi., 633-643/ Ha., 1089-1099/ Gum., 1017-1027/ Gū., 17:15-25; V, 24-32.

137. The ability of the gods to float above the earth without taint is commonly attested in Sanskrit literature, for example, in the beloved story of Nala-Damayantī at *Mahābhārata* 3.54.21-24.

138. *ŚS* Śi., 642/ Ha., 1098/ Gum., 1026/ Gū., 17-24; V, 31.

139. A brief description of the awaiting city is at *ŚS* Śi., 646/ Ha., 1102/ Gum., 1030/ Gū., 17:28; V, 38. A fuller description of the throne and the palace occupies the introductory prose to *ŚS* Gū., chap. 18; V, 77-133.

140. *ŚS* Śi., 651/ Ha., 391/ Gum., 1035/ Gū., 17:33; V, 41. Basava's use of erotic imagery is minimal, but his sense of separation and longing is also expressed at *ŚS* Śi., 647-648/ Ha., 1103-1104/ Gum., 1031-1032/ Gū., 17:29-30; V, 38f. The use of separation as an aesthetic and religious motif, though in a more erotic mode, is prominently displayed in the *Gītāgovinda* of Jayadeva recently edited, translated, and discussed as the *Love Song of the Dark Lord: Jayadeva's Gītāgovinda*, ed. and trans. Barbara Stoler Miller (New York: Columbia University Press, 1977).

141. *ŚS* Śi., 674-675/ Ha., 1131-1132/ Gum., 1059-1060/ Gū., 17:58-59; V, 66ff.

142. Compare Duryodhana's folly and disastrous anger, at *Mahābhārata* 2.43, with the scene at *ŚS* Gū., 18, prose introduction; V, 76-80.

143. Basava's problems in discerning a true devotee and acting appropriately towards him have provided the intrigue for the stories of Maruḷuśaṅkara, Mōḷigeya Mārayya, and Nuliya Candayya's *liṅga*. His simple devotion fails to discriminate among all who claim to be devotees of the Lord. See his *vacana* to this effect at *BV* 719: (K) p. 287; (E) p. 237.

144. *ŚS* Śi., 684/ Ha., 1140/ Gum., 1069/ Gū., 18:9; V, 89.

145. The actual sequence of events in the *Śūnyasaṃpādane* is less clear than this narrative implies. There Prabhu first seems to have been received without undue animosity and even enthroned (*ŚS* Gū., 18:1-12; V, 18-91). Then the large group of *jaṅgamas* defected (*ŚS* Gū., 18:13; V, 92f). Probably the intent was to portray two factions—one joyful at Prabhu's investiture, the other apprehensive and jealous. In any case, both factions were later reconciled to his leadership (*ŚS* Gū., 19:82: V, 214f.)

146. *ŚS* Śi., 690/ Ha., 1147/ Gum., 1075/ Gū., 18:15; V, 94.

147. Those who had remained included:

Cennabasava—*ŚS* Śi., 691/ Ha., 1148/ Gum., 1076/ Gū., 18:16: V, 95.
Basava—*ŚS* Śi., 694/ Ha., 1051/ Gum., 1079/ Gū., 18:21; V, 99f.
Mōḷigeya Mārayya—*ŚS* —/ —/ —/ Gū., 18:58 (18:53); V, 130f.
Maḍivāḷa Mācayya—*ŚS* Śi., 729/ Ha., 1186/ Gum., 1114/ Gū., 19:7; V, 149f.
Haḍapada Appaṇṇa—*ŚS* Śi., 730/ Ha., 1187/ Gum., 1115/ Gū., 19:8; V, 150ff.

Soḍḍala Bācarasa—*ŚS* Śi., 736/ Ha., 1193/ Gum., 1121/ Gū., 19:14; V, 156f.

148. *ŚS* Śi., 702-710/ Ha., 1159-1166/ Gum., 1087-1094/ Gū., 18:29-36; V, 107-112.

149. *ŚS* Śi., 715-120/ Ha., 1172-1177/ Gum., 1100-1105/ Gū., 18:40-50; V, 117-125.

150. *ŚS* Śi., 723/ Ha., 1180/ Gum., 1108/ Gū., 19:1 and prose; V, 144f.

151. *ŚS* Śi., 726-742/ Ha., 1183-1199/ Gum., 1111-1127/ Gū., 19:4-20; V, 147-163.

152. *ŚS* Śi., 743/ —/ Gum., 1128/ Gū., 19:22; V, 164f. Compare similar responses at *ŚS*. Śi., 750, 752, 754/ Ha., 1207, 1209, 1212/ Gum., 1135, 1137, 1139/ Gū., 19:29, 19:31, and 19:33; V, 170f, 172f, and 174f.

153. *ŚS* Gū., 19:34-81; V, 175-214.

154. *ŚS* Śi., 786/ Ha., 1145/ Gum., 1172/ Gū., 19:78; V, 210f.

155. Such passages predicting future events occur near the end of many Vīraśaiva and other Indian works. Compare the present *kālajñāna* with the final chapters of the *Cennabasava Purāṇa* at *CBP* (K-E), pp. 219-21. In the present work, predictive descriptions are given for the attainment of absolute unity (demise) of several *śaraṇas*:

Basava—*ŚS* —/ —/ —/ Gū., 20:20-21; V, 318f.

Cennabasava—*ŚS* Śi., 899/ Ha., 1359/ Gum., 1269/ Gū., 20:45ff (20:33ff); V, 335ff.

Bahurūpa Couḍayya—*ŚS* —/ —/ Gum., 1279/ Gū., 20:61ff); (20:49ff); V, 345ff.

Haḍapada Appaṇṇa—*ŚS* Śi., 914/ Ha., 1374/ Gum., 1288/ Gū., 20:69f (20:57f); V, 351f.

Soḍḍala Bācarasa—*ŚS* Śi., 916/ Ha., 1376/ Gum., 1290/ Gū., 20:71f(20:59f); V, 353f.

Akkanāgāyi—*ŚS* Śi., 919/ Ha., 1379/ Gum., 1293/ Gū., 20:74f (20:62); V, 355ff.

Mōḷigeya Mārayya—*ŚS* Śi., 921/ Ha., 1381/ Gum., 1295/ Gū., 20:76f (20:64f); V, 357f.

Ḍōhara Kakkayya—*ŚS* Śi., 923/ Ha., 1383/ Gum., 1297/ Gū., 20:78f (20:66f); V, 358ff.

Allama Prabhu—*ŚS* Śi., 925/ Ha., 1385/ Gum., 1299/ Gū., 20:85ff (20:68ff); V, 363ff.

156. *ŚS* Śi., 861/ Ha., 1321/ Gum., 1249/ Gū., 20:1; V, 299f.

157. *ŚS* Śi., 861, 864/ Ha., 1321, 1324/ Gum., 1249/ Gū., 20:1, 20:4; V, 299f and 304.

158. *ŚS* Śi., 904/ Ha., 1364/ Gum., 1275 /Gū., 20:51 (20:39); V, 338f.

159. Prabhu's encounter with Gōrakṣa is also told at *PLL* (sam), pp. 105-13. The cult of the Gorakhnathīs or Kānphaṭas has been thoroughly described and their principal text, the *Gorakṣaśataka*, translated by George Weston Briggs, *Gorakhnāth and the Kānphaṭa Yogīs* (Calcutta: Y.M.C.A. Publishing House, 1938). Briggs tends to date the reputed founder of the group, Gorakhnātha, to the thirteenth century or later (pp. 228-50). Such dates would argue against either his encounter with a twelfth century Allama Prabhu or against such an early date for Prabhu. Certainly the yogic cult and traditions about its founder

were well formed by the fifteenth century composition of the *Śūnyasaṃpādane*. If a twelfth-century Prabhu did engage in some sort of yogic context with a great *siddha*, the specific identification of that accomplished one could have later been confused with a growing Gorakhnātha influence. On the other hand, the entire tale may well be a fifteenth century invention reflecting actual struggles of the Vīraśaivas against competing, and sometimes more stringent, yogic groups in that late era.

160. See the editors' comments at *ŚS* Gū., vol. V, p. 373.

161. See the prose to *ŚS* Śi., 932/ —/ Gum., 1306/ Gū., 21:2; V, 388.

162. Prabhu's "spaceless trance" (*nirvayala samādhi*) is mentioned at *ŚS* —/ —/ Gum., 1309 prose/Gū., 21:8 prose; V, 394.

163. *ŚS* —/ —/ Gum., 1306/ Gū., 21:5; V, 390.

164. Elsewhere, Basava's wife is identified variously as Gaṅgāmbike or as Māyidēvi, e.g. at *BP* (K) 4:14-16; 10:22-28; 19:21, 30; 41:42, 49; and 58:7 for the former and *BP* (K) 10:43 and 58:6 for the latter. Desai, *Basavesvara*, pp. 263-64, is inclined to see the traditions about Nīlamma, reputedly a step-sister of the king Bijjaḷa, as rather late. Her remaining in Kalyāṇa appears in a different light if she indeed was the sister of the king.

165. The quarrel and exodus are told at *ŚS* —/ —/ Gum., 1317 prose and 1321 prose/ Gū., 21:18 prose and 21:40 prose; V, 405f and 417ff.

166. Nīlamma's refusal to leave Kalyāṇa and join her husband takes on a different significance, however, if she indeed was the sister of king Bijjaḷa.

167. *ŚS* —/ —/ —/ Gū., 21:40 (21:22); V, 419f. The rest of Nīlamma's story appears in the prose to *ŚS* —/ —/ Gum., 1321/ Gū., 21:40 & 21:45; V, 417ff and 422ff.

168. The unitive state is described for several of the *śaraṇas*.

Basava—*ŚS* Śi., 947/ Ha., 1407/ Gum., 1324/ Gū., 21:48 (21:27); V, 426f.

Nīlalōcane—*ŚS* —/ —/ —/ Gū., 21:57 (21:36); V, 435.

Akkanāgi—*ŚS* Śi., 950/ Ha., 1411/ Gum., 1328/ Gū., 21:63 (21:42); V, 440ff.

Maḍivāḷa Mācayya—*ŚS* Śi., 958/ Ha., 1417/ Gum., 1336/ Gū., 21:78 (21:52); V, 453ff.

Cennabasava—*ŚS* Śi., 959/ Ha., 1418/ Gum., 1337/ Gū., 21:79 (21:53); V. 455f.

169. *ŚS* Śi., 933/ Ha., 1393/ Gum., 1311/ Gū., 21:12; V, 398ff.

CHAPTER THREE

THE SOTERIOLOGY OF THE ŚŪNYASAMPĀDANE: Objectivist v. Subjectivist

The preceding chapter summarized the *Śūnyasaṃpādane* and found that several types of religious associations, including objectivist and subjectivist ones, appeared and found prominent proponents in that text. Attention to all the issues debated there would provide a useful but compendious, analysis of Vīraśaiva idea·sı A more manageable and equally useful analysis can focus, however, only on the Eight Coverings (the *aṣṭāvaraṇa*)[1] which are characteristic of contemporary Liṅgāyata practice. Attention to these eight "Aids to Faith" will provide an understanding of the tensions within the text which pull toward a particularist-subjectivist religious organization and those which pull toward objectivism, toward universalism, and toward a radically subjectivist individualism in the arguments of Cennabasava, Basava, and Allama Prabhu respectively.

For purposes of analysis, these Eight Coverings may themselves be classified into three categories:[2]

I. Human Assistants on the Path of Faith
   1. *guru*—family or village priest who initiates one
   2. *jaṅgama*—wandering ascetic or monastic

II. The Religious Talisman
   3. *iṣṭaliṅga*—small stone bestowed at initiation (*dīkṣā*) and worn always by each Liṅgāyata

III. The Minor Sacramental Substances
   4. *pādodaka*—water made holy by contact with the feet of the *guru* or of the *jaṅgama*
   5. *prasāda*—food consecrated by having been first offered to the *guru* or the *jaṅgama*
   6. *vibhūti*—holy ash prepared from cow-dung by a special ritual process
   7. *rudrākṣa*—prayer beads made from a special seed

8. *mantra*—the one sacred formula holy to Lord Śiva: *oṃ namaḥ śivāya*

With particular emphasis on the first three coverings and with incidental analysis of the last five, the present chapter will explore the *aṣṭāvaraṇa* for the light that scheme sheds on the relative objectivism/subjectivism of Vīraśaiva practices and organization.

THE AṢṬĀVARAṆA SCHEME

Guru and Jaṅgama: Human Assistants on the Path of Faith

For contemporary Liṅgāyatas, one of the richest external sources for development of one's spiritual potential is the religious specialist—the *guru* or the *jaṅgama.*[3] Such priestly specialists provide teaching and guidance to lay Liṅgāyatas and officiate at important ceremonies in the life of these laypersons. In addition, they perform important functions in sacralizing certain other external aids to a faithful life. For example, the water which has been used to bathe their feet (*pādodaka*) and the food which has first been offered to them (*prasāda*) acquire a sacred nature and soteriological power by virtue of that contact with their persons. These two types of religious specialists serve as the primary locus of salvific potency which is attained by external and objective means.

The exact nature of the specialization between *guru* and *jaṅgama* is far from clear, and whatever clarity may be obtained is complicated by the divergent patterns found when northern and southern Karnāṭaka are compared.[4] In general, however, some functional distinction may be made. The *guru* tends to be a married householder who inherited his clerical authority as well as the client families for whom he performs priestly functions—chiefly life-cycle rituals.[5] The *jaṅgama,* as the name implies,[6] is often a wandering celibate whose presence at sacred occasions may be required but who himself serves less as a ritual celebrant than as a focus for ritual worship.[7] Generally, he has no established clientele under his pastoral charge but offers his services wherever they are needed, usually in exchange for several days' board and lodging.

A detailed delineation of the several functions of these specialists would be highly desirable, but for the present one shared characteristic provides ample grounds for exploration. As persons specifically dedicated to spiritual pursuits and religious occupations, they provide valuable aid to Liṅgāyata laypersons who seek greater knowledge of religious truth and also greater assurance of their own relation to that truth. In their teaching activities, in their celebration of rituals, and in their consecration of various sacramental substances these religious specialists provide objective focus to Liṅgāyata piety. They serve as embodied dispensers of the Lord's grace or, at least of the assurance of that grace.

In a purely subjectivist soteriology, there would be no such priestly specialists at all. Each individual would be responsible for working out his or her own relation to the Lord and to the Lord's grace. Rather than reliance on objective signs of salvific standing such as life-cycle rituals performed by special individuals, unassisted attainment of inner grace and ethical purity would be incumbent on each Liṅgāyata.

In contrast to such a subjectivist pattern, the mere existence of priestly specialists represents a somewhat objective soteriology. Having priests set apart to perform specific functions which are then of benefit to other individual Liṅgāyatas and specifically having their clerical authority resident upon their office rather than upon their own inner and ethical characteristics represents a significant step toward an objectified scheme of salvific attainment.[8]

The *Śūnyasaṃpādane* is replete with debates about the necessity of the religious specialists, particularly *guru* and *jaṅgama*, in the quest for spiritual attainment by the individual Liṅgāyata. In these debates, however, the text adopts no single, consistent answer to the problem. The necessity of a *guru* for progress on the spiritual path is strongly asserted by Cennabasava and equally rejected or circumvented by Allama Prabhu. A mediating position is advanced by Basava who tends to appreciate the assistance of the *guru* but insists that that assistance is for perfection of the Liṅgāyata's subjective purity rather than for the award of external salvific merit. A careful analysis of those episodes where the necessity of the *guru* is at issue will illuminate the tensions within the text which pull toward either subjective or objective models of salvific attainment.

Iṣṭaliṅga: the Religious Talisman

The Vīraśaiva community derives its alternate name, Liṅgāyata, from the group's distinctive practice of always wearing about the neck a small stone symbol (the *liṅga*).[9] That symbol serves both as a sign of and as a means to spiritual perfection for practicing Liṅgāyatas. The *liṅga* provides a focus for daily, individual worship as each faithful Liṅgāyata contemplates the image in the privacy of his or her home at least once during the course of the day.[10] In addition, the symbol has considerable potency in sacralizing all with which it contacts—the wearer's body as well as food and water which are offered to it prior to consumption.[11] The *liṅga* serves as the primary inanimate focus of salvific potency which is attained by external and objective means.

In Vīraśaiva usage, the term *liṅga* has several connotations which, in turn, give rise to several attitudes toward the *liṅga*. The major distinction within these connotations is between the *liṅga* as a concrete, visible object and *liṅga* as an abstracted concept referring to some internal, or spiritual reality. In other words, as with most religious terms, the word *liṅga* refers both to some objective, visible thing and to some non-objective "Reality" symbolized by that concrete object.[12]

In careful Vīraśaiva parlance, the concrete, objective stone *liṅga* may be of two types. The first of these is the large, fixed stone *liṅga* which serves as a focus of public worship in (non-Vīra-)Śaiva temples. The fixed stone symbol is designated either as *sthāvaraliṅga* (standing *liṅga*) or as *Śaivaliṅga*. The other concrete, objective *liṅga* is the small, mobile stone which is carried always on the person by Liṅgāyatas and which serves to focus their private, daily worship. This mobile emblem is designated either as *iṣṭaliṅga* or *karasthala*(-*liṅga*).[13] In both these senses, *liṅga* is a wholly concrete and particularized object, visible to the eye, perceptible to the touch, and available as a source of soteriological assistance to the devoted seeker.

For Vīraśaivas the abstract concept of an invisible, internal reality symbolized by *liṅga* may also have diverse connotations. On the one hand, the reference may be to a cosmic absolute which provides an ontological basis for existence. This absolute may be variously designated as *mahāliṅga*, *jaṅgamaliṅga*, *niṣkalā liṅga*, *śūnyaliṅga*, or by one of several other names. On the other hand, the individualized or personalized presence of this cosmic reality may be represented as residing within the very nature of the individual devotee. This internalization of the cosmic reality and of the concretized symbolization of that reality may be called either *prāṇaliṅga* or *bhāvaliṅga*. In both these senses, *liṅga* is something quite different from a concrete and particularized object, and is rather a fundamental component of Vīraśaiva metaphysics.[14]

All the important figures of Vīraśaivism's formative period seem agreed that the fixed, stone *sthāvara-* or *Śaivaliṅga* was not an appropriate focus for their piety. Its relation to the larger body of (non-Vīra-)Śaivas provided too close a relation to existent religious and societal forms for the ardent reformatory thrust of Vīraśaiva experience. Likewise, all seem agreed that the abstract concept of *liṅga* as both cosmic and individual metaphysical reality could not be rejected from Vīraśaiva religious life. The full internalization of ultimate power and being could be seen as nothing but the culminating goal of Vīraśaiva faith and practice. On the other hand, the individualized and mobile, but concrete symbol of Vīraśaiva membership, the *iṣṭaliṅga*, provided a basis for widely differing interpretations and opposing assessments of the object's value in the soteriological scheme of Vīraśaiva faith.

In a purely subjectivist soteriology, of course, there would be no cult objects, such as the *iṣṭaliṅga*. Each individual would be responsible for working out his or her own relation to the Lord through some direct and internal contact with the divine. Rather than reliance on objective means to and signs of salvific standing, unassisted attainment of inner grace and ethical purity would be incumbent on each Liṅgāyata.

In contrast to such a subjectivist pattern, the mere existence of the concrete *liṅga* symbol represents a somewhat objective soteriology. Having a specific object set apart which can provide a focus or conduit for achieving some measure of salvific standing represents a significant step toward an objectified scheme of salvific attainment.

The *Śūnyasaṃpādane* is replete with debates about the necessity and usefulness of the *liṅga* object in the quest for spiritual attainment by the individual Liṅgāyata. In those debates, however, the text adopts no single, consistent answer to the problem. The utility of the *iṣṭaliṅga* for progress on the spiritual path is strongly asserted by Cennabasava and equally rejected or circumvented by Allama Prabhu. A mediating position is advanced by Basava who tends to appreciate the assistance of the *liṅga* object but insists that that assistance culminates only in the perfection of the Liṅgāyata's experienced unity with some ultimate reality. A careful analysis of those episodes where the utility of the *liṅga* is at issue will illuminate the tensions within the text which pull toward either subjective or objective models of salvific attainment.

The Minor Sacramental Substances

Besides the religious specialist, both under the title *guru* and under the similar but distinct term *jaṅgama*, and besides the small, stone *liṅga* symbol worn always about the neck, there are five other more or less important objective aids to faith within Liṅgāyata practice. Two of these, of secondary importance, are *prasāda*—comestibles first offered to the deity in the form of *guru*, *jaṅgama*, or *liṅga* prior to being consumed by the devotee—and *pādodaka*—the water used to wash the *guru* or *jaṅgama's* feet and then drunk by the devotee. Three other substances or devices—*vibhūti*, *rudrākṣa*, and *mantra*—are of tertiary but undeniable significance. *Vibhūti* is the sacred ash prepared under the supervision of priests by special ritual processes and smeared on the forehead of the devotee; *rudrākṣas* are rough, round seeds strung together and used in counting recitations in the fashion of telling the beads of the Rosary;[15] and the *mantra*, of course, is the sacred utterance evocative of Śiva's grace and usually limited, for Vīraśaivas, to the six syllables *ōṃ namaḥ Śivāya*.

Not surprisingly, the *śaraṇas*' attitudes toward the efficacy of these secondary and tertiary aids to faith parallel their attitudes toward the primary devices—the priestly specialist and the religious talisman. Allama Prabhu tends to reject outright the usefulness of these devices and, in fact, often condemns them as hindrances to true inner faith. Cennabasava, on the other hand, finds undeniable and explicit value in resort to these objective sources of salvific grace. Basava tends to utilize these sacramental devices rather unselfconsciously. While he appreciates and promotes their benefit for the devotee, he is also sympathetic to Prabhu's concerns and therefore insists upon the need for an internalization of their purport before their true efficacy can be known.

Since an investigation of these *śaraṇas*' attitudes toward the secondary and tertiary sacramental devices provides little insight beyond that gained from an investigation of the three primary devices, a detailed analysis seems unwarranted. Incidental attention to these five relatively minor sacraments does, however, complement an analysis of the three major ones; and they will, therefore, find brief mention where appropriate.

Dialectical Encounters in the Śūnyasaṃpādane

The narrative format of the *Śūnyasaṃpādane* portrays Allama Prabhu's encounters with numerous other spiritual seekers. The primary topic of discussion and debate in a number of these encounters, especially in the earlier encounters, is the nature and necessity of guidance by a human teacher for one engaged in spiritual pursuits. While, in Liṅgāyata tradition, Allama Prabhu is himself considered the *jaṅgama* par excellence, his own experience convinces him that one does not need the assistance of another person in order to attain spiritual beatitude. His encounters with Basava, Cennabasava, and other *śaraṇas* reveal the divergence of opinion which existed in the Vīraśaiva movement concerning the appropriate role of the *guru* and *jaṅgama.*

Similarly, the *Śūnyasaṃpādane* chronicles Vīraśaiva debate about the usefulness and purpose of the *iṣṭaliṅga* and of *liṅga* worship. The introductory portion of that text contains a series of verses attributed to Cennabasava in which the successive incarnations of the Lord into human forms is said to have been for the express purpose of rendering worship to the *liṅga.*[16] Thus, for Cennabasava, the *liṅga* was not simply a useful device of the faith but actually the cause for the holy drama of events at Kalyāṇa. Not surprisingly, Allama Prabhu had a different opinion of the role and function of the *liṅga* and its worship as he argued for a more inner and subjective relation to the divine—a relation devoid of such objective foci.

The dialogue begins from Allama's first encounter with the silent Animiṣa.

Allama Prabhu Visits Animiṣa's Cavern

The issue of whether or not one needs a *guru* for assistance in progress on the path of spiritual attainment presents itself early and often in the *Śūnyasaṃpādane.* Already the issue is addressed in the first chapter which finds Allama Prabhu wandering about in search of spiritual insight and understanding.

It seems to have been Allama's initial assumption that alone he was not adequate to the task of acquiring that insight. For that reason he sought a teacher. Though he had already proved himself an accomplished *śaraṇa* when he taught to the gardener Goggayya the necessity of internal spiritual cultivation,[17] Allama was unable perfectly to follow his own advice. He continued to seek a teacher who could objectify spiritual knowledge for him and who could provide assurance to him of his own progress in attaining that salvific knowledge.

Having stumbled upon the cave of Animiṣa, the Unblinking One, Allama rushed to grasp the *guru's* feet and to secure the *guru's* blessing upon himself. Perceiving the possibility of attaining the Lord's grace from this objectively present source, Allama effusively praised this 'treasure trove' of salvific power.

> Like a long-sought-after vine, on the leg now entwined;
> Like an object long sought, now to hand being brought;
> Like a penniless beggar, stumbling onto great treasure;
> Coming, searching, and seeking, onto pure consciousness
>   peering,
> I behold my Lord of Insight.
> With my outer and inner, bathed in supernal splendour,
> I behold the Light of all Light.
> Contemplating upon his palm the object which has no form,
> I behold my Master beyond norm.
> O Lord of the Hidden Caverns.
>
> —Allama Prabhu[18]

In rather concrete, bodily images of legs and hands, Allama celebrated the reassuring embrace of the vine wrapped about him like the supportive arms of his *guru* affirming his state of grace. He compared that wonderful teacher to a desired object and even to material treasure. The individual's quest for spiritual attainment lay not within himself but within the location, recognition, and veneration of this external assistant—this great treasure. Having found that external assistant, Allama rejoiced.

Allama's hopeful joy proved misplaced, however, as the perfect *guru* sat unmoving and unblinking and made no acknowledgement of his eager pupil. Unable to obtain objective verification of his worthiness for salvation from this taciturn master before him, Allama was chagrined.

> ...
> Visible to the eye;
> Elusive to the touch;
> Receding as you advance;
> Close if you possess.
> ... —Allama Prabhu[19]

The non-objective, non-tactile nature of grace began to dawn upon Allama as he noted its elusive, receding/advancing quality, but he nevertheless continued to perceive beatitude as objectively 'visible to the eye'. Ardently hoping for some objective sign from Animiṣa that grace and salvation were his, Allama stood in awesome observance of the *guru's* every feature. Perceiving no indication that an outward sign of his soteriological status was forthcoming, Allama fell into despair.

> The *guru* still and taciturn, asked to share his wisdom,
> Does not reply in return; addressed, he does not listen.
> Whatever at all can I do, O Lord,
> In this meeting of deaf with mute?
> ... —Allama Prabhu[20]

What disturbed Allama about Animiṣa's inactivity was that it provided no assurance about his own soteriological status and the worth of his spiritual attainment. He had found the perfect *guru* and sat at that one's feet, but no action and no answer were forthcoming. Without some external assurance of his attainment. Allama could not rest. Eventually, however, he began to discern that such objective attainment of spiritual perfection and objective verification of that attainment could not rightly be expected. He was being offered an even greater gift—a subtle and inner knowledge of the Lord's grace. Foregoing the images of the gross senses, such as touch and sight, Allama turned to the subtleties of fragrance to express this non-objective and interior experience of the Lord's gracious person.

> ...
> My knowledge dwells fragrantly inside;
> It's diluted when turned to the outside.
> What could be apt simile
> For this novel unity?
> Without merging my Self into you,
> There would be irredeemably two.
> O Lord of the Hidden Caverns.
> —Allama Prabhu[21]

He discerned that true beatitude lay not in receiving blessings and instructions from a teacher outside himself but within the inner confines of his own heart. Only by realizing that there existed no real distinction between himself as ardent seeker and Animiṣa as accomplished teacher did he come to share in that *guru's* wisdom and spiritual perfection. Thus in the "inward sympathy" of silence Allama overcame all sense of duality between himself and his *guru*. In utter humility he begged the *guru* to become the very breath within him and the director of his inner will.

> If I am your pupil, and you are my Master,
> Destroy the works of my body,
> Expunge the taint of my senses;
> Clothe yourself in my limbs,
> Empty yourself in my breath,
> Lose yourself in my will!
> Come to my palm as a grace healing balm,
> O Lord of the Hidden Caverns.
>
> —Allama Prabhu[22]

Then with plenary joy, as all sense of master and disciple, of outer and inner, and of superior and inferior melted away, Allama exulted in the complete subjective identity between himself and his *guru*.

> For the camphor which has burned in the fire,
> For the salt which has dissolved in the water,
> For the pupil who has entered the *guru*,
> Can there be any further action,
> Any subject-object distinction?
> O Lord of the Hidden Caverns.
>
> —Allama Prabhu[23]

It is noteworthy that Allama's primary image here is one drawn from the ritual worship most common in Brahmanical practice— the offering of libations and other substances into the fire. He compares the merger of the pupil into the *guru* to the sacrificial act in which camphor disappears in the sacred fire. The subsequent indistinguishability of the camphor and the fire in the fragrant smoke recalls to mind the indwelling fragrance with which he earlier compared the true knowledge of student and *guru* as a unity without differentiation. It is this non-quantifiable, non-objective nature of the Lord's grace which Allama learns to understand and appreciate through his contact with Animiṣa.

This same interpretation of efficacious ritual as an inner and subjective event underlay Allama's understanding of another objective focus of Liṅgāyata practice—the *liṅga* on Animiṣa's palm. Allama did not reject the worship of *liṅga* outright. He felt that *liṅga* worship was indeed a useful and desirable activity, but only under certain specific conditions—namely purity and perfection of inner intent. He could, therefore, desire investiture with the objective *liṅga* resting on Animiṣa's palm, but not without reservation.

Touching *liṅga's* toe
At morning's first glow,
Greeting Śiva's own
In the early dawn,
This is the fruit of life—
Such is scripture's advice.
I do not care for
Those who would ignore
Our Lord of the Hidden Caverns.

—Allama Prabhu[24]

Advising daily veneration of the *iṣṭaliṅga* as both a scriptural requirement and a fulfilment of life's very purpose and going so far as to express his disapproval of those who failed to worship *liṅga* regularly, Allama seemed to accede to the view that life's very purpose was worship of *liṅga*. Allama, however, was not content with that simple view of *liṅga* worship's efficacy. He felt that something more than the external ritual of worshipping *liṅga* was required. Without an intense purification of one's inner being and a dedication of the very Self to the higher purpose symbolised by *liṅga's* metaphysical connotations, *liṅga* worship would be but an empty show.

Hearing the claim,
'I am a *bhakta*;'
Seeing the same
Worshipping *liṅga*;

I am amazed
Unless he has razed
The taint of earth,
Of fire and wind and water,
Of sun and moon and ether,
Of the very Self,
O Lord of the Hidden Caverns.
—Allama Prabhu[25]

Allama's provisional allowance of a place and purpose for *liṅga* worship required that that worship be more than mere external ceremony. In fact, the external ceremony could be seen as wholly inappropriate unless it was accompanied by that inner intent and inner preparedness. Allama's reservations extended beyond *liṅga* to the other objective foci of Liṅgāyata worship.

Realizing the wholly inner nature of salvific grace and the utter uselessness of seeking that grace through external persons, action, or object, Allama went so far as to reject all the aids to faith commonly valued by Liṅgāyatas. Neither *mantra*, *vibhūti*, *pādōdaka*, *dīkṣā*, nor *iṣṭaliṅga* was needed when the full presence of the spiritual master was perceived to be within oneself.

If the unseen *guru* comes into sight,
Prayerful petition you need not recite.
You need not touch hand to head;
Holy ash you need not spread;
Nor holy scripture need be read.
The holy shower need not take place,
For here is *liṅga* without rite,
Here is bondage without bite.
Make me able to accept your grace,
O Lord of the Hidden Caverns.
—Allama Prabhu[26]

In Allama's encounter with Animiṣa, several factors acquire prominence. First, while it is true that Animiṣa himself served as the objective focus of Allama's meditative experience, it must be noted that nothing which Animiṣa did or said in any way contributed to Allama's soteriological experience. The entire process of learning, growth, ego disintegration, divine reintegration, etc.

took place wholly within Allama's own person. The *guru* before him did nothing to facilitate that process and in no way acted to validate that experience or to provide assurance of its efficacy.

Allama himself was not unaware of the significance of this experience. From this powerful experience of the Lord's grace as something which overwhelms from within rather than being obtained from without, Allama developed a radically subjective view of the soteriological process. Henceforward, whenever he was able to insert himself into a debate over the role of external aids or aides to faith, he unfailingly rejected the necessity and even validity of external, objective agents in favour of simple, inner spiritual experience.

Basava Unwittingly Initiates Cennabasava

In each of his encounters with other spiritual seekers, Allama Prabhu took a relatively consistent position that the external *guru* and the objective *liṅga* were of little spiritual value. The internal, subjective awareness of the Lord's grace wholly superseded the need for any external assistant or assistance. It would be a mistake, however, to think that Allama's was the only, or even the triumphant, position advanced in the *Śūnyasaṃpādane*. Other *śaraṇas* saw the role of the *guru* and the function of the *liṅga* in an entirely different light, and they did not all suffer the fate of Muktayyakka in their argumentation.

Two relatively independent views of the *guru* and his role in the soteriological process were advanced, defended, and preserved by Basava and by his young nephew Cennabasava. Cennabasava's view, in almost diametrical opposition to Allama Prabhu's, emphasized the absolute necessity of initiation at the hands of an accomplished master. That master, as the divine incarnate in human form, was worthy of homage and veneration, and he alone was capable of communicating salvific grace to the devoted layperson. Basava's view was a much less radical challenge to Allama's. He certainly saw the value and need for assistance in glorifying the Lord, but he could not affirm the inescapable necessity for an objective assistant. Certainly, he could not acquiesce to the demand that he himself provide that assistance, for he was acutely and humbly aware of his own inadequacies. In the debate between these two figures, their respective views of the *guru* clearly emerge.

Cennabasava's insistence that Basava perform the initiation ceremony for him was based upon his general conviction that the *guru* was the Lord incarnate and his specific belief that Basava was such a *guru*—Lord Kūḍalacennasaṅgama in human form. He explained the process of the Lord's incarnation and the objectification of the Lord's salvation through various physical agencies, and he continued by identifying that *guru* form specifically with Basava.

> The Lord (Hara), thinking,
> 'I should make my form manifest,'
> Came to earth in the *guru's* dress.
> For the mind, he became word;
> For the body, he became food;
> As *liṅga* he came to the palm;
> As *jaṅgama* the breath became calm.
> In these four ways,
> Basava himself displays
> Our Lord of the Lovely Waters.
>
> —Cennabasava[27]

He indicated that the devotee gained simple and straightforward spiritual benefit from reliance upon the *guru's* spiritual superiority. In fact, by homage to the *guru*, specifically to *guru* Basava, he (Cennabasava) had gained release from the bonds of *karma* and the cycles of rebirth.

> Having honored the blessed feet
> Of the glorious master,
> The bonds of existence fall away.
> *Guru* is refuge;
> *Guruliṅga* is refuge;
> *Guru* Basava is refuge.
> From him did that *liṅga* issue
> Which eluded Brahmā and Viṣṇu,
> And is called Our Lord of the Lovely Waters.
>
> —Cennabasava[28]

From the above two *vacanas*, Cennabasava's view of the role and function of the *guru* begins to clarify itself. First, it is clear that the *guru* was a very present and objective manifestation of the Lord himself. Secondly, it appears that the Lord, through the *guru*, communicated his salvific power in several quite objective agents, including *mantra*, *prasāda*, and *liṅga*. Further, it is clear that Cennabasava perceived the actual and existent Basava to be just such a *guru*. He was not talking of some incorporeal process by which one gains salvific knowledge from other, more knowledgeable, persons. Rather he intended the actual veneration of the Lord himself present in the physical person of his *guru*, Basava. If nothing else, the objectivist images of earthly manifestation, sacred *mantra*, blessed offering, venerated *liṅga*, homage to the *guru's* feet, and the eminent *liṅga* make this actual physical intent clear in Cennabasava's utterances.

Basava, however, did not wholly subscribe to Cennabasava's perspective. He denied Cennabasava's request for initiation on two counts. First, Basava contended that whatever the merits of having an objectively present source of salvific assurance in the form of the *guru*, he (Basava) was not worthy to serve as such a teacher. He emphatically denied any ability to communicate in objective form the grace of the Lord.

> The men who were saved of old
> Themselves did save themselves.
> They have all reached union with the *liṅga* of Truth.
> To give others instruction is not my call.
> I have not done anything for them at all
> But live as servant to those who grasp the Truth.
> The immortal host will bear witness
> For giving grace I have no fitness.
> O Lord of the Meeting Rivers.
>
> —Basava[29]

Basava was especially aware of the intellectual brilliance of his young nephew and, therefore, was doubly disturbed at the prospect of serving as *guru* for one who was already so far advanced in the faith.[30]

Second and more importantly, Basava contended that Cennabasava's entire quest for a *guru* and for objective assurance of salvific standing represented as much Cennabasava's own soterio logical concerns as a genuine understanding of the Lord's salvific process. Specifically, Basava charged that *guru, liṅga, jaṅgama, prasāda*, instruction (*upadeśa*), and even Basava himself as exalted teacher were objectifications of Cennabasava's soteriological concerns. Unable to provide a genuine affirmation or denial of Cennabasava's own state of grace, Basava felt importuned by his nephew's demands that he do so.

> O Cennabasava,
> It's you who created *guru*;
> It's you who created *liṅga*;
> It's you who created *jaṅgama*;
> It's you who created *prasāda*;
> It's you who created *upadēśa*;
> It's you who set me up (as judge).
> I cannot assent;
> I cannot dissent.
> For that my witness is
> Our Lord of the Meeting Rivers.
>
> —Basava[31]

Contained within Basava's very challenge, however, is a clue to his position on the role of the *guru*, the necessity of initiation, and the function of sacraments. It should be noted that Basava did not utterly deny the efficacy of such external objectifications of the Lord's grace. In fact, having pointed out Cennabasava's role in establishing such objective means of attaining and being assured about salvific grace, Basava admitted that, while he could not honor that request from Cennabasava for *guru's* initiation, neither could he deny it outright. The narrative of the *Śūnyasaṃpādane* indicates that Basava indeed provided a rather veiled initiatory blessing to his nephew by taking the latter's *iṣṭaliṅga* into his own hand, noting that he did not know what to do with it, and returning it to his nephew's palm.[32]

Cennabasava certainly perceived this event to be the objective verification of his soteriological status and praised Basava's role in providing that external assurance of an internal reality. In fact, he suggested that Basava's role in that process was both important and valid despite Basava's own humble reticence.

...
If you do something, it is you who do it.
If I seize upon grace, it is you who give it.
If I give my *liṅga* into your hand
Saying, 'Here, fathom its characteristics!'
And you give it back again
Saying, 'I can discern no features on it!
'Go, give it to your Lord of the Lovely Waters!'
Still I receive the same grace from your honor.
...
—Cennabasava[33]

This contention of Cennabasava, that Basava's role as *guru* was valid despite reservations on his uncle's part, is capable of interpretation in two ways. On the one hand, it may represent a full objectification of the priestly office in which the *guru's* efficacious activities are independent not only of his actual skills and moral worth but also of his very intention to serve as a spiritual guide. Thus, neither Basava's abilities nor his intentions bear upon the soteriological formula. The mere act of receiving the *liṅga* into his hand and returning it to Cennabasava constitutes a wholly valid communication of grace from the office of the *guru* to the office of the disciple.[34]

A second interpretation is that which, in fact, was advanced by Cennabasava. He contended that the external ceremony was important, indeed crucial, for the certification of salvific status as it recognized and verified an already existing condition. The spiritual identity between the disciple and the *guru* was the essential element which made the external ceremony possible.

...
The knowledge that in me shines
Is the unmanifest *liṅga* in your heart.
The radiant *liṅga* that in you shines
Is the saving knowledge on my part.
Separating the one from the other,
You cannot tell a difference.
There's one *liṅga*, one teaching,
And one ritual performance.
How then speak you of nearer and further?
After giving me instruction initially
In my own inner nature,
How can you now say, Sir,

'I can't perform the act ritually'?
If you will initiate me,
I will do you proud;
The great host of the mortal world
Will applaud us out loud.
Look here, Basava, on this I have as my witness
Our Lord of the Lovely Waters.
—Cennabasava[35]

Cennabasava, in this way, introduced an appreciation for the non-objective, internal, spiritual nature of his relation to the Lord and to his *guru* Basava. On the basis of a subjective interpretation and appropriation of the *guru's* teachings and example, Cennabasava was led to know the Lord's power and grace. The objective ritual performed by the *guru* as an external sign of that inner condition was not a mere mechanical process by which substantial grace could be conferred but an outer sign or seal of an inner, subjective reality.

It must not escape attention, however, that Cennabasava in no way implied that the internal, subjective state itself could suffice without the external sign of its efficacy. The initiatory ritual performed by the external assistant may have signified an inner condition, but that condition without the ritual was insufficient and invalid.[36] The external ritual was not something separate from the inner state and, since it was not separate, it could not be foregone.

The objective, external nature of the ritual was highlighted by some of Cennabasava's own imagery. At least part of the benefit from the performance of the ritual by the *guru* was the praise, applause, and affirmation which could be expected from one's fellow worldlings. Clearly, for Cennabasava, the *guru's* performance of the initiatory ritual was an objective and visible sign of his soteriological status. It was so objective, in fact, that the external approbation of one's fellows could justify and legitimize the need for the *guru's* participation.[37]

As was characteristic of Basava's personality throughout the text, that great personage did not adopt a clearly delineable position in rejection either of Cennabasava's objectivist soteriology or of Prabhu's subjectivist one. With a sincere desire to remain on good terms with all and to learn whatever he could from his compatriots, Basava attempted to appropriate as much as possible from the positions of all his peers. Such is the case in the present instance. After having advanced a rather humble statement of the necessity for subjective knowledge of the Lord and having indicated Cennabasava's role in developing a more objectivist soteriology, Basava listened intently to his nephew's position and incorporated it into his own. His restatement of his understanding of the place of the external ritual in which he himself served as *guru* for his nephew provided a summary of Cennabasava's arguments as found suitable for and adopted by the less theoretically inclined Basava.

...
Before there was touch of my hand to his face,
Arguing that *guru* came after, disciple before,
Placing on my palm the *liṅga* called Lord,
He caused me to grant him salvific grace.
Our previous encounter to me having shown,
Cennabasava took me for his very own.
O Lord of the Meeting Rivers.

—Basava[38]

While this *vacana* represents Basava's restatement of Cennabasava's position, it should be noted that the emphasis has again shifted from Cennabasava's objectivism to Basava's less-than-strident subjectivism. While the *guru* role is no longer denied and the importance of *liṅga* and the laying on of hands is preserved, Basava has shifted the emphasis to the utter identification of Cennabasava with himself and the essential inter-penetration of the roles of *guru* and disciple. The objective assistance of the external teacher is not denied, but neither is that given a validity separate from subjective union of *guru* and disciple.

In like manner, Basava adopted neither extreme in his view of the role of the *liṅga*. Rejecting the radical subjectivism of Allama as well as the strident objectivism of Cennabasava, Basava diligently sought to understand the relation between the external symbol of objective grace and the internal state which necessarily accompanied an efficacious external symbol. This humble acceptance of the objective coupled with his genuine appreciation for the subjective led Basava to query his compatriots repeatedly about the nature of *liṅga* worship.

The nature of the bond between *liṅga* and *prāṇa*
I do not know.
The nature of the bond between the breath and sign
I do not know.
In bathing and feeding
The external sign,
Useless days are spent,
But no good is lent.
O Cennabasava,
Tell me how to set
My internal breath
Within our Lord of the Meeting Rivers.

—Basava[39]

Perceiving the uselessness of mechanically bathing an external sign of and source for saving grace, Basava nonetheless perceived that Cennabasava among others attributed great importance to such behaviour. In fact, Basava's own piety included a considerable component of devoted worship of the Lord in one concrete symbol or another. His quandary was the need to discern how the indispensable subjective component related to the objective *liṅga* worship and not the conviction or desire to demean external worship of objective forms.

Cennabasava, on the other hand, was less concerned with this subtle relation of external form and internal life-breath than with the transforming power which he had experienced in the external symbols. Referring to the initiation which he had received *in utero* from Basava, he proclaimed the salvific grace which he had received from that ceremony of initiation.

...
When you placed the ashen dressing
On my body still enwombed,
I received your finest blessing.
Now I, Cennabasava,
Am servant just to you,
O Lord of the Lovely Waters.

—Cennabasava[40]

Besides attesting his devotion to Basava as the master from whom he hoped to learn, Cennabasava praised his uncle's role in providing an objective measure of saving grace through the ceremony performed upon the enwombed embryo. The smearing of the holy ash upon the abdomen of the expectant mother was an objective and utterly external act which nonetheless, in Cennabasava's view, had the power to transform the soteriological status of the nascent human life there enwombed. Though the embryo was not capable of any mental intent in the initiation and though the holy ash itself never actually touched the embryo but only the mother's flesh, still the ceremony served to communicate a measure of objective saving power to the person who grew from that embryo.

Of course, even the objectivist Cennabasava would not argue that the ritual's efficacy was fully exhausted in its external performance. His present coming to a full understanding of the unity of symbol and meaning completed the soteriological process set in motion by the prenatal ritual. That ritual itself, however, had a force and power to set that process in motion and to impel Cennabasava toward spiritual understanding merely by its own communication of objective salvific potential. What was needed now was a ceremony in confirmation of the eventually perfected results of that embryonically received grace. In both cases, the external ritual itself had its own objective and independent soteriological efficacy.

The ability of the external symbol to transform the individual without his or her intention or even acquiescence was further praised by Cennabasava through allusion to a legend in which Basava, through the power of his piety, converted several spies who had put on the *liṅga* as disguise but were themselves non-Liṅgāyata agents of the king Bijjaḷa.

...
When you had declared,
'All who *liṅga* wear
Are one with the Lord,'
Bijjaḷa, the heretic,
As a test, played a trick.
Who but you could make
True *liṅga's* power take
On those who would feign
The *jaṅgama's* mien?
...
On this I have as my witness
Our Lord of the Lovely Waters.

—Cennabasava[41]

Though those who wore the *liṅgas* had no intention of becoming Liṅgāyatas and were, in fact, bent upon the destruction of the *śaraṇa* company, the mere fact that they put on the objective symbol of Vīraśaiva piety was sufficient to transform them. The power of that external symbol to convey objective grace from the Lord to them revealed their espionage, purged their ill-intent, and converted them to true *jaṅgamas*. Such was the power of the external symbol in Cennabasava's eyes.

Allama Prabhu is Kept Waiting by Basava

While Allama Prabhu and Siddharāma stood outside his residence awaiting proper reception, Basava remained inside worshipping the Lord in the form of *iṣṭaliṅga*. The situation posed a genuine dilemma for Basava whose ardent devotion more than once beclouded his efforts at systematic thought. On the one hand stood the *liṅga* as objective focus of worship; on the other, stood the equally objective religious specialist in the form of *jaṅgama* Allama. The *liṅga*, however, was inner in that it was hidden inside Basava's private chamber. Seemingly a more personal and subjective worship would focus on this private symbol. The *jaṅgama*, on the other hand, standing outside Basava's door and visible to the public, was outer and served a seemingly more objective focus of worship.

Basava, without any clear articulation of his reasons, continued to show a general preference for the inner and subjective as he continued his accustomed *liṅga* worship. Cennabasava, however, ever alert for a concrete source of salvific grace, perceived the newly arrived *jaṅgama* to be worthy of attention. In his view, worship of *liṅga*, however useful in ordinary times, paled beside the publicly objective *jaṅgama* outside the door. Compared to the fully objective Allama and the social ritual attendant upon an eminent *jaṅgama*, the simple *liṅga* must have appeared less useful in Cennabasava's soteriological quest. In any case, he readily advised Basava to leave off *liṅga* worship and to receive the *jaṅgama* at the door.[42]

Basava's rationale for rejecting Cennabasava's advice and continuing to concentrate on the *liṅga* while ignoring the great personage outside his door was that a perfect and essential identity existed between the object of worship (*liṅga*), the officiant of spiritual knowledge (*jaṅgama*), and the worshipper (*bhakta*).

Liṅga, *jaṅgama*, and *bhakta* were one in essence and all-pervasively present. Little profit availed from ignoring one in order to venerate the other.

> See, the body of a *bhakta*, the *jaṅgama* wears.
> See, the soul of a *jaṅgama*, the *bhakta* shares.
> *Bhakta* and *jaṅgama* in *bhakta* reside.
> *Jaṅgama* and *bhakta* in *jaṅgama* abide.
>
> ...
>
> The true *jaṅgama* can only signify
> One who's come, the *bhakta* to purify.
> Saying, 'I am Master of wealth, life, and pride,'
> Entering as Master where the *bhakta* abides,
> He accepts the *bhakta's* all—
> His body, his mind, and his soul.
>
> ...
>
> I am just the doorkeeper of the Master's house.
> I cannot keep him in; I cannot keep him out.
> O Lord of the Meeting Rivers.
>
> —Basava[43]

Again, something of the ambiguity in Basava's devotion to the Lord emerges from this *vacana*. Basava did not make a definitive, much less a systematic, statement about the objectivity or the subjectivity of salvific agency through either *liṅga* or *jaṅgama*. Rather, he first emphasized the subjective aspects of an identity between the seeker and the sought, the teacher and the taught. He moved quickly, however, to a definition of the religious specialist which emphasized that one's role in accepting all which the devotee had to offer and, from the outside inwards, purifying the devotee's nature. In the process, noteworthy was the continuation of a distinction between teacher and disciple in which the teacher clearly continued as "Master" over such objective factors as the devotee's wealth. Finally, Basava's whole-hearted but non-systematic devotion restated itself in his helpless plaint that he could not determine what was inside and what was outside anyway. In other words, whether the path to the divine be perceived as internal and subjective or external and objective was not an issue within the purview of Basava's power. His plain devotion to the Lord, whether through worship of *liṅga* or worship of *jaṅgama*, overcame the attempt to discriminate a systematic soteriology.

Eventually, however, persuaded by his nephew's arguments, Basava left off his *liṅga* worship and went to greet the *jaṅgama* at his door. Allama, unfortunately, was not easily to be pleased and rejected Basava's increasingly abject apologies. At first glance it appears that Allama's rejections arose from his pique at being ignored in favour of the *liṅga*. His comments, however, reveal a much less egotistical motive. Though Basava had come with profuse apologies, Allama perceived that these apologies grew out of a sense of external and objective propriety, which, insofar as they were motivated by Cennabasava's advice, they indeed did. Allama, therefore, attempted to deepen Basava's awareness of the utter identity between the objective and the subjective nature of the Lord's grace. Through a series of rejoinders he cleansed Basava's apologies of their externalism. Allama's definition of the true *jaṅgama* illustrates this heuristic motive.

> Who can tell the link of *bhakta* and *jaṅgama*?
> Handing over his wealth, his pride, and his breath,
> One should not think 'Now I am a *bhakta*'! ...
> That one is no true *jaṅgama*,
> Who, entering the *bhakta's* house,
> Receives homage to his feet;
> Who, from bodily desires,
> Eats delicious feasts;
> Who, from base and sinful greed,
> For alms does plead and plead and plead.
> If these are promptly given, obsequity he nurses;
> If these are not forthcoming, furiously he curses. ...
> O Lord of the Hidden Caverns.
>
> —Allama Prabhu[44]

Allama's rejection of Basava's apologies was predicated not upon a wound to his own pride but upon the apparent externalism of Basava's approach. Whereas, after debating the relative importance of the external *liṅga* and the equally external *jaṅgama*, Basava had attempted to dedicate all his belongings to the *jaṅgama* at his door, Allama insisted that merely handing over wealth and pride were still external acts designed to gain an objective measure of grace from the *jaṅgama* who accepted them. Allama's aim was to indicate a more fundamental identity of *jaṅgama* and *bhakta* in which the inherent dualism of Basava's initial dilemma—whether to remain inside worshipping the *liṅga* or to go outside to receive the *jaṅgama*—implied a choice between two, quite objective soteriologies. Allama's goal was to purge Basava of the externalism latent in either of his perceived options—*liṅga* worship or *jaṅgama* worship.[45]

Elsewhere, Allama went so far as to impugn the practice of *liṅga* worship altogether. Not only did objective, external worship fail to attain salvific grace for one, but also the very practice of ritual worship could itself lead to ever-deeper entrapment within the continuing cycle of rebirth and redeath.

> For the learned man,
> Worship of form is the seed of rebirth;
> Worship of *liṅga* is the seed of rebirth.
> *Jaṅgama* and *liṅga* merged become the breath.
> Therefore, under Basava's shelter
> I am protected,
> O Lord of the Hidden Caverns.
>
> —Allama Prabhu[46]

As the entire episode makes it clear, what bothered Allama was not Basava's failure to receive and honor him properly as a great religious teacher, but Basava's attempt to cut off the outer from the inner. By an idolatrous focus on the *liṅga* image within his chamber and the *liṅga* principle within his heart, Basava had shut himself off from the opportunity to grow in spiritual perfection. Holding the unpredictably dynamic *jaṅgama* principle at bay in the form of the itinerant Allama, Basava set up a dichotomy between the outer and the inner which Allama found spiritually unhealthy. The fault was not in worshipping or in failure to worship the wandering priest; the fault lay in holding the dynamic potential for inner transformation at bay.

Suitably chastised, Basava readily confessed the insincere facility with which he had proclaimed a philosophical identity of the static *liṅga* and the moving *jaṅgama* while maintaining a dichotomous notion of inner and outer—of self and other.

> Speaking to another, I proclaim,
> '*Liṅga* and *jaṅgama* are the same!'
> Having put on that show, I falter;

For inwardly I know I'm a liar.
Saying, 'I'm kinsman of both,'
Is a lie for which I'll burn.
O Lord of the Meeting Rivers.

—Basava[47]

Basava admitted that his initial defense of continuing to worship his *iṣṭaliṅga* was based upon an insincere rationalization. In some genuine way, *liṅga* and *jaṅgama* were the same and Allama had now revealed that sense more fully, but that identity was not one which could be adequately understood in purely intellectual terms. The dynamic potential of the *jaṅgama* to call unexpectedly at one's door and upon one's heart created a transforming experience which went far beyond intellectualization. Basava's initial attempt to hold that dynamism outside reflected his imperfect realization of the identity of inner and outer spiritual agency.

On the basis of their continued dialogue, Basava eventually came to share Allama's views on external worship of an objective symbol. He then condemned the external objectivism of his erstwhile worship and the sham which his objectivist piety had been. Rejecting the eightfold worship (*aṣṭāvaraṇa*) and the sixteen forms of service, he lamented his inability to cast his joy and his sorrow upon the non-objective and incomprehensible grace of the Lord which lay within rather than upon the objective and controllable forms of external piety.

Like a laborer impressed,
Who never knows his master,
I perform the eightfold worship;
I do the sixteenfold service.
Not knowing to cast my joy upon the Living Lord,
I am an empty ritualist;
Not knowing the fixed from the moving,
I am a lowly priest for hire.
I am but a shameless deceiver
When I claim as my very breath
The Lord of the Meeting Rivers.

—Basava[48]

It was not only that *liṅga* had a rather partial and conditional efficacy as an object of worship but also that the very worship of *liṅga* itself was a hindrance to full realization of the essential unity of one's inner nature with the divine nature. Far from enjoying even a limited efficacy in securing salvation, the *liṅga* as an object of worship could actually hinder one's soteriological quest. Worship of the external, objective *liṅga* could actually be a contributory factor in entrapping one in a repetitive cycle of birth. The performance of ritual worship would lead to the continued accumulation of karmic merit, and the consequential execution of that merit would necessitate continued worldly lives.[49] Only when one's very self could be seen as identical with the cosmic metaphysical principle of the static and the dynamic absolute could one escape that cycle of rebirth.

Cennabasava Accuses Allama Prabhu of Guru-murder

It should be obvious from the foregoing that Cennabasava's attitude toward the role of the *guru* was quite different from Allama Prabhu's. That difference existed not so much at the philosophical as at the practical level. Cennabasava, like Allama, could argue for the metaphysical identity of master and disciple, but he, nonetheless, insisted on the propriety and importance of homage paid by the disciple to the *guru.*[50] Despite occasional intimations of a philosophical monism, the overall import of Cennabasava's declarations was that the *guru* remained an important focus for homage and for dedicated service by the devotee as one who followed prescribed practices dedicated to the Lord. Besides the inherent dualism implied in the sense of service to the Lord, Cennabasava's objective understanding of the salvific process required that he perceive his rescue as arising from his supplications and homage at the feet of his two *gurus*—Basava and Allama Prabhu.

Unable to abide Cennabasava's preservation of a practical dualism and an objectively available source of salvific grace in the person of the *guru* even within the context of vaguely monistic pronouncements, Allama Prabhu directly challenged the genuineness of Cennabasava's experience and understanding of unity. So long as a reliance on *liṅga* and *jaṅgama* remained in Cennabasava's descriptions, Allama harbored suspicion about Cennabasava's accomplishment.

Becoming bereft of body
While living on *liṅga*,
What is the use?
Performing selfless service
While leaning on *jaṅgama*,
What is the use?
As long as you think
I and thou distinct,
As long as you perform
Rites to the *jaṅgama* form,
There remains a sense of two
In the *bhakti* that you do.
O Lord of the Hidden Caverns.

—Allama Prabhu[51]

The seemingly subjective efforts to discard attachment to one's body and to engage in service of the *śaraṇas* were, in Allama's eyes, not so subjective after all. The performance of service and the display of homage to the objective human teacher betrayed an ineradicable sense of servant and served. For Allama, this lingering sense of the objective reality of beatific potency in the human *jaṅgama* mitigated any true experience of the Lord's wholly present grace within one. Any reliance on external sources of objectively communicated grace was, perforce, a reliance on some duality distinct from the devotee's own inner spiritual resources. Such reliance impugned the full import of genuine devotion—the inner identity of the devotee and the Lord of the universe.

For Cennabasava, however, an experience of grace which had no objective component would be no experience at all. He did not feel that reliance on an external *guru* in any way lessened the intensity and veracity of his knowledge of the Lord. In fact, he praised and rejoiced in his own embodiment which permitted him to know the Lord through such objective symbols as *liṅga*, *prasāda*, and *jaṅgama* and through those to obtain a concrete verification of his soteriological standing.

Because of the body, one sees the *liṅga*.
Because of the body, one sees the *jaṅgama*.
Because of the body, one gets the *prasāda*.

Because of the body, I have seen you,
O Lord of the Lovely Waters.
—Cennabasava[52]

In reply to Allama's challenge that there was no use in trying to escape embodiment while relying upon *liṅga* and *jaṅgama*, Cennabasava concurred. He added, however, that it was precisely because of the availability of the Lord's saving grace through such objective agents that embodiment was to be celebrated and enjoyed. The embodied devotee certainly had available to him or her equally embodied and objective foci of devotion and conduits of divine grace.

In fact, Cennabasava pressed his point further and directly, indeed rudely, challenged the legitimacy of Allama's claim to have received salvific knowledge and proper initiation without the agency of a human *guru*. He went so far as to accuse Allama of violence and harm toward Animiṣa inasmuch as the latter immediately departed from worldly form after Allama had attained self-initiation in that one's presence.

Without a *guru*
Wherefore is there *liṅga* for you?
You killed your master;
Thereby did the *liṅga* come through.
Now this understand:
Animiṣa became your *guru*.
All the three worlds know
'Prabhu breaks his vow!'
O Lord of the Lovely Waters.
—Cennabasava[53]

Cennabasava denied the possibility that Allama had received proper initiation through entirely internal and subjective means. Though Allama was unwilling to admit it or unable to recognize it, he had indeed an objective master—Animiṣa—who had communicated to him a quite physical sign of the Lord's grace—the *liṅga*. The fact that Allama, immediately subsequent to that event, had denied the *guru's* agency in that initiation did not, for Cennabasava, alter the essentially objective nature of the event. Allama's witting or unwitting destruction of his *guru* in that initiatory moment was only complicated by his heinous denial of the *guru's* critical role in the initiation.

In response to Cennabasava's direct challenge to his interpretation of the events surrounding his initiatory experience, Allama made a small capitulation to his challenger's position. He presented his understanding of the role which the objective *guru* and *liṅga* played in his own acquisition of salvific knowledge.

> After the breath of the *guru*
> Became dissolved into *liṅga*,
> That *liṅga* came to my palm.
> See, on my palm
> Is my *guru*, Animiṣa!
> See, in my knowledge
> Is my *guru*, Animiṣa!
> See, before my eyes
> Is my *guru's guru*, Basava.
> Look here, Cennabasava,
> I have done no harm to my *guru*.
> On this I have as my witness
> Our Lord of the Hidden Caverns.
>
> —Allama Prabhu[54]

Here Allama did not deny the potency of the objective *guru* altogether. It was not the actual physical teacher, however, which was important for Allama but the presence of the *guru's* teaching, protection, and spiritual power within Allama's present experience. The embodied teacher had passed into concrete but abstract form in the *liṅga*. Thereby the teacher had come to Allama's palm, but, more critically, he had actually come to Allama's mind as knowledge. In fact, Allama could continue to acknowledge a *guru*, who stood in Animiṣa's spiritual lineage, in the person of Basava. In spite of this rhetorical submission to Cennabasava's position, however, Allama was able to persist in his contention that what was critical was not the external symbol of the Lord's grace but the direct and inner knowledge which each *bhakta* must carry alone and unassisted within himself of herself.

Indeed, Allama could go so far as to demean knowledge which had to be gained from the external teacher. A more genuine knowledge lay within the devotee if only he or she could recognize it.

Knowing knowledge produced by *liṅga* is not real knowing;
Knowing knowledge produced by *guru* is not real knowing.
Thinking, '*Liṅga* is produced by *guru*', is sheer fantasy.
There is no Self but the Self!
But without destroying all one's dependency,
One cannot become one's true Self.
Learn that, O Cennabasava,
About our Lord of the Hidden Caverns.

—Allama Prabhu[55]

As usual this reply by Allama insisted on the unaided, non-objective attainment of inner grace. He rejected the veracity of knowledge which was gained through such external means as the contemplation of *liṅga* or the teaching of a *guru*, and insisted instead that saving knowledge must come to oneself through oneself. Even when confronted with a direct challenge to the legitimacy of his spiritual attainments, Allama's ultimate response was this characteristic rejection of any valid source of salvific knowledge which depended upon external or objective aids, such as cult objects and priestly specialists, could one ever hope fully to know the true nature of one's Self and only such Self-knowledge was soteriologically valid.

The requirement for that supersession of external aids is illustrated by another of Allama's pronouncements wherein he indicated the unpleasant side-effect of reliance on external aids to faith—continued bondage to the world of saṃsāric redeath.

Worldlings are caught in human suffering;
The gods are caught in divine pleasure;
Sages are caught in ascetic fervor;
Worshippers are caught in intimate union;
Rudra's host are caught in Śiva's heaven;
Liṅga wearers are caught in *liṅga's* string;
Those who rely on foot-water's grace
Return forever to birth's disgrace...
O Lord of the Hidden Caverns.

—Allama Prabhu[56]

Allama was not merely arguing for the inefficacy of external aids to faith; he was contending that any reliance on such external aids was itself an unenlightening and binding activity. Not only did he argue the binding nature of the Brahmanical rituals devoted to the Vedic gods and of yogic discipline, but also he insisted that the external, objective aids around which the Vīraśaiva cult was organized were themselves ensnaring and unenlightening devices. The *iṣṭaliṅga* about the neck was suspended by a noose which would ensnare and choke the devotee. The water from the *guru's* foot was not the nectar of liberating enlightenment but a draught of stuporous intoxicant for which the "morning after" consisted of continued rebirth and resuffering. Only through the full and inner knowledge of the reality symbolized by the external aids to faith could reliance on them cease and cyclical rebirth be escaped.

Siddharāma Objects Then Acquiesces to Initiation

The issue of whether or not Siddharāma must be initiated into the Vīraśaiva fold and be invested with the *iṣṭaliṅga* provides the clearest ground for debate about the value of objective sources of and signs of grace.[57] Siddharāma's highly visible and externalist activities in the erection and endowment of temples had earlier been attacked by Allama Prabhu, and Siddharāma had heeded his master's advice. In pursuit of a more subjectivist understanding of the faith experience, Siddharāma encountered a seeming anomaly within the Vīraśaiva tradition. If inner and individual experience was so crucial, why should Liṅgāyatas wear the outer tign of the faith—the *iṣṭaliṅga*? Beyond that, why should he, Siddharāma, be invested with the *liṅga* sign? Was it not enough that he had left off temple building and temple worship in favor of a more direct and inner piety? Why now revert to the objective externalism of wearing the *iṣṭaliṅga*?

O Prabhu,
Is *liṅga* body or a sign on the body?
Is *liṅga* soul or a sign for the soul?
Is *liṅga* knowledge or a sign of knowing's edge?
Liṅga as soul and soul as *liṅga*,
I do not understand.
Teach me the way that bodily form,
With *liṅga* in the hand, may be known to your soul.
Have grace for me,
O Lord of the Faultless Jasmines.
—Siddharāma[58]

Siddharāma had understood from Allama that the large, fixed *sthāvaralingas*, which it had been his wont to construct, were external hindrances to the genuine inner merger of the thing symbolized by the *liṅga*—i.e. the cosmic Lord—with the soul of the individual devotee. Having learned this valuable lesson from Allama, Siddharāma was now puzzled at that saint's suggestion that initiatory investiture with the small, stone *iṣṭaliṅga* would be of benefit. He requested to be told how that small, stone *liṅga* in the hand could be any more known to the soul than could the large, fixed symbols of his previous devotion.

Allama, of course, shared a position rather close to Siddharāma's and raised similar questions in the assembly of the *śaraṇas*. Cennabasava, not unexpectedly, accepted the challenge and defended the need to wear *iṣṭaliṅga*. His defense was not in support of the purely mechanical soteriological operation of external symbols, and he brought his philosophical sophistication to bear in explaining the essential identity of the individual's inner nature and the basis of cosmic ontology. In sum, however, Cennabasava's position reduced itself to a plain insistence that all who would be saved must wear the *iṣṭaliṅga* on the body.

> A kite, flitting in the sky,
> Must have the tethering guy.
> A hero one can never be,
> Unless one strives courageously.
> A buggy cannot roll a bit,
> Unless earth serve as road for it.
> Detachment just cannot be won,
> Unless one put the *liṅga* on.
> Prabhu, I must simply say,
> '*Liṅga* is the only way!'
> O Lord of the Lovely Waters.
>
> —Cennabasava[59]

Indicating his understanding that what was most important was not the *liṅga* itself but the inner self of the individual who wore the *liṅga*, Cennabasava compared that inner self to highly visible objects such as the colorful kite and the luxurious buggy. He carefully chose his examples, however, in order to illustrate that each of these items was useless without some relatively simple auxiliary object. Just as the kite needed the kite-string to make it fly, so did the faithful person need the holy Śaiva thread (*śivadāra*) about the body. Just as the buggy needed the earth to support it, so did the faithful one need the firm stone basis (*iṣṭaliṅga*) for his pious contemplations. Like the kite without a string or the cart without a solid road, the spiritual seeker without the *liṅga* would fall helpless into a quagmire of samsaric attachment to sensory illusions.

Allama was not convinced by Cennabasava's insistence on the absolute necessity of *liṅga* and restated his reservations on behalf of Siddharāma.

> Body has parts; breath has minute parts;
> Will is *liṅga* without parts.
> See, there's nothing save
> What has come, what is possessed, what is unified.
> After Śiva and Śakti's whole
> Become bodies and soul,
> What need could there be to know
> A sign separate from the Lord.
> O Lord of the Hidden Caverns.
>
> —Allama Prabhu[60]

Referring to the three types of individualized *liṅga—iṣṭa-*, *prāṇa-*, and *bhāvaliṅga* which reside on the body, in the breath, and in the will respectively—Allama indicated that these had no reality unless achieved and integrated into the very being of the person's individual self. Symbolizing this union in terms of the Lord as Śiva and the individual soul as His consort, Śakti, Allama indicated the supersession of external signs produced by a union of these two. To him, Cennabasava's talk of the utility, indeed the necessity, of a physical *liṅga* symbol upon the body betrayed a failure clearly to perceive this identical unity of universal absolute and particular soul.

Allama was not, on the other hand, blind to the vast importance which the objective *liṅga* sign had for many of his fellow *śaraṇas*. In fact, it was in response to their demand for an objective sign of inner grace that he finally advised Siddharāma to proceed with the initiation ceremony and to wear thenceforth the *liṅga* on his person.

So what? If a jewel is bright radiant,
It still must be set in gold shining band.
So what? If a fruit is juicy and sweet,
It still must hang from a fruit-bearing tree.

Therefore, if *liṅga* touches not
The palm's central spot,
There can never be knowledge's unity.
Therefore, touch with *liṅga* is *bhakta's* dogma for true purity.
O Cennabasava, let Siddharāma have *liṅga's* saving touch
As a pleasing salve for the popular mind of the *śaraṇa* band.
O Lord of the Hidden Caverns.

—Allama Prabhu[61]

Like the shining jewel or the succulent fruit, the *iṣṭaliṅga* was an important and highly visible object which would attract the attention of all people. For Allama, however, that jewel and that fruit were meaningless unless they were set in the proper context and provided with appropriate support. Likewise, the *liṅga* by itself had no genuine value or soteriological power; only the *liṅga* suspended from the nurturing limbs of the true devotee had such power. The value in contact with *liṅga* was only when that contact was a genuine and thorough-going contact with one's most inner nature. In the eyes of the *bhaktas* who constituted the *śaraṇa* band, however, *liṅga* as an external and visible sign was deemed important, and Allama acquiesced to their demands. It was not really for Siddharāma's benefit but for the benefit of the other devotees that Allama urged Siddharāma to forego his misgivings and consent to investiture with the *liṅga* at the hands of Cennabasava.[62] In that way, Prabhu affirmed the *liṅga* as an external symbol of one's inner state of grace, but he did not indicate the availability of objective grace through the *liṅga* object itself. He did not see that concession to worldly desires to be a potent source of salvific transformation.

The debate about the necessity of initiation for an accomplished *yōgi*, but non-Vīraśaiva, such as Siddharāma provides a wealth of data concerning the importance of the *liṅga* as an objective sign of grace bestowed by the *guru* and about the boundaries of the community of believers who could call themselves Vīraśaivas. The *guru* and the *jaṅgama*, as the agents who bestow an objective measure of grace and signify that bestowal with the *liṅga* emblem, are important to the debate raging around Siddharāma. The debate does, however, provide an opportunity for Siddharāma to state his views of *guru* and *jaṅgama* and for Cennabasava to clarify his views.

After the debate had been resolved and Siddharāma had been duly initiated into the Vīraśaiva company, that great *yōgi* was forthright and forceful in attributing his new-found non-dualistic knowledge and his inner beatitude to the initiation which he received from his *guru*.

> When the erroneous clause,
> 'This world and that are two,'
> Has been brought to pause,
> It is surely because,
> Having died at *guru's* arm,
> I am raised by five-worded charm;
> I have worshipped *liṅga* every way;
> I have worn beads and ash-mark everyday.
> After throwing burdens aside
> And making one from two,
> After breaking sin and pride,
> I became one with you.
> What then is this world; what is that?
> The limbs of the *bhakta* are body for *liṅga*.
> Where true *bhaktas* dwell, that is Rudra's land.
> When upon me fell the touch of *guru's* hand,
> All this came about.
> O Lord of the Faultless Jasmines.
>
> —Siddharāma[63]

For Siddharāma, the knowledge that there was no duality of this world and another and no duality of disciple and teacher came to him through a wholly objective process in which the exalted teacher, the *guru*, laid his hand upon Siddharāma's head, invested that disciple with *liṅga* and *mantra*, and gave him external, objective assurance of his salvific standing. Siddharāma's praise was not for the nature of non-dualist knowledge, but for the *mantra*, *liṅga*, *rudrākṣa*, *vibhūti*, and most of all, *guru's* gracious touch. Without that initiatory action by the *guru*, Siddharāma would not have obtained those objective signs of the Lord's saving grace and would not have had any inkling of non-dualistic consciousness.

Siddharāma's views on the nature and role of the priestly assistant are interesting in their own right, but for present purposes they appreciate in value by their relation to and reflection of the views of Cennabasava. In debating the necessity of initiation with Siddharāma and in explaining that ceremony after the fact, Cennabasava recapitulated his own views on the absolute necessity of the external *guru* who could communicate objectively quantified and signified salvific grace. Through the identification of the *guru* and *jaṅgama* with the other signs of grace—*liṅga*, *mantra*, *prasāda*, etc.—Cennabasava explained how a devotee such as Siddharāma could experience identity with the Lord.

> The Lord became *guru*; his wondrous form he showed.
> That *guru*
> Became *liṅga* on the palm,
> Became *mantra* in the mind,
> Became *prasāda* for the body,
> Became *jaṅgama* in the breath.
> Serene Siddharāma became one
> With our Lord of the Lovely Waters.
>
> —Cennabasava[64]

For Cennabasava then, the *guru* was indeed a wholly appropriate objective focus of veneration, for the *guru* was none other than the Lord incarnate. Whatever interiorization of divine grace into the life and breath of the devotee may have taken place was predicated upon the presence and actions of the external and objective source of the Lord's grace—the *guru*.

Cennabasava, of course, did not subscribe to a simplistic and mechanistic theory of the soteriological process. He saw that mere external penance and even *guru* veneration could be unefficacious unless accompanied by genuine experience of the Lord's presence.

> In the forest groves making penitential heat
> Until the end of time,
> Is that worth one day at the *guru's* feet?
> Serving the *guru's* feet until the end of time,

Is that worth one day's *liṅga* worship sublime?
Until the end of time, worshipping *liṅga's* stone,
Is that worth one day's inviting *jaṅgama* home?
Until the end of time, meeting the *jaṅgama's* wants
Is that worth one hour among your *śaraṇas*' haunts?
O Lord of the Lovely Waters.
—Cennabasava[65]

Cennabasava thus made even a brief experience of the Lord's presence superior to the empty and mechanical practice of objective ritual. It is worthy of notice, however, that the primary image which he chose for symbolizing the full presence of the Lord was again an objective one. Rather than ending with a plea for a brief, but genuine, inner experience of grace, he located genuine grace within the objective focus of the community of *śaraṇas*. In other words, to the extent that such objective means of grace as *guru* and *liṅga* were incomplete and were superseded by some additional element, that element was the community of believers, the company of the saints. The ultimate component in Cennabasava's soteriological scheme was, thus, a characteristically objective one—the Vīraśaiva community.

Basava and Cennabasava Pay Homage to Allama Prabhu

The reception of Allama Prabhu into the inner court of Basava's home at Kalyāṇa and his reception and veneration there by the host of *śaraṇas* provided a specific context within which reflection upon the role of the human religious specialist was in order. Bringing Prabhu into the court, establishing him upon an elevated seat, and paying homage to his feet, both Basava and Cennabasava expressed their interpretations of their actions.

Having first praised the Lord of his inner heart for coming in bodily form to his inner chamber, Basava described his own joyous worship of his illustrious *guru*.

Becoming delimited, the *guru* took form
And descended to the throne of alchemic stone.
I washed his lotus feet with water of pure bliss,
Annointed him with perfume sweet,
Offered him uncooked rice which the immortals eat,
Covered him with heart-lotus petals,

Censed him with fragrant knowledge,
Offered him devotion's sweet nectar,
Bathed him with unbridled pleasure,
Served him thrice-purified *pān*.
In total unity grace has come to me
From Prabhu the saint.
O Lord of the Meeting Rivers.
—Basava[66]

Again Basava's warm devotion was quite comfortable with an external expression of veneration and gratitude toward an accomplished saint of the Lord. None of Prabhu's insistence on subjective formlessness entered into Basava's *vacana*. The delimited human *guru*, sitting on a material throne, and being offered material sustenance and sensuous pleasures was, for Basava, a worthy focus of unashamed veneration. The nature of that veneration, however, should not escape attention, for it was with flower petals from the heart, fragrance from the mind, and nectar from devotion that Basava felt comfortable worshipping his *guru*. Furthermore, the grace which he felt that he had received was from total unity with that *guru*. It was not so much an objective grace somehow 'communicated' by the *guru* to the devotee as a shared subjectivity. Thus, while Basava's praise of Prabhu fully affirmed the propriety and efficacy of worship of the *guru* by the devotee, it, nonetheless, insisted that the grace attained by that worship was attained in inner and subjective identity with the *guru's* spiritual magnitude.

Cennabasava's praise of Prabhu, on the other hand, reflected a slightly more objective, though by no means mechanistic, process by which grace was obtained.

If I see *śaraṇas* who have you within,
Then constantly trusting, my mind bows to them.
If I should see such,
Compassion's nectar pours out upon me.
My lowly mind does, to their lotus feet.
Eightfold worship and sixteenfold service.
Seeing your *jaṅgama* Prabhu,
Ever worshipping him as you,

My mind never grows weary.
O Lord of the Lovely Waters.
—Cennabasava[67]

Cennabasava's view was by no means wholly externalistic or mechanistic. The worship which he gave was certainly accompanied by mental intent and, in fact, may have consisted of nothing except mental intent. Clearly he supported the necessity of the mind's bowing and of the mind's doing worship and service, but the image which he chose to express the communication of grace upon the devotee should not be overlooked. It was "compassion's touch" which would be "poured out" upon the devotee. Unlike Basava's emphasis on a shared grace through inner identity, Cennabasava chose the external image of touch and the pouring out of an objective quantity of grace to express the process by which the devotee received beatitude from the *guru*. This objectivist interpretation of the salvific process is consistent with that precocious nephew's perspective throughout the *Śūnyasaṃpādane*.

Nuliya Candayya Loses his Iṣṭaliṅga

The debate over the utility and necessity of the *iṣṭaliṅga* as an external source of objective grace came to a head in the story of Nuliya Candayya the rope-maker. As a pious Liṅgāyata, Nuliya Candayya unquestioningly wore the *iṣṭaliṅga* around his neck while he engaged in his daily labor. When the *liṅga* inadvertantly fell into the water while he was cutting reeds and Nuliya Candayya was faced with a choice between continuing in his dedicated labor or stopping the search for the small stone, he chose the former course of action. Reasoning that the stone *liṅga* merely symbolized an all-pervasive metaphysical reality, he arrived at the conclusion that the stone *liṅga* was quite auxiliary to genuine piety.

Where great *liṅga* goes
Is everywhere.
If doubt ever arose,
'Has great *liṅga* left,'
Could body survive
Of *ātman* bereft?
Look Maḍivāḷa,
While *jaṅgama* thrives,

No gap can arise
From our Lord of the Lovely Liṅga.
—Nuliya Candayya[68]

The omnipresence of *liṅga* in its cosmic, metaphysical sense, implied that there was no possibility of being separate from it. Beyond that, its indispensability meant that existence apart from it would be inconceivable. The very fact that the body continued to function and the person to perceive existence implied that one was not separate from the genuine *liṅga*. Separation from the small stone symbol aside, the genuine potency of the *liṅga* principle must still reside in one who continued to exist. The objective symbol was proved unessential by the very indispensability of genuine *liṅga*.

Cennabasava, predictably, could not abide this conclusion of Nuliya Candayya's argument. While recognizing the crucial subjective component of *liṅga's* power, he ardently insisted that, without the external *iṣṭaliṅga* symbol, the devotee's service and spiritual life would be in vain.

The *guru's* grace is *liṅga*;
Liṅga's truth is *jaṅgama*;
Yet this is outer practice.
Right knowledge of *jaṅgama*
Comes just from inner practice.

If body has no *liṅga*,
Jaṅgama will not receive
The service one freely gives.
Therefore, rejecting the one,
Relying on the other
It seems is rather like
Soul without body,
Śiva without Śakti,
Flame without a wick.
Can there be *bhakti*
Void of the body?
Born with deformity
Can one be the king?
Is one devotee
If he's void of *liṅga*?

No, he'll never see
True divinity!
O Lord of the Lovely Waters.
—Cennabasava[69]

Cennabasava's rather sophisticated philosophical understanding of the non-dualism of reality demanded that he recognize the necessity for inner culture before the outer symbol had any real meaning. It was not unusual for him as he did in this *vacana*, to insist upon the perfection of inner practice as the devotee appropriated the grace provided by the outer symbol. He could not, however, go along with Nuliya Candayya, Allama Prabhu, and others in dispensing altogether with the value and necessity of the external, objective symbol. Rather he insisted that the absence of the objective *iṣṭaliṅga* symbol rendered one incapable of true service and devotion to the Lord. Just as a physical impurity would make one unfit for rule, so would the absence of the *liṅga* make one unfit for true *bhakti*. The presence of that symbol might require a corresponding inner practice, but the absence of the external symbol was, in itself, a spiritually debilitating infirmity. The external symbol provided the opportunity for and the signification of a perfected inner spirituality.

In response to Nuliya Candayya's stubborn rejection of his lost *liṅga* and Cennabasava's insistence on the external symbol as essential to salvation, Allama Prabhu both stated what he saw as the appropriate role for the external *liṅga* and described the integral nature of external and internal when *liṅga* had been truly incorporated into one's being. In the first case, he advised Nuliya Candayya to put the *liṅga* on, not because of its own potency in providing objective grace but because his recalcitrant rejection of *liṅga* revealed an even graver danger in idolatrous dedication to dedicated labor.

Unless the eyes see, mind cannot perceive;
When the mind perceives, feet may then proceed;
Unless the feet move, work is not achieved.
When I speak of feet, I mean your every act.
The deeds that you do are all *liṅga*, in fact.
Therefore, acting without the symbol
Is profanity, pure and simple.

O Candayya, take heed!
Purity one does need
For our Lord of the Hidden Caverns.
—Allama Prabhu[70]

Prabhu granted a provisional purpose to the objective *liṅga* symbol in that it helped one to focus one's eyes, one's mind, and one's every activity upon the reality of the Lord. His primary reason for advising Nuliya Candayya to put on the *liṅga*, however, was in order to avoid the subtler but equally pernicious idolatrous objectivism which Nuliya Candayya's strident rejection of *liṅga* implied. That objectivism further manifested itself in the value which Nuliya wished to substitute for *liṅga* worship—dedicated labor in a vocation as service to the Lord. The danger was that Nuliya Candayya would begin to think of that labor as something which earned him quantities of objective grace. Prabhu wished to avoid that Pelagian soteriology and, perhaps reluctantly, acceded to the common *śaraṇa* insistence on wearing *iṣṭaliṅga*.

Prabhu went on to make it clear that, whatever value resided in wearing the external *liṅga*, true salvific grace could be had only through an integral union of one's individual nature with the cosmic reality symbolized by *liṅga* and resident not in the stone *liṅga* but in the devotee's heart.

Corporeal *liṅga* is mental *liṅga*;
Mental *liṅga* is affective *liṅga*;
Affective *liṅga* is service to *jaṅgama*.
And what I call 'service' is partless true essence.
Once you know the true,
If one ask of you
What side you argue,
Then you ought to show
The partless essence true.
The sort of bliss one gains
When thus he takes the pain
Is truth without part
Which *liṅga* does impart.
O Cenna, explain to Candayya
About our Lord Gūhēśvara!
—Allama Prabhu[71]

The *iṣṭaliṅga*, *prāṇaliṅga*, and *bhāvaliṅga*—corporeal, mental, and affective *liṅgas* respectively—culminated in an understanding and experience of a single and indivisible true essence resident in the self and the cosmos. The fullest experience of that integral union with cosmic reality in the subjective individual was specifically the sort of experience which could be obtained through *liṅga*. It could not, however, be obtained simply from objective *liṅga*. Rather the *liṅga* principle had to be experienced by a full realization of one's inner integrity with the internalized *liṅga* itself; mere bodily *liṅga* was useless in providing this experiential realization.

Allama Prabhu Feasts Insatiably on Basava's Offerings

One of the *Śūnyasaṃpādane's* more dramatic illustrations of the Lord's absolute demand on the devotee's entire person was the feast at which Basava attempted to satiate Allama Prabhu's terrific hunger. After serving up course after course of food, Basava realized that only the whole and unreserved offering of himself would appease the Lord in Prabhu's form. Interestingly it was Cennabasava who suggested the total offering of subjective being to the Lord, again indicating that his characteristic objectivism was, by no means, an empty mechanicalism.

Within the context of that dramatic episode, each of these principal *śaraṇas* reiterated his view of the role of the religious specialist in the life of the devotee. Characteristically, Prabhu's statement deemphasized the external, objective *guru* and emphasized the internal, subjective identification of master and disciple.

Follow not the crowd in praising out loud
The touch of *guru's* hand.
It can't cleanse the fault in which had been caught
The invisible senses.
Smudging out a bit the senses' nonsense,
Writing *liṅga* writ,
Is within the reach of
Pupil, but not teacher.

Disciple without *guru*, *guru* without pupil,
Need no mutuality.
I say, 'O hail! All hail! O Cennabasava.'

He has attained unity
With our Lord of the Hidden Caverns.
—Allama Prabhu[72]

Perhaps in as direct language as he used anywhere, Prabhu here attempted to disabuse the listeners of their misplaced confidence in the *guru's* miraculous powers. Directly and forcefully he indicated that the touch of the *guru's* hand in the initiatory ceremony had no power to remove the fault of sensory involvement and entrapment in the world of ignorance, birth, and death. In fact, the ability to efface the marks made by the senses on one's inner subjectivity lay not in the hands of the *guru* at all. It was only the devotee himself or herself who could eradicate the senses' tyrannical control and become free to experience the '*liṅga's* writ'—the Lord's unconditioned and unconditional grace.

There was no need for mutual intercourse—adoration and dispensation—between the disciple and the *guru*. In the perfect identity of these two's inner, subjective natures the dualistic relationship of teacher and taught dissipated entirely. Prabhu's highest praise, not surprisingly, was reserved for those who realized that devotee needs no preceptor and teacher needs no taught. The *guru*-less disciple (*guruvillada śisya*) and the disciple-less guru (*śiṣyanillada guru*) were utterly beyond the dualistic relations implied by an objectivist soteriology.

Ever aware of the spiritual benefit which he had gained from Prabhu's teachings and, of equal importance, from Prabhu's presence as an objective embodiment of spiritual potency and concrete focus for devoted worship, Basava challenged his *guru's* current diminution of the importance of objective means to salvation.

Without regard for status, pretence, and class,
Entering them nonetheless,
Would you seek the greater?
Would you shun the lesser?
Having descended to the *jaṅgama* race,
Having inducted them into your grace,
There is no way to change what happened to occur.
How could you say things should not be as they are?
You have come wearing two faces—

One of form, one of empty spaces.
Now affirming the one, rejecting the other,
You are at fault, O Prabhu (my father).
O Lord of the Meeting Rivers.

—Basava[73]

Basava's argument was not, at heart, a theoretical one. He merely knew that he and others had received great spiritual benefit from the teaching and ritual activity which Prabhu had undertaken among the *śaraṇas* or *jaṅgamas*. His experience of that benefit was sufficiently transforming that he was unwilling to allow Prabhu any outright denial of the importance and efficacy of external forms and actions for conveying salvific grace. This attempt by Prabhu to deny his one face—that of form—as somehow invalid or, at least, less valid than the unseen, unformed, internal essence struck Basava as a repudiation of the genuine spiritual benefit which many of the *śaraṇas* had experienced by focusing their devotion on an objective form. Particularly, it struck Basava as a repudiation of the depth and genuineness of his own spiritual experiences in the presence of the Lord in objective form—the *guru*.

Cennabasava, as was usual, argued an even more important role for the objective human spiritual assistant. He felt that it was specifically from the surfeit of salvific grace attendant upon such exemplary *gurus* as Basava that one acquired his own soteriological standing.

No one at all do I see
Anywhere in the worlds three
Who knows the path of true *bhakti*.
If they worship just the *liṅga*,
They can't escape *saṃsāra*.
For, as you must know, the *liṅga*
Is simply the *jaṅgama's* face.
Bowing, offering, serving, one gets a divine share.
To the savour of his grace nothing can compare.
Accepting the grace of Basava's faith,
I am saved!

Therefore, the fame of the grace of Basava and Prabhu,
In the three worlds, grew and grew.
O Lord of the Lovely Waters.
—Cennabasava[74]

Again the non-dualism of Cennabasava's theoretical position displayed itself in his insistence on the inadequacy of devotion to the objective *liṅga* form. The purely external worship of the inanimate *liṅga* failed to recognize the true object of devotion and the actual source of saving grace. That true source was not, for Cennabasava, however, the inner subjective nature of the devotee. It was, rather, the equally objective and wholly present human assistant—in this case *guru* Basava. Through Basava's ardent devotion and unfailing service to the Lord in *jaṅgama* form, Basava had acquired a surfeit of the Lord's gracious merit far in excess of what was necessary for his own salvation. A lesser devotee, by devoted service to the human repository of grace—Basava, could acquire a share in that salvific stockpile. It was specifically by such a sharing in Basava's divine merit that Cennabasava felt himself to have attained soteriological standing. The efficacy of supererogatory grace from Basava and from Prabhu was precisely the component of the *śaraṇa* movement which Cennabasava felt contributed to its growth and fame in the world. It was because the other *śaraṇas* could share in a measure of that objective grace that Vīraśaivism could, should, and would spread and prosper.

Prabhu, of course, was little interested in these notions of supererogation. He maintained his insistence on the subjective quality of any saving knowledge.

The saint who knows himself
Does not need the six schools,
Does not need the three schools,
Does not need the written tools—
Veda, Śāstra, Purāṇa,
Hymnals, and dictionaries.
Because on their bodies
They wear no phylacteries—
Guru, liṅga, jaṅgama, prasāda, and *pādōdaka*.
Because they've come to unity
With the fivefold remedy—

Guru, liṅga, jaṅgama, prasāda, pādōdaka—
All creatures bow down;
All voices resound,
'Live thou evermore!'
All souls implore,
'Thy loveliness outpour!'
All fourteen worlds repeat,
'Victory, victory!' at the feet
Of your beloved Basava.
O Lord of the Hidden Caverns.

—Allama Prabhu[75]

In face of true knowledge of the Lord's saving grace within himself, Prabhu rejected the necessity of the classical philosophical schools of Brahmanical philosophy (the *darśanas*) as well as the standard sources of scriptural authority within those schools. His iconoclasm extended far beyond the devices of the Brahmanical tradition, however, and included the fivefold worship of Vīraśaivism. Those saints to whom the world should show respect and from whom others might gain beneficence were, in Prabhu's view, precisely the ones who had realized an inner identity with the symbolic devices of sacramental worship. The image of the fivefold worship could be retained as could the image of offering homage to the feet of Basava, but true spiritual attainment required supersession of these external symbols in favor of full and inner knowledge.

THE THREE VIEWS OF RITUAL WORSHIP

The foregoing investigation of the *Śūnyasaṃpādane's* ideals and attitudes toward the eightfold system of Vīraśaiva sacramental worship has revealed one rather clear result—no single view of the role and function of the eightfold worship held sway. Reflecting both its explicit character as an editorial compendium of the fifteenth century and its implicit similarity to other avowedly religious texts, such as the *Bhagavad Gītā*, in contradistinction to systematic philosophical treatises, the *Śūnyasaṃpādane* displays an irreconcilable diversity of opinions on the nature and function of objective aids to faith.

The full range of soteriological persuasions, ranging from utter and intense subjectivism to a thorough-going defense of objective acquisitions of salvific grace presents itself. The emphasis on inner transformation, on individual-cosmic essential identification, and on rigorous ethical voluntarism is balanced by an insistence that that transformation can be occasioned by external, objective events of which the beneficiary need not even be aware until after the fact, that that identification can never be allowed to blur the utter distinction between finite worshipper and infinite absolute, and that that rigorism pales beside the flow of objective salvation from the divine to the human. That both these perspectives present themselves within the text can hardly be gainsaid. That each perspective has its own proponents and defenders within the textual debate is the only-slightly-less-indisputable contention arising from the present investigation.

Allama Prabhu's View

The radical subjectivist perspective was most forcefully propagated by Allama Prabhu. He was able to muster a certain provisional recognition of the validity of objective ceremonies, but only insofar as these served to aid the less advanced in the faith to attain a true vision of the ultimate dispensability of such objectifications.[76] For the most part, Allama Prabhu was rather bold in rejecting any claims to salvific efficacy on the part of external ceremonies.[77] Unable to secure an objective sign of blessing from his *guru*, Allama Prabhu realized that the *guru* and the disciple are not separate anyway and therefore an objective sign would be superfluous.[78] Utilizing a standard *advaita* metaphor from the Upaniṣads, he argued that the identity of disciple and *guru* was like the irreversible dissolution of salt in water.[79] Because of that inner identity there was no need for external prayers, for the use of holy ash, for the reading and study of scripture, or for holy bathing.[80] The wholly inner identification of the finite devotee with the infinitude of the absolute was itself a subjective transformation of salvific import.

This attitude was summarized by one of Allama Prabhu's *vacanas* from the early portions of the *Śūnyasaṃpādane* and was recapitulated throughout the text.

> If the unseen *guru* comes into sight,
> Prayerful petition you need not recite.

You need not touch hand to head;
Holy ash you need not spread;
Nor holy scripture need be read.
The holy shower need not take place,
For here is *liṅga* without rite,
Here is bondage without bite.
Make me able to accept your grace,
O Lord of the Hidden Caverns.
—Allama Prabhu[81]

When the full presence of the spiritual master was perceived to be within oneself, neither *mantra*, *vibhūti*, *pādōdaka*, *dīkṣā*, nor *iṣṭaliṅga* was needed. This experience of the Lord's powerful grace was something which overwhelmed from within rather than being obtained from without. Having developed this radically subjective view of the soteriological process, Allama Prabhu henceforward consistently rejected the necessity and validity of external, objective agents and unceasingly defended the essential efficacy of direct and inner spiritual experience.

Cennabasava's View

The explicitly objectivist perspective was most boldly advanced by Cennabasava. Admittedly, his philosophical interpretation of the nature and operation of the soteriological process tended to utilize *advaita*-type identifications of subjective and objective realities,[82] but the very attempt to evolve a consistent philosophical explanation of the sacramental system's operation betrayed a concern for an objectified and rationalized soteriology rather than a reliance on the subjective transformation wrought by spiritual experience. For the most part, Cennabasava was rather bold in advancing and defending the claims for salvific efficacy resident in external ceremonies. He interpreted Basava's initiation ceremony as a genuine and efficacious external ceremony which provided him with salvific status.[83] He never tired of praising the *guru* who and who alone could provide grace to the devotee.[84] That grace could be communicated in a variety of ways—prayers, initiation ceremonies, wearing the holy ash, ritual bathing, etc.[85] The gracious salvation which one could obtain in objective quantities from the *guru* through these various sacramental means was the sole saving grace.

Cennabasava's attitude was summarized in one of his *vacanas* from the *Śūnyasaṃpādane.*

The Lord became *guru*
His wondrous form he showed.
That *guru*
Became *liṅga* on the palm,
Became *mantra* in the mind,
Became *prasāda* for the body,
Became *jaṅgama* in the breath.
Serene Siddharāma became one
With our Lord of the Lovely Waters.
—Cennabasava[86]

Cennabasava expressed a sophisticated and systematized understanding of complex philosophical doctrines which culminated in an advaitic union between the seeker and the sought. Unlike Allama Prabhu, however, Cennabasava did not carry that philosophical non-dualism to an outright rejection of objective sign and external ceremony. On the contrary, he emphasized the specifics of the ceremonial cult and interpreted those substances and personages to be of a single essence themselves. The non-dualism he proposed was one of purpose and essence for an objective cult, but that cult had an undeniable efficacy and necessity. In contrast to Prabhu's rejection of external ceremonialism in favor of inner transformation, Cennabasava reemphasized the utility of the ceremony and of ceremonial substances in an objective soteriological economy.

Basava's View

Imbued with a powerful and sincere desire to experience the Lord's saving grace in every corner of his limbs, Basava recognized the deficiency of any wholly objectivist practice. His longing for a full and genuine experience of the Lord rendered any sole reliance on an objectivist cult impossible.[87] At the same time, Basava was acutely aware of the benefits which he had received from other of the *śaraṇas*, and simultaneously his own inner joy at the Lord's presence demanded expression in the form of worshipful service to the divine.[88] Basava's attitude toward the value of an external cult of objective grace was, therefore, medial between the attitudes of Allama Prabhu and of Cennabasava. He valued external assistants in his own salvific quest and sought external forms to express his joyful spirituality, but he also demanded that that spirituality be genuinely transformatory of his innermost being.[89]

Even his rather poignant complaint against the vacuity of ritualism was not a rejection of ritual worship per se but an attempt to rid that worship of its mechanical hypocrisy and to imbue it with a pervasive inner spiritual intensity.

> Like a laborer impressed,
> Who never knows his master,
> I perform the eightfold worship;
> I do the sixteenfold service.
> Not knowing to cast my joy upon the Living Lord,
> I am an empty ritualist;
> Not knowing the fixed from the moving,
> I am a lowly priest for hire.
> I am but a shameless deceiver
> When I claim as my breath
> The Lord of the Meeting Rivers.
>
> —Basava[90]

Basava was not, however, of the opinion that the quest for inner spirituality and outer worship were antithetical. Once the genuine sense of inner spirituality had dawned, then the external cult became suffused with a glorious joy. The performance of ritual worship accompanied by genuine inner intent was both an opportunity for celebration and a means for the enhancement of that inner accomplishment.

> Becoming delimited, the *guru* took form
> And descended to the throne of alchemic stone.
> I washed his lotus feet with water of pure bliss,
> Annointed him with perfume sweet,...
> Offered him devotion's sweet nectar,
> Bathed him with unbridled pleasure,...
> In total unity grace has come to me
> From Prabhu the saint.
> O Lord of the Meeting Rivers.
>
> —Basava[91]

Basava's rejection of empty ritualism was clearly not a rejection of all ritual worship. Genuine, heart-felt service of the Lord was an opportunity and a pleasure which could be joyfully embraced. Requisite only was that that service be genuinely motivated by inner spirituality and not by ulterior motives and empty formalism.

Summary of the Three's Views

In fine, Allama Prabhu rejected the objective cult in favor of subjective spirituality; Cennabasava defended and propagated the objective cult as a valid means of attaining salvific grace; and Basava, disdaining the hypocrisy of empty ritualism, nonetheless rejoiced in the performance of genuine and heart-felt worship of the Lord through objective means.

NOTES

1. The *aṣṭāvaraṇa* scheme is described briefly and clearly in S.C. Nandimath's *Handbook of Vīraśaivism* (Dharwar: L.E. Association, 1942), pp. 54-64. Also of value is the Kannada celebration of the *aṣṭāvaraṇa's* greatness, the *Aṣṭāvaraṇagaḷa Mahatva* [Mailāraśaraṇaru racisīda] (Dharwar: Murughāmaṭha, 1971).

2. This classification is the present researcher's and is for purposes of analysis. The tradition itself recognizes a division into three levels of importance, as follows:

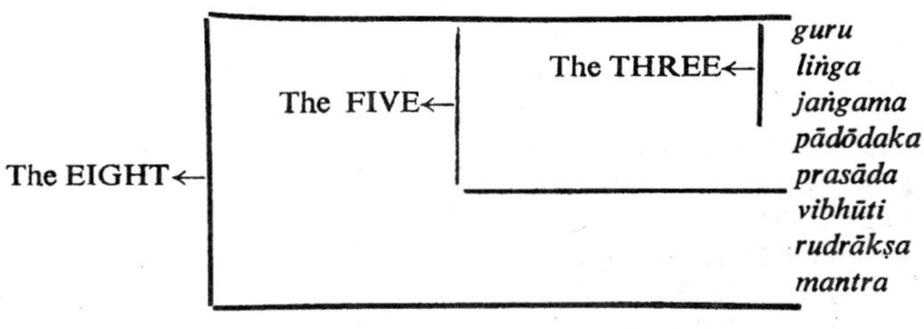

One contemporary Liṅgāyata gives her interpretation of the interrelations of the *aṣṭāvaraṇa*: "Guru, Liṅga and Jaṅgama are the worshipped ones; Vibhūti, Rudrākṣi and Mantra (the holy ash, Rudrākṣi beads and the sacred spell) are the means to win the revered one. The fruits that a worshipper gets in return for his worshipping them are Pādōdaka and Prasāda." See Māte Mahādēvi (née Ratnamma), *A Guide to Lingayatism* (Dharwar: Suyidhana Sugrantha Maale, Jaganmata Akkamahadevi Ashrama, 1973), p. 33.

3. A third title for a religious specialist is *svāmiji*. The *svāmiji*, though also celibate and often of a *guru* lineage, is chiefly characterized by his office as the

head of a monastery and spiritual guide for its members. See Māte Mahādēvi's *Guide*, p. 37. Clement Marro discusses the role of the *svāmiji* or, as he calls that one, the *sthira jaṅgama* in his "Role and Position of the Guru and of the Jangama in Lingayatism", *Bangalore Theological Forum* 6.2 (1974 July-December): 40-46.

4. A rough distinction is attempted by R.E. Enthoven at *ERE*, s.v. "Lingayats", p. 70. William McCormack has noted the variant patterns between northern and southern Karnāṭaka in his "On Lingayat Culture", in A.K. Ramanujan, ed. and trans., *Speaking of Śiva* (Baltimore: Penguin Books, Inc., 1973), p. 178. Again Marro's recent work illumines. He notes the crucial distinction by which the *guru* performs the initiation ceremony and then yields to the *jaṅgama* whose task it is to lead the initiate to utter release from worldly ignorance. The *guru* makes one a *bhakta*, but the *jaṅgama* makes that *bhakta* a *jñānin*, a *jīvamukta*. Finally, however, Marro assents that the distinction between the two is solely one of emphasis, not of substance. See Clement Marro, "Role of the Guru", pp. 32-39.

5. In theory, at least, *guru*-hood is not merely hereditary but also is an ethical, moral category. Thus Māte Mahādēvi asserts in her *Guide*, p. 37. In fact, heredity seems by far the most important determinant of priestly status.

6. The word derives, obviously, from the root *gam*. Ramanujan has developed the implications of that derivation in Introduction to *Speaking of Śiva*, pp. 20ff.

7. However, the existence of married, sedentary *jaṅgamas*, constituting an hereditary caste roughly identical to *gurus* is attested by Enthoven, *ERE*, "Lingayats", p. 70 and by McCormack, "Lingayat Culture", p. 178.

8. The literary tradition does not specifically argue for the idea of *ex opere operato*; individual Liṅgāyatas, however, will often scorn the private moral life of a *guru* or *swāmiji* but nonetheless point with pride to the good works accomplished by virtue of his office. The explicit Christian doctrine, dating from at least the thirteenth century, was formalized at Trent in 1547 and appears in *Concilium Tridentinum: Diariorum, Actorum, Epistularum, Tractatuum*, vol. 5, new collection, ed. Societas Goerresiana (Freiberg: Herder, 1964), p. 995, being document no. 395 in Session Seven entitled "Canones de sacramentis in genere".

9. A description of the *iṣṭaliṅga* as well as a picture of one is given by Swami Lingananda (né Sangamesh), *Emblem of God*. trans. S.M. Angadi (Dharwar: Suyidhana Sugrantha Maale, 1973), facing page 68.

10. The ritual of *liṅga* veneration is outlined, instructions are given for its performance, and chants to accompany it are provided by M.G. Nañjuṇḍārādhya, *Ṣaṭsthala Liṅgapūjāvidhi*, 2nd rev. ed. (Mysore: Prabōdha Pustakamāle, 1971).

11. Some of the *liṅga's* salubrious functions are presented in the primary textual defense of its veneration, the *Liṅgadhāraṇacandrikā*.

12. Lingananda has gone to lengths to demonstrate the abstract philosophical content of the *liṅga* symbolic category. See Lingananda, *Emblem*, pp. 16-41. The term's use within the articulated *ṣaṭsthala* philosophy also illustrates its non-concrete connotations. See, for example, Ramanujan's Appendix I to his *Speaking of Śiva*, pp. 169-174.

13. In fact, the case can be made that it is only when such specific terms as *iṣṭaliṅga* or *karasthalaliṅga* are used that the tradition refers to the concrete *liṅga* in the hand. The term *liṅga* itself may, most generally, refer to some abstract metaphysical reality. This contention is developed, at least insofar as it applies to Basava's ideas, by R. Blake Michael, " '*Liṅga*' as Lord Supreme in the *Vacanas* of Basava", *Numen* 29.2 (1982 December).

14. Vīraśaiva cosmologies utilize this valence of *liṅga's* meanings. A fine explication thereof appears as H.P. Malledevaru's *Essentials of Vīraśaivism* (Bombay: Bharatiya Vidya Bhavan, 1973).

15. In fact, the practice of counting the prayers of the Rosary on beads probably originated in India and spread into the Muslim and Christian worlds sometime around the eleventh century. The practice already was common to Śaiva groups in India prior to the rise of Vīraśaivism and is one more indicant of Vīraśaiva continuities with wider Indian practice. See Eithne Wilkins, *The Rose-Garden Game: The Symbolic Background to the European Prayer-Beads* (London: Victor Gollancz Ltd., 1969), pp. 31f. Also of value is Franz Michel William, *The Rosary: Its History and Meaning*, trans. Edwin Kaiser (New York: Benzinger Brothers, Inc., 1953).

16. *ŚS* —/ —/ Gum., introductory passages; pp. 3-4/ Gū., introductory passages; I, 49-54.

17. *ŚS* —/ —/ —/ Gū., 1:29; I, 76f.

18. *ŚS* Śi., 33/ Ha., 33/ Gum., 32/ Gū., 1:31; I, 80f. Compare also Basava's *vacana* at *ŚS* Śi., 877 or *BV* (K), 1178 which begins with the same image of the vine-entwined seeker.

19. *ŚS* Śi., 36/ Ha., 36/ Gum., 35/ Gū., 1:34; I, 83f. The translation is by Nandimath, Menezes, and Hiremath. The images of the entwining creeper from the previous *vacana* and the elusive object of desire in this one are combined in Jayadeva's lines:

When spring came, tender-limbed Rādhā wandered
Like a flowering creeper in the forest wilderness,
Seeking Krishna in his many haunts
The god of love increased her ordeal,
Tormenting her with fevered thoughts,
And her friend sang to heighten the mood.

See *Love Song of the Dark Lord: Jayadeva's Gītagovinda*, ed. and trans. Barbara Stoler Miller (New York: Columbia University Press, 1977), p. 74.

20. *ŚS* Śi., 37/ Ha., 37/ Gum., 36/ Gū., 1:35; I, 84f. The image of Animiṣa as the unspeaking tarbaby recalls the Buddha's Aryan silence on which Raimundo Panikkar has commented in *El silencia del Dios* (Madrid: Guadiana de Publicaciones, 1970), pp. 233-280. Such uses of silence force the seeker to rely upon his or her own inner devices for spiritual advancement rather than on another's merit. The use of silence as a meditative technique and also as a teaching device is discussed by Alice Borchard Greene, *The Philosophy of Silence* (New York: Richard R. Smith, 1940). Within the devotional tradition of India, it is Kabīr who most effectively and consistently utilizes the image of silence. He echoes Prabhu's experience when he mentions the radical muteness imposed on the believer by an encounter with the Lord's presence in the *guru*:

I became mute and witless/ and my ears no longer heard,
My legs became paralysed/ when the Satguru's arrow struck me.

See *Kabīr*, vol. I, trans. Ch. Vaudeville (Oxford: Clarendon Press, 1974). p. 154.

21. *ŚS* Śi., 37/ Ha., 37/ Gum., 36/ Gū., 1:35; I, 84f. Compare the Bengali hymn which ends:

I have neither knowledge/ Nor have I *yoga*;
I only follow the scent.
Ah, where shall I find Him/ To whom I have given my heart?

See A.J. Apasamy, ed., *Temple Bells: Readings from the Hindu Religious Literature* (Calcutta: YMCA Publishing House, n.d.), p. 33.

22. *ŚS* Śi., 40/ Ha., 40/ Gum., 39/ Gū., 1:38; I, 87f. Note the Sāṅkhya-Yoga like progressive withdrawal from actions, senses, mind, and intellect. The goal of the process for Prabhu, however, was not isolation of pure consciousness, but an emptying of the Self so that it could be refilled by the Lord's own presence.

23. *ŚS* Śi., 42/ Ha., 42/ Gum., 41/ Gū., 1:40; I, 90. In this *vacana,* as contrasted to the last one, the direction of merger is the merger of the pupil's nature into the *guru's*. Compare Kabīr's images of salt lost in flour and the moth burnt up in the flame at *Kabīr*, p. 157:

Kabīr, when I have found a perfect Guru,
the salt has vanished in the flour:
Caste, family, and lineage are no more,
what name then will you give me?
To find the Gurù is a great boon:
without Him, you are lost,
As the moth attracted by the lamp's flame
falls into it in full knowledge!

24. *ŚS* Śi., 57/ Ha., 268, 913/ Gum., 56, 476/ Gū., 1:58; I, 105. The morning worship of the Lord's image is described in similar phrases by Māṇikka Vāsahar:

Hail to Thee, treasure rare,/ Source of all prosperity,
Dawn has come, at Thy feet,/ Flowers themselves, fair flowers lay we.
Praising Thee, we await/ Smiles that blossom fair and sweet
In Thy face, as we fall/ Prone adoring at Thy feet.

See F. Kingsbury and G.E. Phillips, ed. and trans., *Hymns of the Tamil Śaivite Saints* (Calcutta: Association Press, 1921), p. 111.

25. *ŚS* Śi., 59/ Ha., 192, 271/ Gum., 58/ Gū., 1:60; I, 106f. Tirunāvukkarasu Svāmi begged for the ability to raze his attachment to the things of the world and to experience the Lord's true power at Kingsbury, *Tamil Hymns*, p. 67:

Immersed in painful cherishing/ Of child and wedded wife,
No room is there in me to feel/ Thy power, Lord of my life,
O whereunto came I to birth?/ To cherish this false world?
Or watch it, bubble-like, appear,/ Then be to nothing hurled?

26. *ŚS* Śi., 39/ Ha., 39/ Gum., 38/ Gū., 1:37; I, 86f. This rejection of external sacramental objects will be discussed in greater detail in a later section. Compare this radical Śaiva rejection of scripture and other orthodox authorities to the generally tamer Vaiṣṇava acceptance thereof. See, for example, *Gītagovinda*, p. 71:

For upholding the Vedas,/For supporting the earth,...
Homage to you, Krishna/ In your ten incarnate forms!

Also compare *ŚS* Śi., 61/ Ha., 272, 918/ Gum., 60/ Gū., 1:62; I, 108.

27. *ŚS* Śi., 252/ Ha., 318, 598/ Gum., 247/ Gū., 4:14; II, 45f.

28. *ŚS* Śi., 256/ —/ Gum., 251/ Gū., 4:18; II, 49.

29. *ŚS* Śi., 241/ Ha., 303/ Gum., 648/ Gū., 4:2; II, 28f. The translation of the first two lines belongs to Bhoosnurmath and Menezes. The remainder is an original effort by this researcher. Again a parallel passage which indicates the difficulty in locating a *guru* who is worthy and willing to initiate one occurs at *Kabīr*, p. 188:

Such a one cannot be found/ to give us initiation
and pull us out by the hair,/ as we sink in the Ocean of Existence!

30. Basava indicates as much at *ŚS* Śi., 243/ Ha., 305/ Gum., 238/ Gū., 4:4; II, 31f and again at *ŚS* Śi., 260/ Ha., 322/ Gum., 255/ Gū., 4:22; II, 53f.

31. *ŚS* Śi., 245/ Ha., 307/ Gum., 240/ Gū., 4:6; II, 35. It should be noted, however, that Bhoosnurmath and Menezes' translation provides a different impression. They begin:

Thou only did'st the Guru make; Thou only
the Liṅga and the Jaṅgama. Thine is
The Grace, and the Initiation Thine!

The current translation is supported, however, by another of Basava's *vacanas*:

Entering the world,/ Remembering the hope/ Of humanity;
You set up worship five-fold—/ *Guru, liṅga, jaṅgama, pādōdaka*, and *prasāda*./ O Cennabasava.... —Basava

ŚS Śi., 511/ Ha., 622/ Gum., 805/ Gū., 8:84 (8:79); III, 104-07.

32. Introductory prose which precedes *ŚS* Gū., 4:9; II, 38.

33. *ŚS* Śi., 246/ Ha., 312/ Gum., 241/ Gū., 4:7; II, 36f. Though the specific pattern of an initiation ceremony is absent, the metaphor of the characterless and imperceptible essence occurs in the Upanishadic passage Chāndogya U. 6:12.

34. It should be noted, however, that, while the qualifications and intentions of the initiator are peripheral to sacramental efficacy, the initiate's intent is crucial. The objective power of the sacramental act is not a mechanical transfer of grace into an empty vessel.

35. *ŚS* Śi., 244/ Ha., 306/ Gum., 239/ Gū., 4:5; II, 32ff. More briefly, the transforming infusion of knowledge's light was described by *Kabīr*, p. 199:

When I was, Hari was not, now Hari is and I am no more:
All darkness vanished,/ when I saw the Lamp within my heart.

36. Cennabasava's continued insistence on the necessity of external signs and ceremonies is illustrated not only by his debates with Siddharāma but also by his reaction to Ghaṭṭivāḷa's challenges at *ŚS* Gū., chap. 15; IV, 193-259.

37. Allama Prabhu later conceded the utility of external ceremony for precisely this reason—its basic appeal to worldly approval. See *ŚS* —/ Ha., 739/ Gum., 500/ Gū., 10:48; III, 256f.

38. *ŚS* Śi., 260/ Ha., 322/ Gum., 255/ Gū., 4:22; II, 53f. The importunate disciple who demands instruction or initiation from a reluctant master is a frequent image. Naciketas, in the Kaṭha Upaniṣad, is one such. Tulsī Dās'

Vinaya Patrikā reflects a similar attitude in its persistent address to Rāma by name.

Murmur 'Rām, Rām' repeat 'Rām, Rām', pray 'Rām, Rām', O my tongue!...
Tulsī, your good lies in fulfilling on your own side this vow with
undistracted persistence!

From Tulsī Dās, *The Petition to Rām: Hindi Devotional Hymns of the Seventeenth Century*, ed. and trans. F.R. Allchin (London: George Allen and Unwin Ltd., 1966), p. 134.

39. *ŚS* Śi., 264/ Ha., 326/ Gum., 259/ Gū., 4:26; II, 57f.

40. *ŚS* Śi., 242/ Ha., 304/ Gum., 237/ Gū., 4:3; II, 29f. A similar efficacy for sacred ashes and for the *mantra* is indicated by Tirunāvukkarasu Svāmi at Kingsbury, *Tamil Hymns*, p. 67:

If men speak not His name in letters five,
Nor e'er the fire-formed Śiva's praise repeat,
And never walk in reverence round His shrine,
And pluck no flowers for offering ere they eat,
If they for healing wear no sacred ash,
I'll tell you whereunto such men were born,
'Twas that foul plagues might torture them to death,
Then death bring rebirths endlessly forlorn.

41. *ŚS* Śi., 269/ —/ Gum., 264/ Gū., 4:31; II, 66ff.

42. Cennabasava's advice appears at *ŚS* Śi., 300/ Ha., 370/ Gum., 295/ Gū., 5:13; II, 134f. Since the *jaṅgama* will give his grace to those who revere him, it is foolish of Basava to ignore this opportunity. Tukārām argues the same point at Appasamy, *Temple Bells*, p. 95:

What messenger need go to the ant's house? At the sight of sugar
they come running to it.
Does the giver stand waiting when no beggar is near?
It is the beggar who runs to better himself. ...
One who means to better himself, says Tuka, he listens to
God's praises, he cultivates a pleasure in this.

43. *ŚS* Śi., 293/ Ha., 355/ Gum., 288/ Gū., 5:6; II, 122f. The demands of hospitality are prominent in Sanskrit literature and also find expression in the vernaculars. For example, the sacred *Kural*:

How stupid those misers are who fail to practise the law of hospitality!
They succeed in being poor in the midst of plenty.
Hospitality is equivalent to a religious sacrifice.

From Tiru Valluvar, *Kural: The Great Book of Tiru-Valluvar*, trans. C. Rajagopalachari (Bombay: Bharatiya Vidya Bhavan, 1975), p. 11.

44. *ŚS* Śi., 295/ Ha., 357/ Gum., 290/ Gū., 5:8; II, 125ff. The hypocritical holy man is frequently the butt of humor and abuse. Kabīr is explicit in his dislike of the insincere *sādhus* at *Kabīr*, p. 280:

You have turned Sādhu: what of that?
you have put on four rows of beads,
Outwardly you have donned a pinkish robe,
but inside you are full of filth!

45. See Allama Prabhu's advice at *ŚS* Śi., 327/ Ha., 418/ Gum., 322/ Gū., 5:40; II, 162ff. Unworthy followers have been the bane of many spiritual

leaders. Like Prabhu, Kabīr despaired of ever teaching anything to the fool, at *Kabīr*, p. 272:

Trying to teach a fool,
you'll soon come to the end of your wits:
Coal will never turn white, even with ten hundredweights of soap!

46. *ŚS* Śi., 436/ Ha., 906/ Gum., 728/ Gū., 7:35; II, 353f. Tayumanavar expresses the same impossibility of worshipping in form for the devotee who has the Lord within. See Appasamy, *Temple Bells*, p. 84:

I will not worship Thee in a form. Thou art inconceivable!
Thou Thyself art in a flower!
My heart does not venture to pluck that dewy blossom.
As I join my palms to worship Thee, my heart blushes to see Thee within.
O Lord, my salute is only half done. How can I worship Thee?

47. *ŚS* Śi., 323/ Ha., 412/ Gum., 318/ Gū., 5:36; II, 158f. Utter self-depreciation in face of the Lord's grace is expressed by *Kabīr*, p. 190:

Kabīr, I searched the whole world,
but I found none (so) bad:
Kabīr is the worst of all, none is worse than Kabīr!

48. *ŚS* Śi., 330/ Ha., 432/ Gum., 325/ Gū., 5:43; II, 164f. Again, Basava's disdain for empty ritualism finds resonance with *Kabīr*, p. 272:

Kabīr, those dull-witted ritualists
are but stone from head to foot:
What is the worst of all, none is worse than Kabīr!

49. Again the *jīvanmukti* doctrine appears. It is also intimated by *Kabīr*, p. 258:

Infallible is the Touchstone of Rām,
no falsity will stick to it:
He alone will stick to that Stone
who, though living, be dead!

50. See, for example, Cennabasava's idea at *ŚS* Śi., 440/ Ha., 505/ Gum., 732/ Gū., 8:4; III, 21ff. The sense of overcoming duality which Cennabasava attempted to express was powerfully described by *Kabīr*, p. 199:

Him whom I went out to seek, / I found just where I was:
He now has become myself/ whom before I called 'Another'!

51. *ŚS* Śi., 475/ Ha., 586/ Gum., 769/ Gū., 8:43 (8:38); III, 66f.

52. *ŚS* Śi., 467/ Ha., 549/ Gum., 761/ Gū., 8:35 (8:30); III, 59. The body is more often an image of the mobile temple with the soul or mind depicted as the devotee inside that temple. One of Basava's more famous *vacanas* reflects this imagery at *BV* 820: (K), p. 333; (E), p. 274. The idea also appears in Appar's saying at Appasamy, *Temple Bells*, p. 74:

Our body is the shrine and the firm mind the devotee.
We have cleansed the shrine with truth, and erected God, the jewel of our minds, as the image. ...
We have worshipped Him.

53. *ŚS* Śi., 497/ Ha., 522/ Gum., 791/ Gū., 8:65 (8:60); III, 88f.

54. *ŚS* Śi., 498/ Ha., 523/ Gum., 792/ Gū., 8:66 (8:61); III, 89f.

55. *ŚS* Śi., 496/ Ha., 521/ Gum., 790 (789)/ Gū., 8:64 (8:59); III, 88f.

Again alluding to Śiva's inestimable *liṅga*, Tirunāvukkarasu Svāmi indicated that true knowledge lay only within. See Kingsbury, *Tamil Hymns*, p. 55:

I sought Him and I found./ Brahm sought in vain on high. Viṣṇu delved vainly underground./ Him in my soul found I.

56. *ŚS* Śi., 487/ Ha., 512, 614/ Gum., 781/ Gū., 8:55 (8:50); III, 77f. The entangling weight of *līnga's* string serves as the image for Tirunāvukkarasu Svāmi's verse at Kingsbury, *Tamil Hymns*, p. 59:

Then though men tie on me two weighty stones,
And sink me in the ocean's depth, e'en then
The cry 'Hail, Śiva', would salvation be.

The utility of bathing and of holy water is questioned by that same saint at Kingsbury, *Tamil Hymns*, p. 57:

Why bathe in Gaṅgā's stream, or Kāverī?
Why go to Comorin in Koṅgu's land?
Why seek the water of the sounding sea?
Release is theirs, and theirs alone, who call
In every place upon the Lord of all.

57. In fact, the three later editors of the *Śūnyasaṃpādane* felt this debate to be so crucial, that their editions were largely motivated by a desire to fill the lacuna in Śivagaṇaprasādi Mahādevayya's version when he omitted the initiation issue.

58. *ŚS* Śi., 568/ Ha., 736/ Gum., 480/ Gū., 10:1; III, 206f.

59. *ŚS* —/ —/ Gum., 398/ Gū., 10:12; III, 217f.

60. *ŚS* —/ Ha., 681/ Gum., 400/ Gū., 10:14; III, 219f.

61. *ŚS* —/ Ha., 739/ Gum., 500/ Gū., 10:48; III, 256f.

62. Compare St. Paul's admonition to those strong in the faith that they should not act in a way which might be harmful to those who were weaker in the faith, e.g. at Romans, chaps. 14 and 15.

63. *ŚS* —/ —/ Gum., 612/ Gū., 10:53; III, 265f.

64. *ŚS* —/ —/ —/ Gū., 10:63; III, 275f.

65. *ŚS* —/ —/ Gum., 610/ Gū., 10:98 (10:95); III, 307f. The importance of association with others of good intent is emphasized by *Kabīr*, p. 276:

Kabīr, the mind is like a bird,/ flying in all the ten directions;
Depending on the company he keeps, / he will feed on this or that.

66. *ŚS* Śi., 395/ Ha., 862/ Gum., 686/ Gū., 11:2; III, 331ff. Basava's joy in worshipping the *guru* apart from himself is not so virulent as is Tukarām's. See Appasamy, *Temple Bells*, p. 39:

Cursed be that knowledge which makes me one with Thee;
I love to have precepts from Thee and prohibitions.
I am thy servant; Thou art my Lord; let there be still between us such difference of high and low; let this wonderful truth be established, destroy it not.
Water cannot taste itself, nor trees taste their own fruit; the worshipper must be separate, thus alone pleasure arises from distinction.

67. *ŚS* Śi., 397/ Ha., 364/ Gum., 688/ Gū., 11:9 (11:4); III, 336f. Again veneration of and association with the saints is praised by *Kabīr*, p. 182:

Kabīr, blessed that day/ when you meet the Saints!
Embrace them closely to you/ and all your sins will be washed away!

68. *ŚS* —/ Ha., 931/ Gum., 886/ Gū., 14:2; IV, 144f.
69. *ŚS* —/ Ha., 975/ Gum., 930/ Gū., 14:46; IV, 186ff.
70. *ŚS* —/ Ha., 972/ Gum., 927/ Gū., 14:43; IV, 183.
71. *ŚS* —/ Ha., 974/ Gum., 929/ Gū., 14:45; IV, 185f.
72. *ŚS* Śi., 761/ Ha., 1219/ Gum., 1146/ Gū., 19:46; V, 184f.
73. *ŚS* Śi, 776/ Ha., 1236/ Gum., 1162/ Gū., 19:68; V, 202f. An awareness of the Lord's diverse forms and a desire to see them directly was also expressed by *Kabīr*, p. 204:

I had come into this world/ and many forms there were to see:
Says Kabīr, O Saints,/ I caught sight of the Incomparable (form)!

74. *ŚS* Śi., 789/ Ha., 1249/ Gum., 1175/ Gū., 19:82; V, 214ff.
75. *ŚS* Śi., 799/ Ha., 1259/ Gum., 1135/ Gū., 19:92; V, 226ff. Both the import and the images of Tirunāvukkarasu Svāmi's verses are strikingly similar to Prabhu's. See Kingsbury, *Tamil Hymns*, p. 57:

Why chant the Vedas, hear the Śāstras' lore?
Why daily teach the books of righteousness?
Why the Vedāngas six day o'er and o'er?
Release is theirs, and theirs alone, whose heart
From thinking of its Lord shall ne'er depart.

76. Examples of Prabhu's attributing a provisional value to the sacraments
@*ŚS* Śi., 128/ Ha., 109/ Gum., 127/ Gū., 3:12; I, 229.
@*ŚS* Śi., 498/ Ha., 523/ Gum., 792/ Gū., 8:66 (8:61); III, 89f.
@*ŚS* —/ Ha., 739/ Gum., 500/ Gū., 10:48; III, 256f.
@*ŚS* Śi., 761/ Ha., 1219/ Gum., 1146/ Gū., 19:46; V, 184f.
@*ŚS* Śi., 774/ Ha., 1234/ Gum., 1160/ Gū., 19:66; V, 199ff.

77. Prabhu specifically rejects the efficacy of external ceremonies:
@*ŚS* Śi., 57/ Ha., 268, 913/ Gum., 56, 476/ Gū., 1:58; I, 105.
@*ŚS* Śi., 295/ Ha., 357/ Gum., 290/ Gū., 5:8; II, 125ff.
@*ŚS* Śi., 327/ Ha., 418/ Gum., 322/ Gū., 5:40; II, 162.
@*ŚS* Śi., 436/ Ha., 906/ Gum., 728/ Gū., 7:35; II, 353f.
@*ŚS* Śi., 475/ Ha., 586/ Gum., 769/ Gū., 8:43 (8:38); III, 66f.
@*ŚS* —/ Ha., 681/ Gum., 400/ Gū., 10:14; III, 219f.

78. Prabhu identifies *guru* and disciple:
@*ŚS* Śi., 37/ Ha., 37/ Gum., 36/ Gū., 1:35; I, 84f.
@*ŚS* Śi., 40/ Ha., 40/ Gum., 39/ Gū., 1:38; I, 87f.
@*ŚS* Śi., 93/ Ha., 74/ Gum., 92/ Gū., 2:18; I, 167f.
@*ŚS* Śi., 99/ Ha., 80/ Gum., 98/ Gū., 2:24; I, 178f.
@*ŚS* Śi., 327/ Ha., 418/ Gum., 322/ Gū., 5:40; II, 162f.
@*ŚS* Śi., 523/ Ha., 634/ Gum., 817/ Gū., 9:13; III, 143f.
@*ŚS* Śi., 623/ Ha., 1079/ Gum., 1007/ Gū., 17:3; V, 12f.
@*ŚS* —/ —/ —/ Gū., 20:90 (20:73); V, 367f.

79. Prabhu uses the salt and water metaphor at *ŚS* Śi., 42/ Ha., 42/ Gum., 41/ Gū., 1:40; I, 90. The Bṛhadāraṇyaka Upaniṣad uses the analogy at II. iv. 12 and elsewhere.

80. Prabhu condemns these sacramental substances:
@*ŚS* Śi., 61/ Ha., 272, 918/ Gum., 60/ Gū., 1:62; I, 108.
@*ŚS* Śi., 487/ Ha., 512, 614/ Gum., 781/ Gū., 8:55 (8:50); III, 77f.
@*ŚS* Śi., 799/ Ha., 1259/ Gum., 1185/ Gū., 19:92; V, 226ff.

81. *ŚS* Śi., 39/ Ha., 39/ Gum., 38/ Gū., 1:37; I, 86f.
82. Cennabasava argues for such identifications:
@*ŚS* Śi., 244/ Ha., 306/ Gum., 239/ Gū., 4:5; II, 32ff.
@*ŚS* Śi., 440/ Ha., 505/ Gum., 732/ Gū., 8:4; III, 21ff.
@*ŚS* Śi., 502/ Ha., 796/ Gum., 527/ Gū., 8:75 (8:70); III, 96.
@*ŚS* Śi., 833/ Ha., 1293/ Gum., 1219/ Gū., 19:132 (19:137); V, 262f.
83. Cennabasava praises the initiation he received from his uncle.
@*ŚS* Śi., 244/ Ha., 306/ Gum., 239/ Gū., 4:5; II, 32ff.
@*ŚS* Śi., 265/ Ha., 327/ Gum., 260/ Gū., 4:27; II, 58-61.
@*ŚS* Śi., 954/ Ha., 1414/ Gum., 1331/ Gū., 21:71 /(21:45); V, 447.
84. Cennabasava insists on the *guru's* unique powers.
@*ŚS* Śi., 246/ Ha., 312/ Gum., 241/ Gū., 4:7; II, 36f.
@*ŚS* Śi., 252/ Ha., 318, 598/ Gum., 247/ Gū., 4:14; II, 45f.
@*ŚS* Śi., 256/ —/ Gum., 251, Gū., 4:18; II, 49.
@*ŚS* Śi., 789/ Ha., 1249/ Gum., 1175/ Gū., 19:82; V, 214ff.
85. Cennabasava defends these sacramental agencies.
@*ŚS* Śi., 242/ Ha., 304/ Gum., 237/ Gū., 4:3; II, 29f.
@*ŚS* Si., 269/—/ Gum., 264/ Gū., 4:31; II, 66ff.
@*ŚS* Śi., 497/ Ha., 522/ Gum., 791/ Gū., 8:65 (8:60); III, 88f.
@*ŚS* Śi., 397/ Ha., 864/ Gum., 688/ Gū., 11:9 (11:4); III, 336f.
@*ŚS* —/ Ha., 975/ Gum., 930/ Gū., 14:46; IV, 186ff.
@*ŚS* Śi., 663/ Ha., 1119/ Gum., 1047/ Gū., 17:45; V, 51.
86. *ŚS* —/ —/ —/ Gū., 10:63; III, 275f.
87. Basava rejects a wholly objectivist soteriology.
@*ŚS* Śi., 241/ Ha., 303/ Gum., 648/ Gū., 4:2; II, 29f.
@*ŚS* Śi., 245/ Ha., 307/ Gum., 240/ Gū., 4:6; II, 35.
@*ŚS* Śi., 264/ Ha., 326/ Gum., 259/ Gū., 4:26; II, 57f.
@*ŚS* Śi., 323/ Ha., 412/ Gum., 318/ Gū., 5:36; II, 158f.
@*ŚS* Śi., 330/ Ha., 432/ Gum., 325/ Gū., 5:43; II, 164f.
88. Basava's joyous sense of worship is expressed.
@*ŚS* Śi., 293/ Ha., 355/ Gum., 288/ Gū., 5:6; II, 122f.
@*ŚS* Śi., 437/ Ha., 729/ Gum., 907/ Gū., 7:36; II, 354f.
@*ŚS* Śi., 511/ Ha., 622/ Gum., 805/ Gū., 8:84 (8:79); III, 104-07.
@*ŚS* Śi., 395/ Ha., 862/ Gum., 686/ Gū., 11:2; III, 371ff.
@*ŚS* Śi., 682/ Ha., 1139/ Gum., 1067/ Gū., 18:7; V, 87f.
@*ŚS* Śi., 776/ Ha., 1236/ Gum., 1162/ Gū., 19:68; V, 202f.
89. Basava's longing for inner spiritual experience appears.
@*ŚS* Śi., 264/ Ha., 326/ Gum., 259/ Gū., 4:26; II, 57f.
@*ŚS* Śi., 547/ Ha., 658/ Gum., 378/ Gū., 9:39; III, 171ff.
@*ŚS* Śi., 863/ Ha., 1323/ Gum., 1251/ Gū., 20:3; V, 302f.
90. *ŚS* Śi., 330/ Ha., 432/ Gum., 325/ Gū., 5:43; II, 164f.
91. *ŚS* Śi., 395/ Ha., 862/ Gum., 686/ Gū., 11:2; III, 331ff.

CHAPTER FOUR

THE ECCLESIOLOGY OF THE ŚŪNYASAMPĀDANE: Universalist v. Particularist

The preceding chapter demonstrated clearly that the *Śūnyasaṃpādane*, as a record of debates about important practices in the spiritual life of the Vīraśaiva community, offered no single ideal form of theory and practice. The solutions which it offered for the ritual and theological problems of the community were various and often simply contradictory. Certainly it provided no unanimity of opinion concerning the nature and the function of the various rituals and ritual substances of the Vīraśaiva tradition.

Similarly, the *Śūnyasaṃpādane* provides no unanimous answer to the problem of determining precisely who belongs to the community and what the benefits of that membership are. At times, it seems to argue that all who wish to join the Vīraśaiva fold should be accepted readily simply on the basis of stated intent. It contends that the mere fact of association with the community of believers will result in the acquisition of salvific merit, for the community itself is an agent in helping individuals to attain a measure of the Lord's saving grace. In other words, it supports a universalist objectivism of the church sort.

At other times, however, the next supports a particularist subjectivism of the sectarian sort. Its position seems to be that membership in a group of like-minded saints is a difficult undertaking and is not easily to be attained. One must demonstrate both the moral purity and the ritual competence required for membership in a narrowly and strictly defined band. Here the text contends that only the already perfected individual, who has attained and deserves salvific standing, can belong to the group. Hence membership in the group provides no salvific merit in itself; rather membership is a sign of perfection already attained.

In short, the *Śūnyasaṃpādane* seems to support alternatively both the notion that Vīraśaivism should be a universalistic church which is itself an objective source of salvation and the idea that the community should be a particularistic sect into which are admitted only those who have acquired a saving grace themselves. The text portrays the community both as a vessel of salvific potency and as a community of the elect.

These issues have already been discussed obliquely in the foregoing investigation of the *aṣṭāvaraṇa* scheme in the *Śūnyasaṃpādane*. In addition, the text often directly debates the definition and purpose of community membership. In both cases, the pattern which emerges for defining the conditions and the functions of membership in the community demonstrates divergent perspectives again championed, one each, by Allama Prabhu, Basava, and Cennabasava. Prabhu, for one, sees little value in concern for the community at all. He does not condemn the society of saints, but he does persistently question its utility to the solitary believer in search of mystical attainment. For Prabhu, the only meaningful community is a community of One—the Lord identified with His follower; but for both Basava and Cennabasava the larger human community is meaningful, albeit in rather different ways.

They, notably, do not share the same perspective on the boundaries of that community. Cennabasava seeks to have the group defined rather narrowly on the basis of a supposed inner perfection as witnessed by the outer signs of the faith. Thus only those of demonstrated ethical and ritual purity are to be admitted to the association of the saints. Basava, on the other hand, is rather uncritical in his hospitable welcome to all who wish to join in the company of good men and women. Thus any who profess to be or desire to be followers of the Lord are more than welcome into the group which enjoys Basava's economic and political patronage.

Again these distinct perspectives emerge in the context of an ongoing debate as Allama Prabhu encounters the various *śaraṇas* within the narrative of the *Śūnyasaṃpādane*. A rehearsal of five of these episodic debates heightens the position taken by each saint on these important issues. Following that, a systematic recapitulation of each one's position concludes the chapter.

DISPUTES OVER MEMBERSHIP IN THE ŚARAṆA BAND

Allama Prabhu's Mystical Experience

Several of the later episodes discuss more explicitly the boundaries of membership in the *śaraṇa* association, but from the very first—Allama Prabhu's encounter with Animiṣa—the parameters of the debate begin to emerge and Allama's perspective is advanced. In that encounter, it should be remembered, Allama did not go to a practising association of saints to gain wisdom and insight. Rather he went out into a lonely field and sought even greater privacy as he entered the hidden cavern which he discovered there.

Deep within that cavern, Allama discovered the unwavering *yōgi* Animiṣa and, at his feet, sought initiation into the fellowship of mystical lore. Animiṣa, however, indicated no awareness of Allama's presence. It remained finally for Allama himself to initiate himself by taking the *liṅga* emblem from Animiṣa's palm. In other words, the entire process of spiritual attainment was, for Allama, an individual quest unassisted by association with a group of like-minded seekers. In fact, it was only by shunning any such association and going alone into the private depths that he attained spiritual insight.

In one *vacana*, he expressed his disdain for the community of those who boasted of spiritual attainment to each other while failing to realize that attainment as an actual and private fact.

> Chasing, touching, gripping,
> Saying, 'I have caught it',
> Stumbling and slipping,
> They have only lost it.
> Those countless ones all thought,
> 'I have it with me!'
> In fact, they have only caught
> A lifeless body.
> I alone have found it
> Through coming together with
> Our Lord of the Hidden Caverns.
>
> —Allama Prabhu[1]

For Allama, those who trumpeted to each other their spiritual attainments were simply mutually deluded. Rather than gaining a true experience of the Lord they had acquired the lifeless corpse of mutual support and admiration. Only the individual and solitary seeker truly knew the Lord's grace, and both his acquisition and his nurture of that grace took place without any essential reference to the community of *śaraṇas* who sought or claimed to seek similar spirituality. Interestingly, Allama set forth no criteria for membership in the *śaraṇa* band, for he did not see any association as worthy of criteria. The only meaningful criteria were those which referred to an individual and personal spiritual attainment. This attitude continued to characterize Allama's position throughout the ensuing debates.

Cennabasava's Initiation

Cennabasava's efforts to secure initiation at the hands of his uncle Basava were not motivated merely by a desire to experience the efficacious power of the initiation ceremony and of the *liṅga* emblem. He also sought to possess an indisputable certificate of membership in the band of the *śaraṇas*. Undergoing the *dīkṣā* ceremony would provide public testimony to his right to associate with the other saints, and wearing the *liṅga* would bear tangible witness to that certification.

Similarly, Basava's reluctance to participate in the ceremony was not based entirely upon his feelings of inadequacy in the priestly role, nor was it based entirely upon his objections to an overemphasis on the concrete symbols of Vīraśaiva sacramental practice. In large part, his reluctance was founded upon his simple inability to perceive the importance of the ceremony. He made no stringent requirements for membership in the group of saints who enjoyed his patronage. His easy and open acceptance of all who wished to associate with the saintly band found expression in his *vacana* addressed to Cennabasava.

> Before the beginning, before the beginningless,
> Because no one was able to tell
> Of *liṅga* and *jaṅgama* well,
> Śiva sent me to mortality
> To explain their linked unity.
> Now when I see *liṅga* wearers,

Whoever could they be except
Our Lord of the Meeting Rivers?
...

—Basava[2]

For Basava, all who wore the *liṅga* were worthy of uncritical acceptance into his fellowship and his patronage. Thus whomever he saw wearing the *liṅga*, he accepted without questioning that one's worthiness to wear the symbol. His universalist perspective on Vīraśaiva membership meant that association with the assembly was not to be restricted to those who somehow deserved admission, but was open to all who professed a desire to associate. The most obvious means of indicating that desire, of course, was the wearing of the *liṅga* emblem, but as subsequent debates will show, even one who did not bear that symbol but professed a desire for inclusion in the assembly was welcome.

Cennabasava, on the other hand, had a much more restrictive sense of what membership in the *śaraṇa* association required. The demonstration of ethical and ritual worthiness prior to inclusion in the group underlay even his arguments for his own inclusion therein and his pressures upon Basava to initiate him. Alongside his arguments that the initiation ceremony and the subsequent wearing of the properly blessed *liṅga* would bestow salvific benefit stood his confident assurance that the band of saints would find him acceptable.

Fret not, fret not! I do now affirm
In front of all the saints,
'I from you shall learn.'
...
When you placed the ashen dressing
On my body still enwombed,
I received your finest blessing.
Now I, Cennabasava,
Am servant just to you,
O Lord of the Lovely Waters.

—Cennabasava[3]

Cennabasava indicated that he had already received the essential blessing from his uncle at the pre-natal initiation ceremony. He was thus, in some sense, already in possession of the Lord's grace. What he desired was not so much another ceremony's salvific benefit as its certification of his worthiness for life within the association of saints. He conceded to Basava that the pre-natal ceremony was efficacious, but he also acted to assure Basava that his inclusion within the assembly of initiated saints would not be an embarrassment. Hence arose his emphasis on affirming his rectitude and worthiness in front of the saintly assembly. In fact, Cennabasava pushed his assurance even further. Not only, he avowed, would he not be an embarrassment to his uncle, but also he would bring positive acclaim upon them—initiator and initiand.

> ...
> The knowledge that in me shines
> Is the unmanifest *liṅga* in your heart.
> The radiant *liṅga* that in you shines
> Is the saving knowledge on my part.
> Separating the one from the other,
> You cannot tell a difference.
> There's one *liṅga*, one teaching,
> And one ritual performance.
> How then speak you of nearer and further?
> After giving me instruction initially
> In my own inner nature,
> How can you now say, sir,
> 'I can't perform the act ritually'?
> If you will initiate me,
> I will do you proud.
> The great host of the mortal world
> Will applaud us out loud.
> Look here, Basava, on this I have as my witness
> Our Lord of the Lovely Waters.
> —Cennabasava[4]

Again Cennabasava's arguments were based not so much on his need to be initiated—an event accomplished before birth anyway—as on his worthiness for inclusion in the saintly band and his assurance that he would bring acclaim to himself, to his teacher-initiator, and to the movement as a whole. Properly initiated and accepted within the boundaries of a stringently defined organization, he would make the entire world stand up and take notice of his spiritual and ethical accomplishment.

What is clear from his arguments, however, is that Cennabasava perceived the boundaries of full inclusion within the saintly assembly to be relatively narrow and rigid. Even he, who had been initiated *in utero* needed certification of his spiritual worthiness by a second ceremony which would certify his full inclusion into the group. His demand for that ceremony was not based upon a professed desire to attain the Lord's grace, as Basava might have demanded, but upon his already existent worthiness foı that grace. Membership in the saintly assembly was, for Cennabasava, membership in a society of those who had already attained and demonstrated spiritual perfection. It was membership in a group narrowly defined by the particular excellences of ethically and ritually virtuous individuals—individuals such as himself.

Siddharāma's Initiation

While Cennabasava had been initiated *in utero* and had to make his case for a second initiation in the presence of the other saints, Siddharāma's problem was a different one. He, like Cennabasava, had demonstrated his general ethical rectitude and moral worthiness by his many acts of charity and piety while he was living near Sholapur. He thus had the internal qualities and certain external manifestations required for membership in a narrowly defined association of saintly persons. He did not, however, possess all the appropriate external signs for entry into the association of the Vīraśaiva adepts. Notably, he had not received initiation and did not wear the *iṣṭaliṅga*.

When Allama Prabhu and Siddharāma had arrived at Kalyāṇa, the latter's entry into the city itself had been the cause of some consternation; and, as the period extended while this uninitiated person remained not only in the city but also in close proximity to the very leaders of the movement, the concerns of the *śaraṇas* grew more acute. Cennabasava was one of the most vocal of those insisting on the need for Siddharāma to undergo initiation so that he could be permitted to remain within the saintly company.

> If you have heard of connubium's bliss,
> Until you are wed before a witness,
> So what?
> If you would say,
> 'My eyes can see,'

When there's no lamp,
What use would they be?
...
Without body, can there be *jīva*?
Without Śakti, can there be Śiva?
...
This is the cause
The face is not fit to see
Of one who is lost
From *iṣṭa* proximity.
O Lord of the Lovely Waters.

—Cennabasava[5]

Cennabasava's defense of the necessity of an external ceremony of initiation reflects the generally objectivist attitude toward ritual discussed in the preceding chapter. As external light is necessary for the inner person to see and, as a union unblessed by a wedding ceremony is no marriage at all, so is the one who lacks external signs of worth unfit for inclusion within the association of the saints. Cennabasava's point, however, was an even sharper one. The one who does not demonstrate all the proper characteristics of the worthy member, including both inner merit and its external symbols, presents a visage which is odious to the saintly company. Even more stridently had Cennabasava insisted on the association's disapproval of the *liṅga*-less person in an earlier *vacana*.

Kūḍala Cennasaṅga's *śaraṇas*,
Who know that Form itself is formless,
Do not approve of such as lack the *aṅga-liṅga* bond,
Because their company is loss.

—Cennabasava[6]

The person whose outer body was *liṅga*-less and whose inner mind did not recognize the interdependence of the body and the Ultimate could not expect to be welcomed into the company of a group of perfected and dedicated virtuosi. The bounds of *śaraṇa*-hood were narrow and rigid; they excluded all who failed to conform to both the outer signs and the inner purity required for membership.

Allama could agree with only part of that formula. It was possession of a pure and perfected inner nature that was necessary. He could not, however, agree that the bearing of an external sign was a trustworthy indication of inner perfection; nor did he think that membership in a group of mortal human beings was an important consideration anyway. He wondered why Cennabasava should make such a fuss about defining membership in the group when what mattered was the wholly individual relation of the person to the Lord.

> What is all this fuss about worshipping the Lord
> For one who has known Him?
> What use is the bedstead in the amorous tryst?
> What use is shamefulness in the ecstasy of bliss?
> What use, the alchemic stone for gold of pure test?
> What use is *liṅga's* sign for Siddharāmayya?
> His very breath inside
> Is our Lord of the Hidden Caverns.
>
> —Allama Prabhu[7]

Allama supported Cennabasava's argument that the true saint would have an inner nature which was a rare conjunction of purity and perfection. The external signs of that perfection, however, were not important to Allama. The issue which plagued Cennabasava's sensitivities was hardly discernible to Allama. Membership in an external association of those who worshipped the Lord was as entirely superfluous consideration. The perfected individual saint, like the lump of pure gold, needed no external reference for his spirituality. That reference lay entirely within.

Cennabasava was not to be swayed by Allama's arguments. He felt that those of spiritual purity, moral rectitude, and ritual acceptability should not have to associate with less adept persons, even though those might be sincere seekers of the Lord's grace. Without both the inner and outer characteristics of this narrowly defined spiritual band, a person would sully all with which he came into contact.

> With an eye between his brows
> But no *liṅga* on his limbs,
> Food cooked in his house
> Is just like dogmeat.
> Just there the wise will not eat.
> If you eat in the house of a non-devotee.

You'll be reborn in a dog's womb, that's a certainty!
Seeing them eat in a house where you're not,
O Śiva, no doubt my mind is distraught.
O Lord of the Lovely Waters.

—Cennabasava[8]

Thus even the signs of prodigious yogic accomplishment, such as possessing a third eye on the brow, were not sufficient to qualify one for membership in the Vīraśaiva assembly. It was only the rigidly defined characteristics of Vīraśaiva cultic practice which, as external signs of an internal perfection, could qualify one for full participation in the life of the Vīraśaiva community. Without those narrowly defined signs of membership in the Vīraśaiva community, one remained an outsider whose very presence was unclean and dangerous. The relaxation of commensal rules which Vīraśaivism propagated within the community certainly did not apply outside the bounds of that group. In fact, those rules may have been even more rigidly applied to Vīraśaivas vis-à-vis non-Vīraśaivas than among castes within the Brahmanical community as a whole. Certainly, for Cennabasava, sharing of food and other contacts with non-members of the community were to be avoided. The community which he envisioned was a rather narrow and strictly defined community of the elect—the morally righteous and ritually pure.

The object of all this debate, Siddharāma, originally was somewhat offended by the insistence that he be initiated and invested with *iṣṭaliṅga*. He contended, with reason, that he was not some loathsome sinner but an accomplished practitioner of *yōga* and a follower of the Lord's ways. The insistence that he undergo a specific initiation into an exclusivist group both undermined his own self-esteem and failed to accord with his understanding of the *śaraṇas*' goals. Their generally non-dualist emphasis and in-group egalitarianism seemed weakened by this rejection of the outsider's worth.

After listening to the principals in the debate, however, Siddharāma modified his perspective. He dropped his objections to a specific boundary, separating in-group and out-group, and began to long, without reservation, for inclusion within the group of accomplished saints

When shall I be in the company of your saints?
When shall I be in the minds of your own?
When shall I be a watchman at your home?
When shall I be in the midst of your crowd?
When shall I be a slave to your name?
When, O God?
When, O Lord of the Faultless Jasmines?
—Siddharāma[9]

Siddharāma's mood of ardent longing to be included among the saints of the Lord reflected the image of the community which Cennabasava had propagated. The exclusivist community whose boundaries were inflexible and difficult to cross began, probably because of its exclusivity, to exert an attraction. Membership in the group became a goal worthy of seeking, and meeting the criteria of that membership became a task worth pursuing. Insofar as the community's attractiveness motivated people to reform their behaviour and to seek after the Lord's grace, the community exerted a soteriological power; but it was a power which operated essentially among those still outside the group. Only after one had experienced that attractive power and had fulfilled the rigid requirements of membership could one be admitted to the select body. Membership in the community of saints was not available merely for the asking; it had to be earned.

Ghaṭṭivāḷayya's Rigorism

Even more radical in his vision of the community as a narrow group of accomplished adepts was Ghaṭṭivāḷayya. He challenged those who were already members of the *śaraṇa* organization to demonstrate the truth and depth of their piety rather than to continue living on the beneficence of Basava's charity. He claimed that many among the *śaraṇas* were less saints than hypocritical freeloaders.

Watering at the mouth
For Basava's charity,
Acting with great display,
They see not the disparity
Of their false devotion.

What do they expect anyway?
(Such as these) I say
Are not for our Lord of the Simple Pleasures.
—Ghaṭṭivāḷayya[10]

Ghaṭṭivāḷayya's obvious quarrel was with the uncritical acceptance which Basava lavished on all who wished to join the community. Ghaṭṭivāḷayya suspected not only the depth of their spiritual accomplishment but also the veracity of their claims to seek the Lord. He felt that they sought only the food and shelter which Basava offered.

Beyond that challenge to Basava's easy acceptance, however, Ghaṭṭivāḷayya also argued that even Cennabasava's rigorist particularism was insufficient for defining a truly spiritual community. He felt that Cennabasava relied too heavily on the external signs of faith—especially wearing the *liṅga*—and was lax on requiring a genuine and inner faith on the part of the members. Specifically, he challenged the community's focus on wearing the *liṅga* by taunting them until they had stripped his own *liṅga* away and, even then, he continued to claim that his inner purity was superior to their external ostentation.

See, the community is not pleased
Because my *iṣṭa* is missing.
Why quibble over things like these
When their consciousness is missing?
Not (for such as them)
Is our Lord of the Simple Pleasures.
—Ghaṭṭivāḷayya[11]

Ghaṭṭivāḷayya's position was thus somewhat akin to that of Allama Prabhu who demanded an inner spiritual perfection of the individual seeker. Prabhu, however, saw little or no importance for the association of the saints. The entire matter was one of personal attainment and individual spirituality. Unlike him, Ghaṭṭivāḷayya exhibited a great concern for the nature of the community. He demanded that it be made up of individuals who were perfected inwardly and not merely those who exhibited the external signs of the faith, but he did not demean the attempt to discern that inward perfection in those who could belong to the community

The reason for Prabhu's disagreement with Ghaṭṭivāḷayya's concern for correctly defining the community, was that he felt that that concern betrayed a lingering sense of dualism in Ghaṭṭivālayya's spiritual attainment. The effort to discern who was inside and who was outside the boundaries of the community revealed a continuing sense of one's self and others as well as a lingering division between the inner and the outer signs of spiritual attainment. For Prabhu, such dualities had fallen away entirely and so, he felt, should they for others.

> Ghaṭṭivāḷayya, thinking
> 'I know it all!'
> Should you speak rudely?
> For one who knows truly
> Should there be false pride?
> You must put aside
> The duality of true and false.
> Community itself is enough;
> What need have you of other stuff?
> For one with a sense of universality
> There can be no talk of truth and falsity.
> O Lord of the Hidden Caverns.
>
> —Allama Prabhu[12]

In saying that community is sufficient, Prabhu was not so much elevating the importance of the community per se as rejecting Ghaṭṭivāḷayya's attempt to introduce a divisive dualism into the community as well as into the implications of his spirituality. The effort to separate the worthy members of the community from those who should not be admitted betrayed an egoic sense which not only would destroy the harmony of the community, but also would destroy the possibility of spiritual attainment for Ghaṭṭivāḷayya himself. Based on an egoic sense of who belongs and who does not and on a dualist sense of true and false contact with the divine, Ghaṭṭivāḷayya's spiritual pursuit betrayed a fatal inability to accept the unity of body and spirit, of self and other, and of seeker and Lord which Prabhu found crucial.

For Prabhu himself, the non-dualist perspective which arose from spiritual attainment was an entirely individual matter, but it was not an egoic attainment. It was not divisive or particularistic merely because it was individual. His attitude toward the community's definition was essentially one of non-interest. The community could define itself as it pleased and he would not interfere. He would, however, interfere in the spiritual progress of any individual *śaraṇa* who betrayed an incomplete sense of non-dualism. Ghaṭṭivāḷayya, through his particularist exclusivism, exhibited just such a dualist perspective and therefore evoked Prabhu's displeasure.

Mahādēviyakka's Liberation

The final episode of interest in highlighting Vīraśaiva attitudes toward membership in the community involves the woman saint Mahādēviyakka. Having rejected the normal role of woman in medieval Indian society as wife and mother, she set out as a wandering and naked ascetic. Probably the tremendous force of will and sacrifice required for her to undertake that life led her to hold a rather rigorous definition of *śaraṇa* membership. She possessed a definite sense that only those of considerable spiritual attainment could be admitted to the society or even to the seat of that society—the city of Kalyāṇa.

> Not just anyone can go to Kalyāṇa!
> One just cannot possibly go there
> Until he has utterly destroyed
> Desire and passion's snares.
> One can't go there
> Until he has purified
> Himself both in-and outside.
> One can't go there
> Until he has let go
> All sense of ego
> But, having purified my inside,
> Having put duality away,
> I can truly say
> Hail, all hail to Kalyāṇa—
> City which I've seen,
> O Lord of the Lovely Jasmines.
>
> —Mahādeviyakka[13]

It should be noted that Sister Mahādēvi's feeling that admission to Kalyāṇa was a privilege to be earned by only a few accomplished saints grew not so much from a sense of superiority on her part as from a desire to measure up to their rigid standards. She sang the praises of the city's inhabitants before she herself had arrived there. Her *vacana* was thus more a poem of longing and hope that she would be able to find acceptance in Kalyāṇa than an egoic celebration of her inclusion among the elect while others stood outside the company. Nonetheless, the attitude which she expressed treated the community of *śaraṇas* at Kalyāṇa as an elect band of those whose minds were pure and whose passions were stilled. Her ardent hope was that she might measure up to the strict standards of membership and find acceptance for herself.

If membership in the community had depended entirely upon Basava's opinion, then Mahādēviyakka need not have worried herself. His vision of the Vīraśaiva community as a body of those who sought fuller knowledge and more perfect service of the Lord led him to accept all who expressed a desire for membership and exhibited some willingness to grow in spiritual perfection within a faithful community.

> What need of a body
> For one who's pleased with the formless?
> What need of pride
> For one who's pleased with the mindless?
> What need of a merkin
> For one who's pleased with the cloakless
> O Prabhu, look here!
> There are no restraints at all
> On that saint we call
> Sister Mahādēvi!
> O Lord of the Meeting Rivers.
>
> —Basava[14]

Basava saw before him a woman whose nakedness attested to a release from the usual bonds of pride and egoic restraint. He felt little need to know more about Mahādēviyakka's spiritual experiences. She had presented herself before the assembly and in utter humility had requested membership in that blessed band. Any further demand upon her would have defeated the purpose of the assembly itself as a group of seekers dedicated to the Lord's service and to better knowledge of Him.

Allama Prabhu, on the other hand, felt it necessary to test that woman's level of religious attainment. Nonchalant toward her external signs of humility—pre-eminently her nakedness—he sought to know more about her inner state of preparedness for the religious life. Hence he chided her that even her strategically placed braids were a sign of malingering pride which betrayed a resilient sense of duality between herself and others.

> Is it true when you claim
> 'Having laid the blame, I left'?
> The error of your mind
> Does not become certainty
> When you leave off your dress
> And take on nudity.
> The clothing of your tresses
> Is still a cover for your body.
> You haven't left disgrace behind.
> This clothing is not fit
> For our Lord of the Hidden Caverns.
>
> —Allama Prabhu[15]

Prabhu's concern was not for maintaining the quality of the *śaraṇa* community as a whole. He made no mention of Mahādēviyakka's unworthiness to join the saintly band. What he did assert was that she stood in imperfect relation to the Lord's grace. On an individual level, she was less perfected spiritually than she might have been. Her pride in her nudity as a sign of spiritual attainment was betrayed by her continued modest placement of her tresses and that in turn betrayed her less-than-perfect realization of the non-duality of soul and Lord. It is noteworthy, in this context, that Prabhu asked not that she make herself worthy of inclusion into the community; he asked that she make herself as spiritually perfect as possible.

Moved by Prabhu's challenge to her genuine spirituality, Mahādēviyakka remorsefully sought the forbearance of the other *śaraṇas*. She desired more than ever to find acceptance in the saintly band and to know the Lord's grace as fully as possible.

> What is to be done for me?
> I am a puppet of this world,

A reservoir of worldly pollution.
A dwelling place for morbid passion.
. . .
Every soul is a seed sown,
But mine bears inedible fruit.
Bear with my faults.
Ye saints, ye gods are God alone—
The Lord of the Lovely Jasmines Himself!
—Mahādēviyakka[16]

Having relinquished vestigial pride, Mahādēviyakka found acceptance within the assembly of *śaraṇas* and became one of their more accomplished and celebrated members. She also attained Prabhu's approval of her own individual spiritual accomplishment when he discerned that she had overcome all dualistic sense and fully realized the Lord within herself.

You have, dear sister, transcended the sense
Of twain, in Guhēśvaraliṅga, sister mine.
—Allama Prabhu[17]

THE THREE VIEWS ON SOCIETY MEMBERSHIP

From the preceding review of several episodes from the *Śūnyasaṃpādane*, there emerged three distinct views on the nature of the Vīraśaiva assembly. These three views—represented by Basava, Allama Prabhu, and Cennabasava—held that membership in the society was open to all earnest seekers, that membership in the society was a bogus concern beside the individual spiritual attainment of the seeker, and that membership was to be restricted to those who had already demonstrated a high degree of saintly perfection.

Parallel to these disagreements over the boundaries of *śaraṇa* membership, were differing views on the functions of that membership. Basava saw the saintly assembly itself as a potentially salvific device. In that association, the spiritual seeker could find guidance and nurture for his or her continued spiritual attainment. Allama Prabhu again saw the assembly as essentially unimportant. Admittedly, one could receive guidance from other adepts, but at base the quest for salvific attainment was an individual search and had little relation to the saintly band. Cennabasava perceived membership in the assembly to be a token of an already attained moral and ritual purity. The opinion of one's fellow members was exceedingly important, but the basis for earning their regard lay in finding perfection prior to admission to the elect cadre.

The views of these three leaders bear review.

Basava's View

Basava's easy acceptance of all sincere seekers into the *śaraṇa* fold is perhaps best illustrated by his relative absence from the debates. Often it was as a result of his actions in accepting seekers into the fold that others became ensnared in arguments about those novices' relative worthiness, but Basava himself seldom intervened in the debates. One notable exception was the case of Mahādēviyakka where Basava rushed forward to receive her while others presented objections. His attitude toward receiving her and others was probably best summarized in his debates with Cennabasava over the latter's desire for initiation.

> Now, when I see *liṅga* wearers,
> Whoever could they be except
> Our Lord of the Meeting Rivers?
>
> —Basava[18]

Basava saw his purpose in life to be one of explaining and teaching to the mortal world about Śiva's salvific plan for them. Given that mission, it was his task to nourish and succor all who seemed capable of coming to know the Lord fully. Hence he set the boundaries of membership into those under his patronage rather broadly and accepted members rather uncritically. One need only put on the *liṅga* or otherwise indicate a desire and willingness to grow in spirituality, and Basava would accept that one.

Basava saw great benefit deriving from this association with other saintly characters. That benefit accrued to him as he had the opportunity to serve others of the Lord's devotees, and it also accrued to others, even sinners, who came into contact with the assembly. Basava's joy at his own opportunity to associate with and serve the devotees found expression in his *vacana*.

O Lord,
Could I describe
The joy of being with your saints?
I can't describe
The worth of talking with your saints.
Like an axle in the hub,
In the saintly company
Make me utterly dumb
Among your sainted devotees.
I am the cow of your righteousness.
O Lord of the Meeting Rivers.
—Basava[19]

Basava found his fullest joy in serving the saints of the Lord. Not only did he learn from discussions of their spiritual struggles and attainments, but also he found the opportunity to serve them, to provide for them, and to nurtue them. Like the magical cow which grants all wishes, Basava strove to provide for all the needs of the saints who sought refuge in his household and sought to know the Lord within that association.

Beyond the opportunity it provided for him to serve the members, the saintly association, in Basava's opinion, served to lead others to the experience of the Lord's saving powei. Even the vilest sinner could find purification of his sins and transformation of his nature through association with the saints.

Going to the house of a true devotee
Taking and eating what's proffered him,
Even one sunk in utter depravity
Is purified from his gravest sin
If he but ask and then eat.
'When one's mind is trapped in sin,
'He should go to the *bhakta's* den;
'He should eat the holy food,
'Or, at least, drink from water good.'
That's why I cry,
'Hail, hail to the true *bhakta*!'
O Lord of the Meeting Rivers.
—Basava[20]

It is noteworthy that Basava did not ascribe such salvific potency to association with just anyone. It was association with the true devotee which could bring purification from sin and transformation of one's being. Neither, however, did Basava seek to define rigidly who that true devotee was. He was more interested in pointing out the utility of coming into contact with the *śaraṇa* assembly through any of its members and finding, in that contact, a transforming power. His urging to any who sought spiritual beatitude was "Get yourself into association with the saints!" He felt that that association itself would bring about good results and hence should not be restricted to the few who were already perfected but should be shared as broadly as possible.

Allama Prabhu's View

In contrast to Basava's broad definition of *śaraṇa* eligibility stood Prabhu's insistence on locating the genuine spiritual accomplishment within each individual seeker. It was not so much that Prabhu was attempting to limit membership among the *śaraṇas* to a chosen few as the fact that he felt association per se to be a relatively useless means of spiritual advancement. He hoped to lead each *śaraṇa* to ever deeper levels of spiritual insight and religious experience. He therefore probed and prodded each seeker without quarter. Clearly he considered many who claimed to be *śaraṇas* to be shallow and superficial followers of the Lord, and from time to time he stated that view.

> Will Śiva's *śaraṇas* approve if you say,
> '*Bhakti* is mine or his or yours'?
> Though you speak words sweetly
> And smear your ash neatly,
> Will you be a *bhakta* by that?
>
> ...
>
> Discerning the subtle aim
> Of the *jaṅgama* who came,
> Rising to greet him,
> Bowing (to his feet) then,
> Stumbling and fearful,
> Mumbling and tearful,
> If one knows his service proper,
> That is *bhakti*—one's true shelter!
>
> ...

Those who are ablaze
With ego's red flame
Just can never please
Our Lord of the Hidden Caverns.
—Allama Prabhu[21]

Prabhu's effort was not one of excluding unworthies from the assembly of saints; his desire was to expunge unworthiness itself from the hearts of individuals. Thus he quickly moved the debate from a question of *śaraṇa* approval to one of genuine egoless service. He demanded more than external conformity to the ritual observances of the community—the wearing of the sacred ash, and he demanded more than an egoic desire to be associated with those who sought the Lord. What he demanded was an humble and contrite heart, dedicated to the service of the Lord and of His *jaṅgamas*. Yet the reward of fulfilling that demand was not simple admission to an assembly of religious adepts but true and dependable refuge in service to the Lord.

Emphasizing the quality of inner attainment necessary for the individual to know the Lord, Prabhu placed little value in association with the band of *śaraṇas* itself. Association with that group, in and of itself, would not provide one any special or more direct access to the Lord's salvation. The signs of that association, for example wearing the *liṅga*, were not themselves efficacious of one's spiritual advancement. In fact, their chief value lay merely in appeasing the demands of the human association of *śaraṇas* with no real effect on one's salvific status.

. . .
Therefore, touch with *liṅga*
Is *bhakta's* dogma
For true purity.
O Cennabasava,
Let Siddharāma have
Liṅga's saving touch
As a pleasing salve
For the popular mind
Of the *śaraṇa* band.
O Lord of the Hidden Caverns.
—Allama Prabhu[22]

In capitulating to the demands of the community for Siddharāma's initiation, Prabhu was not confirming the soteriological capacity either of the *liṅga* or of membership in the society of *śaraṇas*. He was merely recognizing the existence of the community and of its sentiments. His argument had been and remained that Siddharāma was individually and internally perfected in spiritual pursuits and, hence, membership in that group of people was optional for his salvific status. Both the definition of the community's boundaries and a determination of the functions of community membership were highly optional considerations for Prabhu. What mattered most was the state of one's individual spiritual accomplishment.

Cennabasava's View

In conscious contrast to Basava, who accepted all wearers of *liṅga* uncritically into the *śaraṇa* assembly, Cennabasava was unable to overlook the shortcomings of certain pretenders to *śaraṇa*-hood. He demanded some degree of moral rectitude and a high level of ritually correct observance from those who wished to be *śaraṇas*.

> Saying, 'All which has *liṅga* on the body
> 'Is Lord Saṅgama Himself',
> Though it is fine for Basava
> Is not the right faith for me.
> . . . —Cennabasava[23]

Cennabasava almost seemed to envy Basava's easy acceptance of those who wished to be members of the spiritual community. He recognized the high degree of self-effacing service which Basava poured out upon those who claimed to be followers of the Lord. Cennabasava himself, however, could not match that level of positive regard which Basava showered rather uncritically upon the *bhaktas*. For Cennabasava, some stricter and clearer criteria of membership were needed. One of the things which he demanded from prospective members of the community was that they exhibit genuinely moral and upright behaviour. Even stronger, however, was his insistence that they subscribe to the code of ritual practice which he advocated for the Vīraśaiva community. Thus he insisted without fail that prospective members, including himself, must have been duly initiated and bear the *iṣṭaliṅga* upon their persons before they could join the assembly.

It was this insistence upon a high degree of moral and ritual perfection prior to membership which informed Cennabasava's view of the function of the community itself. For him, true benefit could be had from living in association with other perfected beings, but he ever contended that that benefit belonged only to those who were already well-advanced in spiritual and religious achievement. Hence he saw the city of Kalyāṇa as a haven for the perfected and a dwelling place for the elect. It was the glories already accomplished by the residents of Kalyāṇa which he praised, not their possible future perfection due to association with other seekers. Thus he praised Kalyāṇa as a heavenly city peopled with saintly persons.

> I shall proclaim completely the glories of that blessed city, Kalyāṇa. May it thrive accompanied by its fame. There, you will find no others except those who are true, pure, immortal, and perfected; those who are great *jñānis* and Śiva's own *yōgis*; those who are endowed with experience of Śiva himself and bear the *Śivaliṅga* as their very breath; and those who study the *Śaivāgamas* and know how to worship Śiva properly—those who are partisans of Śiva united with His *prasāda* and *pādōdaka*.
>
> —Cennabasava[24]

Cennabasava saw the assembly of folks at Kalyāṇa not as a group of those collected under their shared desire to learn about and to serve the Lord, but as a group of those elected by their spiritual and religious pre-eminence. The community at Kalyāṇa was a community of the saints. They gathered together as a party of the Lord's devotees and stood over and against all who were without their degree of perfection. In other words, they were a particularly rigorist and exclusivist assembly of the sectarian sort. In his view, theirs was not a universalist and inclusivist church open to all but a particularist and exclusivist sect restricted to those who had earned their admission.

NOTES

1. *ŚS* Śi., 60/ Ha., 917/ Gum., 59/ Gū., 1:61; I, 107f. A similar idea was expressed by Tayamanavar when he argued that none can contain or imprison the Lord's greatness. See A.J. Appasamy, *Temple Bells: Readings from Hindu Religious Literature* (Calcutta: Y.M.C.A. Publishing House, n.d.), p. 39:

Place has no power to prison His presence;
No one can say, 'He is here, He is there';
Not in this place, not in that, is the Godhead,
Unbounded by places, He bides everywhere.

2. *ŚS* Śi., 243/ Ha., 305/ Gum., 238/ Gū., 4:4; II, 31f.

3. *ŚS* Śi., 242/ Ha., 304/ Gum., 237/ Gū., 4:3; II, 29ff. The *Kural* asserts the necessity of listening to and learning from a master in order to avoid the conceit of self-learning. See Tiruvalluvar, *Kural: The Great Book of Tiru-Valluvar*, trans. C. Rajagopalachari (Bombay: Bharatiya Vidya Bhavan, 1975), p. 83:

Listening to the expositions of learned men gives one the humility of speech that appertains to true learning. Mere study is apt to leave one conceited.

4. *ŚS* Śi., 244/ Ha., 306/ Gum., 239/ Gū., 4:5; II, 32ff.

5. *ŚS* —/ —/ —/ Gū., 10:17; III, 222f. Cennabasava's insistence on proper marriage as a fitting symbol for the culmination of spiritual bliss runs counter not only to the experience of Prabhu and Siddharāma but also to that of many other *bhaktas* elsewhere. The love of one who is not one's proper spouse (*parakīyā*) permeates the imagery of northern Indian Vaiṣṇava poetry.

6. *ŚS* —/ Ha., 680/ Gum., 402/ Gū., 10:16; III, 221. The translation is by Bhoosnurmath and Menezes, but their punctuation has been altered.

7. *ŚS* —/ —/ —/ Gū., 10:10; III, 216. Again the motif of love as perfect union is more characteristic of later Bengali devotional literature than of the Vīraśaivas. For example, love as perfect union needing no platform except the restless waves is expressed in the following *sahaja* poem from Bengal. See Chandidās, *Love Songs of Chandidās: The Rebel Poet-Priest of Bengal*, trans. Deben Bhattacharya (New York: Grove Press, Inc., 1967), p. 153:

On the earth/ rests the water,/ on water/ rest the waves/ and on waves/ afloat is love .../

Love, love and love./ This four-letter word/ carries a multiple/ of opinions./ But if you adore it/ and go deeper and deeper,/ you will find that/ it is only One—Wholly love.

8. *ŚS* —/ Ha., 568/ Gum., 430/ Gū., 10:29, III, 233f.

9. *ŚS* —/ —/ Gum., 444/ Gū., 10:36; III, 240f. This plaintive yearning for the Lord's presence finds resonance in much of *bhakti* literature. Besides the longing of the souls as *gopīs* for the Lord as Kṛṣṇa, a more explicit longing to enjoy the Lord's salvific presence occurs in Tulsī Dās, *Petition to Rām: Hindi*

Devotional Hymns of the Seventeenth Century, trans. and ed. F.R. Allchin (London: George Allen and Unwin Ltd., 1966), pp. 149-150:

Wherefore, O Hari, have you forgotten me?

You know your own greatness and my sins, yet—Lord—you have not given me your support. ...

I have no fear of falling into hell, even though I'm quite defeated in my efforts,

But my heavy affliction is this, O Lord of Tulsī Dās, that your Name has not consumed my sins!

10. *ŚS* —/ —/ —/ Gū., 15:10; IV, 213f. The *Kural* likewise condemns the hypocrite who is disguised for the attainment of food. See *Kural*, p. 48:

The feeble-minded wearing the brave trappings of strength is like a miserable cow putting on the skin of a tiger to save itself from being impounded while feeding stealthily on the corn in a stranger's field.

11. *ŚS* —/ —/ —/ Gū., 15:27; IV, 226.

12. *ŚS* —/ —/ —/ Gū., 15:18; IV, 219f.

13. *ŚS* Śi., 589/ Ha., 993/ Gum., 951/ Gū., 16:4; IV, 286f.

14. *ŚS* Śi., 594/ Ha., 998/ Gum., 956/ Gū., 16:9; IV, 291f.

15. *ŚS* —/ —/ —/ Gū., 16:15; IV, 296f. This wearing of long hair is a familiar characteristic of male Śaiva ascetics. The image evokes Śiva's own long matted hair as the currents of Gaṅgā. Sundaramūrti Swāmi has appealed to Śiva's androgynous nature in his efforts to balance devotion with the exigencies of domestication represented by women. Specifically he refers to Śiva's locks as the Gaṅgā. See F. Kingsbury and G.E. Phillips, *Hymns of the Tamil Śaivite Saints* (Calcutta: Association Press, 1921), p. 81:

Thou art half woman Thyself;/ Gaṅgā is in Thy long hair.

Full well canst Thou comprehend/ Burden of women so fair.

16. *ŚS* —/ —/ —/ Gū., 16:39; IV, 314f. A similar disgust with fruitless embodiment was expressed by Tulsī Dās, *Petition to Rām*, p. 216:

What gain was there in obtaining this human body, When in speech, thought or deed, never even in dreams have you been of service in the affairs of others?...

For all who are born in this world fear, sleep, food and copulation are the common lot,/ And you, who have obtained this body—difficult even for the gods to gain/ —Have not worshipped Hari, but have wasted it in pride and haughtiness.

17. *ŚS* —/ —/ —/ Gū., 16:41; IV, 316f. The translation is by Bhoosnurmath and Menezes.

18. *ŚS* Śi., 243/ Ha., 305/ Gum., 238/ Gū., 4:4; II, 31f.

19. *ŚS* Śi., 403/ Ha., 873/ Gum., 695/ Gū., 7:2; II, 311f.

20. *ŚS* —/ —/ —/ Gū., 13:2; IV, 74.

21. *ŚS* Śi., 297/ Ha., 359/ Gum., 292/ Gū., 5:10; II, 129ff. The *Kural* also warns of those who pretend to be devotees but in fact are not even decent human beings. Their external similarity to the true devotee is dangerously deceiving. With irony the *Kural*, p. 107 says:

Strange indeed is the complete physical resemblance of the unscrupulous to the human species. It is the best example of mimesis we know of.

22. *ŚS* —/ Ha., 739/ Gum., 500/ Gū., 10:48; III, 256ff.

23. *ŚS* Śi., 397/ Ha., 864/ Gum., 688/ Gū., 11:9 (11:4); III, 336f.

24. *ŚS* Śi., 272/ Ha., 320/ Gum., 267/ Gū., 4:34; II, 72-82. A comparison with Mahādēviyakka's *vacana* (*ŚS* Śi., 589/ Ha., 993/ Gum., 951/ Gū., 16:4; IV, 286f) which appears above reveals a similar view of the saintly perfection of those assembled at Kalyāṇa.

Chapter Five

CONCLUSION

In the Introduction, preliminary to a detailed study of the *Śūnya-saṃpādane*, a more general study of Vīraśaiva phenomena as presented in the secondary literature was essayed. That general study began by noting several pertinent characteristics of the movement, including many of its important practices. Certain factors about Vīraśaiva institutional arrangement and ritual practice became more intelligible when viewed in light of a typology of religious associations.

For example, the wearing of the *liṅga* by each individual and the direct soteriological relation implied by that practice, the rejection of the temple cult with its priestly specialists, the revulsion at wearing the sacred thread bestowed in the Brahmanical initiation—these and other factors highlighted an antagonistic relation between Vīraśaivism and orthodox Brahmanical Hinduism. On the other hand, Vīraśaiva affirmation of certain values shared by Brahmanical Hindus, Jains, and even Buddhists—values such as strict vegetarianism and teetotalism—illustrated a more intimate relation among the traditions.

Holding these and other characteristics in mind, a review and critique of previous attempts to understand the relation of Vīraśaivism to its broader religio-social context was undertaken. The attempt to discern whether Vīraśaivas are "Hindus" or not was found to be misdirected insofar as it operated with a sharper division between Hindu and non-Hindu than was warranted. More profitable was a view which saw the Vīraśaivas, as well as Brahmanical Hindus, as Indian first—and that means as "Hindu" —and then as some sub-division within that larger descriptive category. Another analytic tool—the attempt to understand the Liṅgāyatas as an Indian sect—was also found inadequate insofar as it utilized a too particularistic and non-generalizable definition of the term "sect". A more formal definition, specifically as developed by the sociological study of religion, provided a hopeful corrective to those problems.

In seeking a fresh perspective on Vīraśaiva institutional patterns and their relation to the movement's broader context, a typological analysis, despite its undeniable perils, was found fundamentally useful. The simple sect-church-mystic terminology originally suggested by Troeltsch, however, did require supplementation. A more formal typology, based upon the abstract dimensions of objectivity/subjectivity of the means of salvation and of particularism/universalism of membership criteria emerged as promising.

COMPETING ASSOCIATIONAL IDEALS IN ANCIENT VĪRAŚAIVISM

The issues which emerged from this review of previous investigations of the movement and the promise which arose from a typological analysis of the competing theories of Vīraśaiva origins provided the basis for a focused study of the movement's institutional structures as exhibited in one period and, in fact, in one text from Vīraśaiva history. The detailed study of that text—the *Śūnyasaṃpādane*—then revealed competing types of religious association reflecting sectarian subjective-particularism, ecclesiastical objective-universalism, and mystical subjective-individualism.

In fact, several competing visions of just what Vīraśaivism was and should be found ardent and able defense from one of the three principal characters in that text—namely, Allama Prabhu, Cennabasava, and Basava. The distinct attitudes of these three *śaraṇas* were explored with respect to their ideas concerning the relative objectivity/subjectivity of the means of salvation and the relative universalism/particularism of their criteria for community membership.

It was found that Allama Prabhu rejected the objective cult in favour of subjective spirituality; Cennabasava defended and propagated the objective cult as a valid means of attaining salvific grace; and Basava rejoiced in the performance of genuine and heart-felt worship of the Lord through objective means only when these were accompanied by a necessary subjective experience. Figure 1 attempts to chart their attitudes on the relative objectivism/subjectivism of soteriological means.

OBJECTIVISM	Cennabasava
MODERATE SUBJECTIVISM	Basava
RADICAL SUBJECTIVISM	Allama Prabhu

FIG. 1. Objective v. Subjective Soteriology

Equally distinct were the views of Basava, Allama Prabhu, and Cennabasava on the appropriate criteria for drawing the boundaries of membership in the *śaraṇa* band. These three *śaraṇas* held respectively the views that membership in the society was universally and inclusively open to all earnest seekers, that membership in the society was a bogus concern beside the individual spiritual attainment of the seeker, and that membership was to be particularly and exclusively restricted to those who had already demonstrated a high degree of saintly perfection. Their ecclesiological ideas are charted in Figure 2.

UNIVERSALISM/ INCLUSIVISM	PARTICULARISM/ EXCLUSIVISM	INDIVIDUALISM
Basava	Cennabasava	Allama Prabhu

FIG. 2. Universalist v. Particularist Ecclesiology

When these two dimensions of religious association—universality/particularity and objectivism/subjectivism—are made proximate, the dynamic of conflict within the Vīraśaiva community emerges. Allama Prabhu rejected the objective cult in favor of subjective spirituality and dismissed debates over membership criteria as meaningless in face of the centrality of individual spirituality for the genuine mystical seeker. Cennabasava defended and propagated the objective cult as a valid means for attaining salvific grace and argued that the criteria for determining who would be allowed to participate in that cult should be strenuous, clear-cut, and rigid. Basava, though rejoicing at the performance of genuine and heart-felt worship of the Lord through objective means, utterly disdained the creeping hypocrisy of empty ritualism and preferred a more subjective and volitional path to salvation coupled with an easy acceptance of all who sought to follow that path.

In other words, none of these three celebrated founders of Vīraśaivism sought to establish a sectarian organization of the subjective-particularist type. In fact, each exerted his energies, in one direction or another, to mould Vīraśaivism into something which was specifically not a sect, at least as that term is understood within typological analysis.

Allama Prabhu's radical subjectivity and, more importantly, his distinct individualism sought a type of religious person, rather than a type of religious group, which corresponded to what Troeltsch had called the mystic. Basava's easy acceptance of all into the *śaraṇa* band led him away from the sectarian type organization toward a more universalistic, though no less subjectivistic and voluntaristic, type organization which corresponds to the denomination or established sect as described by later elaborators upon Troeltsch's ideas.[1] Cennabasava's continued emphasis on a rigorous particularism combined with his delight in the objective availablity of salvific grace to gravitate toward a type of religious organization often overlooked and perhaps best denominated the cultus. Figure 3 summarizes the institutional ideals of these three saintly persons.

	UNIVERSALISM/ INCLUSIVISM	PARTICULARISM/ EXCLUSIVISM	INDIVIDUALISM
OBJECTIVISM	U-O CHURCH	P-O CULTUS ↑ Cennabasava	I-O (Unknown, except perhaps as "fetishism" in the psychological sense)
MODERATE SUBJECTIVISM	U-S DENOMINATION ←Basava	P-S SECT	
RADICAL SUBJECTIVISM			I-S MYSTIC Allama Prabhu ↘

FIG. 3. Three Vīraśaiva Institutional Ideals

DENOMINATIONAL FACTORS IN CONTEMPORARY VĪRAŚAIVISM

Although the present is not the appropriate context for a detailed analysis of contemporary Vīraśaivism, it is worthwhile to note that competing associational ideals are by no means confined to Vīraśaiva antiquity. In fact, two often overlooked and closely related factors—internal Vīraśaiva denominational strife and theories about the origin of the movement—are but contemporary manifestations of the longstanding competition between ideal visions of what Vīraśaivism ought to be.

This matter has been dealt with more thoroughly elsewhere,[2] but for the present it is important only to note in passing that contemporary Vīraśaivism is often portrayed in an only partially accurate manner. Typically, modern works portray the group as a radical and reformatory sectarian movement set over and against the institutions of its broader context within Brahmanical Hinduism. They also commonly present, without caveat, an account of the foundation of the movement in the twelfth century actions of Basava. The matter, however, is not nearly so simple; for, like many things Indian, the origins of the Vīraśaiva movement are subject to disputation.

There are, in fact, two major sets of beliefs among Vīraśaivas about their movement's foundation, and each set of beliefs contributes to a distinct vision of the pattern which Vīraśaiva organizational forms ought to take. Furthermore, the two sets of foundation beliefs and the two ideal visions of Vīraśaiva organization coincide rather closely with a little chronicled but quite real denominational split within Vīraśaivism.

The better known account of the movement's origins deals with the activities of a twelfth-century founder and benefactor, Basava, and his saintly colleagues.[3] This account stresses the direct, unmediated salvation which is available without priestly assistance or ritual performance. Further it stresses the intracommunal nature of Vīraśaiva goals and fulfilments. In short, this account provides the rationale for an exclusivist and subjectivist Vīraśaivism of the sectarian sort.

The other account of the movement's origins claims great antiquity for Vīraśaivism reaching ultimately to the Indus Valley civilization and given added impetus by five great teachers—Revaṇārādhya, Maruḷārādhya, Ekōrāmārādhya, Paṇḍitārādhya, and Viśvārādhya—whose dates are unknown but are reputedly long before Basava's twelfth-century activities.[4] This account allows a relatively greater role for the assistance of priests and the efficacy of rituals in helping one to attain salvation. Further, it places no requirement of voluntary acceptance upon Vīraśaivas but makes its salvific agency available to all who are born within the Vīraśaiva regions or families. In short, this account provides a rationale for a universalistic and objectivist vision of the Vīraśaiva church.

At the level of theory, a reconciliation of these two accounts is not difficult to discern. One could argue that a Śaiva cult which owed its organizational, philosophical, and spiritual existence to several great teachers may well have existed for centuries before Basava. It would have functioned under the institutional guidance of the five great monastic centers and received its guidance from the heads of those monasteries. The twelfth century may have brought a revitalization of that cult under the emotional intensity of Basava's spiritual experience. His position as a royal minister and the patronage he gave to these ardent Śaivas would have aided Basava's revivalist effort and contributed to his eminence in the movement.

This compromise account recommends itself to those who seek a dogged consistency in their history and to Vīraśaivas of good will who seek to overcome denominational strife. It should be noted, however, that this attempt at reconciliation is merely a theoretical device which ignores the normative function of the myths of origin for adherents thereto. The basic Basava and *ācārya* accounts represent not so much different theoretical persuasions as fundamental differences of institutional loyalty. The loyalties divide along lines of an institutional separation not well-known in the West but quite apparent to Vīraśaivas themselves.[5]

Rather than one single affiliation of Vīraśaiva priests and laymen, there are actually two, separate systems of monastic organizational and hieratic loyalty—the so-called *virakta maṭhas* and the distinct *gurusthala maṭhas*.[6] The former are located primarily in cities, emphasize educational endeavors, and expect ascetic rigor from their leaders. For the monks and laymen associated with the *virakta* denomination, the beliefs, organization, and practices reflected in the Basava account serve as normative guide for their basically sectarian type of religious organization. The *gurusthala maṭhas* are more likely to be located in villages, to emphasize such pastoral functions as worship and conflict mediation, and to be served by priestly specialists who are fully incorporated into the social structure of the community. Those who associate with the *gurusthala* denomination's temples derive the norms for their basically ecclesiastical organizational pattern from the *ācārya* (great teacher) theory. Thus the perdurance of these two seemingly contradictory accounts is found to have its basis in the existing social institutions, i.e. religious denominations, formed upon the normative vision of each account.

These factors become especially clear when the apparent ideals of each denomination are compared to the ideals expressed in each foundation myth. The distinction between those ideals, both of denominational form and of foundation myth, is best characterized by the sociological typology of the sect and the church, or ecclesia. Comparison reveals that the sectarian ideal prominent within the Basava foundation account propagates itself institutionally in the ideals and practices of one Vīraśaiva denomination. The particularism and subjectivism of that myth find institutional expression in the denomination exhibiting allegiance to that myth—namely, the "sectarian" *viraktas*. Similarly, the ecclesial ideal prominent within the *ācārya* foundation account propagates itself institutionally in the ideals and practices of the other denomination. The universalism and objectivism of that myth find their actualization in the group which professes that myth—namely, the "ecclesial" *gurusthalins*. Figure 4 charts this typological comparison.

SECT	ECCLESIA (CHURCH)
particularist membership subjective soteriology voluntarism world rejection egalitarianism anti-ritualism	universalistic membership objective soteriology ascription world acceptance hierarchism sacramentalism
VIRAKTA DENOMINATION	*GURUSTHALA* DENOMINATION
monasteries ascetical leaders social services teaching functions voluntary membership	temples married priests conflict mediation liturgical celebrations parish membership
BASAVA ACCOUNT	*ĀCĀRYA* ACCOUNT
rejection of initiation rejection of caste intense inner religiosity spirituality society formed in-group distinctiveness	ceremonial actions silent on social ideals miraculous powers of *ācāryas* geographical sees established indistinct group boundaries

FIG. 4. An Ideal Typology of Vīraśaiva Foundation Accounts and Denominational Affiliations

In fact, it seems that the denominational divisions endure, to a great extent, because of their allegiance to different ideal visions of what Vīraśaivism should be. Those ideals, expressed in the foundation myths, find their way into practice in the two actual denominations of Vīraśaivism; and it is only with damage to a full understanding of Vīraśaivism that one or the other foundation myth and one or the other denominational pattern can be taken as normative.[7] Both ideals represent express actualizations of Vīraśaivism's ideal genius.

PROSPECTUS FOR FUTURE STUDIES

It would seem that the present study has demonstrated at least one thing: the patterns of Vīraśaiva institutional arrangement were, in the fifteenth-century, considerably more diverse than can be indicated by any single typological term such as "sect". Furthermore, it has indicated that recognition of that earlier diversity helps in understanding the major denominational division of contemporary Vīraśaivism. Beyond these conclusions, however, the present study also suggests several aspects of Vīraśaiva organizational history which promise profit for future investigation.

A Diachronic Analysis of Vīraśaivism

The most important and promising, though perhaps also the most difficult, of these directions for further investigation is an effort to move beyond a purely synchronic analysis of the fifteenth century toward a diachronic analysis of institutional developments between the twelfth and fifteenth centuries and from that period to the present. The outline of such a diachronic analysis would see the origins of the Vīraśaiva movement within the intense mystical experience of individuals who eventually came together into some sort of restricted society based on the subjective depth of those experiences. That particularist and subjectivist society would then, over time, evolve a concern for objective signs of its status and for objective means by which others could share in its experiences. Simultaneously, it would evolve toward a greater and greater inclusiveness of individuals within its ranks without demanding the same degree of individual, subjective experience from those newcomers. Specifically, would its demands for subjective experience be loosened beginning with the second generation—the children of the original *śaraṇas*. In short, the individual mystic, in seeking association with like-minded colleagues, would soon find himself the member of a particularistic-subjectivist sect which over time would evolve toward becoming a universalist-objectivist church.

This general tendency within religious institutions is well-known among sociologists of religion and finds considerable, though not universal, acceptance among them.[8] What is intriguing, however, is that the narrative of the *Śūnyasampādane* itself traces just such a development.

The opening chapter deals with Allama Prabhu alone with his *guru* in the cave. Upon leaving the cave, he meets up with and intensifies the subjective religious experience of another loner, Siddharāma. The two then become involved in the activities of a society within the society of Kalyāṇa where sectarian particularist subjectivism seems to be the order of the day. That sectarian order, however, faces constant challenges from Basava to become more universalistic, on the one hand, and from Cennabasava to become more objectivist, on the other. In other words, it evolves toward the church-type of objectivist universalism and Allama Prabhu, the individualist, finds himself reluctantly elevated to leadership within the emerging objective hierarchy of that group.

In fact, it is interesting to observe that the *Śūnyasampādane* not only chronicles such developments within Vīraśaivism's first three hundred years but also participates in that very process of institutional evolution. From the writing of the first version by Śivagaṇaprasādi Mahādēvayya until the composition of Gūḷūra Siddhavīraṇārya's, the objectification of membership in the form of initiation had acquired sufficient importance that it found a prominent place in the latter's version. It was primarily in order to narrate the debate over Siddharāma's initiation that the later editors of the *Śūnyasampādane* undertook their revisions of Śivagaṇaprasādi Mahādēvayya's effort. The *Śūnyasampādane* may not only portray the evolution of Vīraśaivism from sect to church but also may participate in that very evolution as the text developed during the fifteenth century.

Vīraśaivism's Objectivist/Universalist Threat to Brahmanical Hinduism

Finally, it should be noted with regard to types of religious institutions in general and with regard to Vīraśaivism in particular that it is not the sectarian type of organization which poses a problem for other religious institutions within its broader context.[9] This is where previous efforts to characterize the Vīraśaivas as a sect have gone wrong, for they have, by and large, attempted to see the sect as a challenge to Brahmanical authority and to characterize the Vīraśaiva challenge to that authority as sectarian. In fact, it is significant that Vīraśaivism can and sometimes does challenge the authority of the Brahmins, but that challenge comes not from the movement's sectarian—i.e. subjectivist particularistic—tendencies. These could be and have been easily tolerated within the broader Brahmanical context. One more or less aberrant sect minding its own particular subjective business posed no problems for the rest of Hindu society.

Rather, it was precisely when Vīraśaivism began asserting its universalistic claims to the allegiance of all who inhabited its environs and began replacing Brahmanical practice with its own objective and quantifiable means to salvation that it became a challenge to the Brahmins. In other words, the distinctness which scholars have attempted to describe by applying the word "sect" to the Vīraśaivas became an important factor only when the group turned away from the structural characteristics—subjectivism and particularism—of what has been called a "sect" in the general sociology of religion and turned towards components of the church-type organization—namely, objectivism and universalism.

Hence, those critics and apologists alike who would have Vīraśaivism shear itself of all objectivist manifestations or of a certain easy-going universalism in favor of a return to a "pure" form of voluntary rigorism in the form of subjectivist particularism would rob the movement of its competitive vitality. It profits not to romanticize a bygone period or to construct a, perhaps-never-actually-existent, image of pristine sectarian Vīraśaivism if so doing harms the movement's capacity for vital contribution to the religious life of India in particular and of humankind in general. That capacity is enhanced, not diminished, by the multiplicity of associational ideals which the movement has exhibited throughout its history and exhibits in its celebrated text—the *Śūnyasaṃpādane*.

NOTES

1. For example, Joachim Wach, "Church, Denomination and Sect", in his *Types of Religious Experience: Christian and non-Christian* (Chicago: University of Chicago Press, 1951), pp. 187-208.

2. Specifically at R. Blake Michael, "Foundation Myths of the Two Denominations of Vīraśaivism: *Viraktas* and *Gurusthalins*", *Journal of Asian Studies* XLII.2 (1983 February); 309-322.

3. The Basava account is treated fully and critically by P.B. Desai, *Basavesvara and His Times* (Dharwar: Kannada Research Institute, Karnatak University, 1968). The scriptural locus is *Basavapurāṇa* [of Bhīmkavi], ed. R.C. Hiremath (Dharwar: Karnatak University Press, 1968), (in Kannaḍa); elsewhere summarized by G. Würth, "The Basava Purāṇa of the Lingaits," *Journal of the Bombay Branch of the Royal Asiatic Society* 8.24 (1865-66): 65-97.

4. The *ācārya* account is presented by S.C. Nandimath, *A Handbook of Vīraśaivism* (Dharwar: L.E. Association, 1942), pp. 13-18, and in more detail with greater attention to primary sources by M.R. Sakhare, *History and Philosophy of the Lingayat Religion* (Belgaum: By the Author, 134 Thalakwadi P.O., n.d. [1942]), pp. 361-413. One scriptural locus is *Siddhānta Śikhāmaṇi* [of Śivayōgi], ed. Kāśīnātha Śāstri (Mysore: Śrī Pañcācārya Electric Press, V.P. Mahādēvayya, 1972).

5. This little-discussed denominational division is described by H.M. Sadasivaiah, *A Comparative Study of Two Vīraśaiva Monasteries* (Mysore: Prasaranga, Manasa Gangotri, 1967), pp. 91-94, whose work, unfortunately, proceeds to compare two apparently *virakta* monasteries. The division is also mentioned by William McCormack, "On Lingayat Culture", in *Speaking of Śiva,* ed. A.K. Ramanujan (Baltimore: Penguin, 1973), pp. 178-79; discussed in more detail by him in "Lingayats as Sect," *Journal of the Royal Anthropological Institute of Great Britain and Ireland* 93 (1963 January to June): 62-64; and elaborated by Clement Marro, "Role and Position of the Guru and of the Jangama in Lingayatism," *Bangalore Theological Forum* 6.2 (1974 July-December): 43-44. See also Lise F. Vail, "The Lingayat Gurusthala Matha; An Investigation into the Nature and Role of the House-hold Monastery in South India", (Ph.D. dissertation, University of Pennsylvania.

6. The following description of the two denominations is based upon the scanty data mentioned above and, more importantly, upon field observations made during 1975-76 under the auspices of the Rotary International Foundation and with the assistance of Mr. Ravi Hiremath of Karnatak University, Dharwar and during 1982 under the auspices of the National Endowment for the Humanities.

7. Compare Troeltsch's conclusion that the various forms of religious association all represent the original genius of Christianity: "From the beginning these ... forms were foreshadowed, and all down the centuries to the present day, wherever religion is dominant, they still appear alongside of one another, while among themselves they are strangely and variously

interwoven and interconnected", *The Social Teaching of the Christian Churches*, trans. Olive Wyon (New York: Harper and Row, Publishers, 1960), pp. 993-4.

8. Specifically this is the so-called Niebuhr-Pope hypothesis.

9. This characteristic has been noted with reference to the Christian data by Paul M. Gustafson, "Church and Sect or Church and Ascetic Protestantism: Ernst Troeltsch's Problem", *Encounter* 30:2 (1969 Spring): pp. 142-47.

APPENDIX I

LIṄGĀYATAS IN KARNĀṬAKA (ESTIMATE)

The modern state of Karnāṭaka (previously called Mysore) has never been canvassed for caste affiliation data. The two following tables, therefore, are based on the outdated but latest available data on caste affliation in that region. Caste affiliation data from the *Census of India*, 1931 have been utilized for all districts except those in the erstwhile Madras Presidency for which reliance was upon the even older *Census of India*, 1921.

The problems of counting the Liṅgāyatas and the crucial data from 1881 through 1931 were presented by Margaret T. Egnor, "The Lingayats of Mysore: A Study in the Acquisition of Power and Prestige" (Senior Honors thesis, Harvard University, 1970), pp. 161-164a.

For the following tables, the volumes utilized were as follow:

Census of India, 1921. Vol. XIII, pts. i and ii: *Madras*. Edited by G. T. Boag. Madras: Superintendent, Government Press, 1922.

Census of India, 1931. Vol. VIII, pts. i and ii: *Bombay Presidency*. Edited by A. H. Dracup and H. T. Sorley. Bombay: Government Central Press, 1933.

——— Vol. XIII: *Coorg*. Edited by M. S. Mandanna. Calcutta: Government of India Central Publication Branch, 1932.

———. Vol. XIV, pts. i and ii: *Madras*. Edited by M. W. M. Yeatts. Calcutta: Government of India Central Publication Branch, 1932.

———. Vol. XXIII, pts. i and ii: *H. E. H. the Nizam's Dominions* (*Hyderabad State*). Edited by Gulam Ahmed Khan. Hyderabad, Deccan: Government Central Press, 1933.

———. Vol. XXV, pts. i and ii: *Mysore*. Edited by M. Venkatesa Iyengar. Bangalore: Government Press, 1932.

Census of India, 1981. Series 9: *Karnataka*. Part II-A: *General Population Tables*. Edited by B.K. Das. Bangalore: Director of Census Operations Karnataka, 1983.

All data which are estimates or extrapolations have been enclosed within brackets [ ].

TABLE A: 1931

Reporting Category	*Current District*	*Population*	*Liṅgāyatas*	%
Bombay Presidency				
Belgaum	Belgaum	1,076,701	292,942	27
Bijapur	Bijapur	869,220	300,676	35
Dharwar	Dharwad	1,102,677	374,981	34
Kanara	Uttar Kannad	417,835	4,721	1
Coorg (*State*)	Kodagu	130,271	5,068	4
Madras Presidency				
Bellary	Bellary	969,774	[116,561]	[12]
Sandur (State)	Bellary	13,583	[3,512]	[26]
South Kanara	Dakshin Kannad	1,372,241	none reported	nil
Hyderabad (*States*)				
Bidar	Bidar	873,615	124,801	14
Gulbarga	Gulbarga	1,225,008	235,940	19
Raichur	Raichur	937,535	140,128	15
Mysore (*State*)				
Bangalore (Cantonment)	Bangalore	134,113	1,090	1
Bangalore (City)	Bangalore	172,357	5,619	3
Bangalore (District)	Bangalore	908,056	45,573	5
Chitaldrug	Chitradurga	656,569	140,987	21
Hassan	Hassan	596,937	85,600	14
Kadur	Chikmagalur	347,715	65,238	19
Kolar (District)	Kolar	763,934	12,113	2
Kolar (Gold Fields)	Kolar	85,103	253	nil
Mysore (City)	Mysore	107,142	4,576	4
Mysore (District)	Mysore and Mandya	1,403,984	199,730	14
Shimoga	Shimoga	519,987	106,504	20
Tumkur	Tumkur	861,405	103,519	12
ALL KARNĀṬAKA AREA (1931)		15,529,647	[2,367,692]	[15]

TABLE B: 1981

District	*Population*	%	*Liṅgāyatas*
Bangalore (inc. Canton. and City)	4,947,610	[4]	[212,981]
Belgaum	2,980,440	[27]	[810,899]
Bellary (inc. Sandur)	1,489,225	[12]	[181,842]
Bidar	995,691	[14]	[142,240]
Bijapur	2,401,782	[35]	[830,812]
Chikmagalur (Kadur)	911,769	[19]	[171,065]
Chitradurga	1,777,499	[21]	[381,688]
Kodagu	461,888	[4]	[17,969]
Dharwad	2,945,487	[34]	[1,001,655]
Gulbarga	2,080,643	[19]	[400,738]
Hassan	1,357,014	[14]	[194,594]
Kolar (inc. Gold Fields)	1,905,492	[1]	[27,753]
Mandya (from Mysore)	1,418,109	[14]	[191,730]
Mysore (inc. City)	2,595,900	[14]	[350,969]
Uttar Kannad	1,072,034	[1]	[12,113]
Raichur	1,783,822	[15]	[266,618]
Shimoga	1,656,731	[20]	[339,332]
Dakshin Kannad	2,376,724	nil	—
Tumkur	1,977,854	[12]	[237,688]
ALL KARNĀṬAKA (1981)	37,135,714	[15]	[5,772,686]
1991 ESTIMATE	[47,068,518]		[7,316,724]

APPENDIX II

THE GENERAL TYPOLOGY OF RELIGIOUS ASSOCIATIONS AND ITS CROSS-CULTURAL APPLICABILITY

The primary purpose of the present, as of any, research is to understand as fully as possible the events, phenomena, or people which constitute the object of study. Here, the primary goal is to understand, as fully as possible, the intimate faith of Vīraśaivas as mediated to them and expressed by them in the discernible "facts" of their religious tradition. Fundamentally, then, any method which facilitates that understanding is to be utilized. Whether that method is popular, unpopular, irreproachable, disreputable, systematic, or *ad hoc*, is unimportant beside its ability to facilitate understanding. Similarly, any reflection upon methodological considerations remains quite secondary to obtaining results which facilitate the understanding of a people's religious faith and tradition.[1]

On the other hand, the more clearly one perceives the peril and promise of a chosen method, the less prone is he/she to avoidable misunderstanding of the topic studied. For that reason, it seems justifiable to explicate, as clearly as possible, the method used in the present research and, at least, to call to attention both the strengths and the potential dangers of that method. The following attempts, rather succinctly, to explicate the method of constructive typology as it has been used to study patterns of religious association within Christianity, to expose the promises that method holds forth as well as the perils it may conceal, to justify the application of that method to materials from a culture other than Christian, and to adumbrate its specific applicability for coming to understand better the religious life and faith of the Vīraśaivas.

THE EMERGENCE OF A TYPOLOGY OF RELIGIOUS ASSOCIATIONS

While those studying Indian materials have sought a definition of the sect which was specifically appropriate to that cultural context, other efforts have been made to discern the structural aspects of the sectarian type organization which would be general throughout history and across cultural boundaries. A rather clear description of the structural characteristics of the sectarian type organization has emerged from a long tradition of study and analysis utilizing materials from the history of Christianity. That investigation, however, has led to insights into the general structure of social and religious institutions which are applicable outside the realm of Christian studies.

When Christian Church History was still, in some sense, a normative discipline, the word "sect" was primarily used to denote groups which were heterodox or heteroprax when compared to the normative position of the Chruch—that is, the one holy and apostolic Church owing allegiance to the Roman pontiff. Under this denotation, it is clear that the sect has long derived its definition fundamentally by contrast to the Church.[2] In the early twentieth century, however, an attempt was initiated to discern the social-structural as well as doctrinal characteristics of the sects and of the Church without prejudice toward either type of institution.

Though the full articulation of a typology of sect-type and church-type religious institutions was provided by and is associated with the name of Ernst Troeltsch, the germ of such a typology was originally planted somewhat earlier by Max Weber.[3] In his *Protestant Ethic and the Spirit of Capitalism*, Weber specifically stated a typology of religious organizations into sect-type and church-type on which he noted several pertinent characteristics. The sect, or believer's church, is (1) exclusivistic—arising from a feeling of divine election of members and a contempt for those who are less fortunate, (2) voluntaristic—emphasizing the voluntary acceptance of rigid self-denial, or inner-worldly asceticism, by its members, (3) communalistic—stressing the common bonds of regenerate personal believers in the struggle to actualize an ideal kingdom on earth, and (4) separatistic—lacking any official relation to the political authority of the state. The church, on the other hand, is (1) inclusive of all who dwell within the area of its religio-political dominion, (2) ascriptive of their membership and allegiance even from the time of their birth, (3) fundatory in serving as a reservoir and dispenser of supernatural good in the effort to increase the glory of God and bring about the salvation of all—both just and unjust, and (4) integral to the political hegemony of a geographically defined state.[4]

Troeltsch's primary contribution to the understanding of this typology of religious associations was to give it a meticulously executed test against the data of Christian history, and thereby to highlight the importance of the typology for subsequent investigators as well as for Weber himself. In Troeltsch's approach, the course of Christian religious associational history is carefully explored while the typology of religious associations emerges slowly, intuitively, and inductively. When he does finally admit the typology explicitly, he adds important elaborations on Weber's understanding. Among these additions are an analysis of the differing roles played by asceticism in the two associational types. Whereas the church-type organization stresses asceticism as but one component of the religious life, the sect-type advocates a general ascetic denial and control for all its members. In the church-type, asceticism is dualistic and heroic and stresses supererogatory acquisition of virtue and sensory repression. In the sect-type, asceticism is integral and egalitarian and stresses a communal charity and sensory detachment but also worldly participation.[5]

A more crucial characteristic of the typology as elaborated by Troeltsch is the relative objectivity/subjectivity of the means of salvation in the two organizational types. Whether the means of human salvation lie within the hands of the objective human institution—through the priesthood and sacraments of the Church—or whether such salvation is a private and individual matter for the subjective human being—available only directly from a transcendent agency—becomes a crucial typological distinction for Troeltsch.

Refinement and elaboration of Troeltsch's typology by subsequent sociologists of religion have led to numerous complex types and typologies. Ecclesia, denomination, established sect, radical sect, etc. have been utilized in the effort to make the typological scheme more accurate.[6] All these types and typological schemes, however, can probably be reduced to two simpler but crucial dimensions—the relative objectivity/subjectivity of the means of grace suggested by Troeltsch and the relative universality/particularity of membership patterns.

By discerning whether the path to salvation is assisted by piecemeal acquisition of salvific merit provided by objective rites and symbols as received at the hands of professional priests or is a solitary road travelled by each individual seeker whose success is an all-or-nothing proposition, one can assess the relative objectivity/subjectivity of the group's soteriology. By studying the relative inclusion of all people under a specific government or within a specific region versus the exclusion of all but those few who subscribe to a particular set of doctrines and practices, one can assess the relative universality/particularity of a group's associational patterns. Paul Gustafson has argued that these are the only two dimensions really important to the sect-church typology and has proposed replacing that two- or three-fold typology by a four-fold one. His four-fold typology is obtained by cross-factoring these two essential dimensions so that four types emerge: universal-objective, universal-subjective, particular-objective, and particular-subjective. He denotes these four types as UO, US, PO, and PS, respectively.[7]

What Troeltsch called the Church corresponds to the universal-objective (UO) type; his sect, to the particular subjective (PS); and his mystic, to a subjective individualism. The chief advantage of Gustafson's scheme, however, is that it eliminates whatever connotations may adhere to the terms "church", "sect", and "mystic" from the contents of their particular histories within Christianity. His purely formal terms permit a focus on a single important dimension as it cross-factors with the other. Hence a focus on the relative objectivity/subjectivity of means of salvation can shift to an analysis of the relation of that polarity to one based on criteria of institutional membership, namely universality/particularity.

It is precisely such a focus which the present research attempts. The objectivity/subjectivity dimension is explored as it is concretely evidenced by two important factors in the institutional arrangement of Vīraśaivism—priesthood and sacraments. The ideal and practice which correspond to a point on that dimension are then investigated along their implications for placement on the universality/particularity dimension. It is primarily the nature of the priesthood and the sacraments—both in theory and in practice which provides the concrete data for analysis.

In fact, an analysis of the system of priesthood and sacrament employed by any religious group is one of the most fundamental and most available points of analysis in determining the group's degree of fit with the ideal-typological model. The church-type's interpretation of the means of salvation as objectively available and specifically entrusted to its care leads to an emphasis on "the concrete holiness of the sacerdotal office, of Apostolic Succession, of the *Depositum fidei* and of the sacraments, and appeals to the extension of the Incarnation which takes place permanently through the priesthood". The sect-type's emphasis on the subjectivity of the salvific relation between the individual and some transcendent leads to a feeling of egalitarian community of those living under a common imperative without the need for objective sacraments and without the necessity of a priesthood to administer those sacraments and thereby facilitate a piecemeal acquisition of salvation.[8]

In addition to the sect-type (PS) and the church-type (UO) of religious association Troeltsch mentions a third type which is often ignored in contemporary applications and criticisms of Troeltsch's typology. This third type, the mystic-type, emphasizes the subjectivity of salvific experience but does so in the relative isolation and dissociation of individual seekers. Nonetheless, it is not bound by strict and exclusivistic rules and hence is best characterized as individualistic, at least insofar as its path is available to any isolated individual who chooses to follow. Once strictly defined membership criteria arise for a group of mystics, the sectarian type association has begun to replace the loose mystic patterns.

In fact, mystic-type associations are often confused with sect-type ones because both stand over and against the close identification of the church-type with secular authority, and both, to some extent, stress a direct relation between the believer and the Lord. The mystic, however, is primarily an individual whose salvation is supplied directly from an inner communication with transcendence. Associations of mystics are, at best, loose communities of like-minded souls often forced into association by external circumstances. They lack the fundamental fellowship based on the scripturally revealed divine law under which sectarians attempt to organize themselves. Mystics derive their model for association from the voluntarism and ethical communalism of the sect-type, but the salvation of the individual not the construction of a righteous community is their primary goal.[9]

CONSTRUCTIVE TYPOLOGY AND CROSS-CULTURAL COMPARISON

Though the outlines of this typology emerge first in a study of Protestantism and then find elaboration in an historical study of Christian tradition, the presuppositions upon which typological method is based make it suitable for understanding other cultural contexts.[10] The ideal type is a consciously artificial construction which is firmly based upon the individual events of historical development but which subsumes those particulars under a broader class and then specifically accentuates the characteristics which distinguish that class from other classes of phenomena.[11] Since the ideal type is based on historical data, it is never entirely without accuracy in describing the historical phenomena, but neither does the type ever perfectly mirror any single particular. The value of the ideal typical construction is not its perfect description of particulars but its accentuation of pertinent class characteristics. Each individual historical particular can then be examined for its relative degree-of-fit to that ideal type, and explanations for individual variations from the ideal pattern can be sought within the particulars of the historical milieu.[12]

The technical use of the term "sect" as found within the typological schemes of the sociology of religion has several advantages over previously discussed formulations as applied to a study of Vīraśaivism. First and foremost, by looking at data from across cultural boundaries, the schemes permit a structural typology of human associations—especially religious associations—which begins to transcend and, at the same time, illumines the culturally and historically limited particulars. Secondly, the schemes allow an analysis of the internal characteristics of the sect-type movement as well as of the church-type or mystic-type association. It is not necessary to define one type of movement merely in contrast to another which has a presumed normative stability. Thirdly, the method facilitates analysis of the interrelations of the different types including construction of an interval continuum with the capacity for greater and greater particular specificity.[13]

When used for comparing social institutional patterns across cultural boundaries, the typological method may require a revision of its ideal typical constructs in order more accurately to accentuate those characteristics which are truly general and pertinent, but there is no reason to think that types of institutional association which arise within one culture will be entirely without resonance elsewhere. Whatever their particulars of history, economy, climate, etc., all human cultures can be expected to exhibit even greater commonalities for the simple reason that they remain *human* cultures. It is not surprising that the struggle to fulfil both the material needs and the less concrete aspirations of the race produces typological patterns of generality and commonality underlying the diverse particulars of human societal histories. Only the absence of such shared patterns would be wholly surprising.[14]

The present research looks carefully at institutional phenomena in the Indian context and finds that among the explanatory schemes applicable to those phenomena one of the most useful and enlightening is the sect-mystic-church typology evolved by Troeltsch in his study of Christianity and revised by Gustafson into the more abstract UO-PO-US-PS typology.

Though its perils are obvious, the potential profit from the typological method is great. That the phenomena never perfectly correspond to the ideal typical pattern implies no devaluation of the Indian data. Historical particulars, whether Indian or Western, should never be expected to correspond perfectly to a purposely accentuated ideal construction. Neither is the absence of perfect degree-of-fit a telling critique of the typological method in general or of the particular types—sect, mystic, and church—in particular. Rather the method employed should be evaluated on the basis of its explanatory and predictive utility[15] in relation to the particular phenomena of the cumulative religious tradition under scrutiny—in this case, Vīraśaivism.

NOTES

1. One of the most vocal opponents of sustained methodological reflection and an ardent proponent of "getting on with the job" has been W.C. Smith. See his most strident, and some might say petulant, comments at "Methodology and the Study of Religion: Some Misgivings", in *Methodological Issues in Religious Studies*, ed. Robert D. Baird (Chico, CA: New Horizons Press, 1975), pp. 1-30.

2. A brief history of the terms "sect" and "church" as used to denote movements defined as heretical by the authoritative tradition is given by Kawerau in *RTK*, s.v. "Sektenwesen in Deutschland," by [Gustav] Kawerau, pp. 157-58. In the Greek New Testament, the noun αιρεσις occurs nine

times. Three of these (Acts 5:17; 15:5; and I Cor. 11:19) were translated into the Latin Vulgate by *haeresis*. The other six occurences (Acts 24:5; 24:14; 26:5; 28:22; Gal. 5:20; and II Pe. 2:1) were translated by *secta*. Thus for the same Greek word, the Latin has two separate words as does the English. In fact, in English the connotations of the two words are quite distinct—"heresy" denoting doctrines which are aberrant and abhorrent to the established Church and "sect" denoting a specific type of particularly distinct and cohesive organized group. It is important to recognize, however, that for most of Christian history the two terms were less than distinct. Both denoted groups which either doctrinally (heresy) or politically (sect) stood apart from the authoritative ideas and practices accepted by those in power at Rome. The origins of this normative definitional process has been well documented by Walter Bauer, *Orthodoxy and Heresy in Earliest Christianity* 2nd ed., ed. Georg Strecker, trans. Philadelphia Seminar on Christian Origins (Philadelphia: Fortress Press, 1971). An example of the normative definition can be seen in the *Corpus Juris Canonica* XXIV. iii.1-40. There at no. 24, a differentiation is made between heretics and schismatics [sectarians], but it is noteworthy that both are defined from the perspective of the normative Church tradition. The section reads: *haeresis perversum dogma habeat, schisma propter episcopalem dissensionem ab ecclesia pariter separat*. At no. 39, the phrase *sectae haereticorum* seems intended to indicate an institutional connotation for the first word and a doctrinal one for the second, but both receive their valence from relation to the Church's authority and dogma. Understanding this normative relational definition of the word "sect" is important because recent Western scholarship has been attempting to construct a typological definition based upon structural rather than relational elements. It is most intriguing that one of the results of this structural approach has been an identification of voluntarism as an important component of sectarian type associations. In this view, one is never born into a sect but must choose to join it and thereafter must elect to follow the stringent requirements of the group for continuing membership. The appearance of voluntarism as a defining characteristic of the sect reflects a recognition, conscious or otherwise, of the primary meaning of the Greek αιρεσις which simply meant "choice". The connotations of "cutting" or "setting apart" incumbent on the Latin *seco* were originally quite secondary. If this observation is held in mind when pursuing the Indian material, many of the previously addressed questions can be seen in a new light.

3. The development of the church-sect-mystic typology from Troeltsch onward within the sociology of religion presents an abundant literature which has been discussed by Ralph B. Potter, "Some Aspects of the Discussion of Typologies of Religious Association since the Work of Ernst Troeltsch" (Seminar paper, Harvard Divinity School, 1959). Potter has pointed out the three major types of typological literature which have evolved out of Troeltsch's work: (1) attempts at the refinement, subdivision, and multiplication of the types, (2) attempts to discern the dynamics of development from the sect to the church, and (3) attempts to discern the essential, perhaps even metaphysically essential, character of the sect. Potter's typology of typologists has been updated, and an attempt has been made to discern the philosophical

implications of Troeltsch's methodology by Duane Keith Friesen, "The Relationship between Ernst Troeltsch's Theory of Religion and His Typology of Religious Association" (Ph.D. dissertation, Harvard University, 1972).

On the other hand, surprisingly little effort has been directed toward discerning the origins of the typology in Troeltsch's intellectual universe. This omission is particularly surprising in light of Max Weber's attempts to have the issue opened so that his own contribution to the typology might be recognized. The debate can best be entered into at Weber's *Protestant Ethic and the Spirit of Capitalism*, trans. Talcott Parsons (New York: Charles Scribner's Sons, 1958), p. 255 n. 173 (to p. 145), which appeared in his *Gesammelte Aufsätze zur Religionssoziologie*, vol. I (Tubingen: J.C.B. Mohr/Paul Siebeck, 1920), p. 153 n. 1—that is the second German edition from which the translation was made. There he includes a few comments which did not appear in the corresponding note in the first German edition published as "Die protestantische Ethik und der 'Geist' des Kapitalismus", *Archiv für Sozialwissenschaft und Sozialpolitik* 20 [n.s. vol. 2] (1904): 64 n. 126. These comments emphasize the dichotomy between Church and sect; claim credit for first stating the dichotomous typology; and continue by acknowledging that Troeltsch "accepts it [the typology] and discusses it in more detail," and that the idea was derived "at about the same time" and presumably "independently" by Kattenbusch. With respect to Troeltsch, it should be noted that the second edition was prepared for publication when Weber and Troeltsch were at odds over a wartime incident, and that Weber may have been pushing his claim for rather petty reasons. The incident is discussed by Marianne Weber, *Max Weber: A Biography*, trans. and ed. Harry Zohn (New York: John Wiley and Sons, 1975), p. 524. That Weber and Troeltsch's closeness both domestically and socially often led to intellectual conflicts is demonstrated by Weber's decision in 1908, after publication of Troeltsch's first chapter on the Christian Churches, to follow an independent scholarly course outside Christian tradition. Ibid., p. 331. Whatever the relations between the two scholars, Weber is perhaps premature in claiming credit for the sect-church typology; certainly he is erroneous in the acknowledgement which he does make.

Weber attributes a discussion of the typology contemporaneous with his own to a Kattenbusch article on "Sekte" in *RTK*, but there is no *RTK* article entitled "Sekte". The distinction between sect and church is discussed in the *RTK*, s.v. "Sektenwesen in Deutschland", by Kawerau; and one of the articles by Kattenbusch does deal briefly with the topic, namely *RTK*, s.v. "Symbole, Symbolik", by F. Kattenbusch, pp. 204 and 206-207. Both these gentlemen were relying on several sources current in German scholarship of the time. Many of the characteristics which were later selected and accentuated in the sect-church typology were beginning to be enunciated as, for exmaple, by Ernst Kalb, *Kirchen und Sekten der Gegenwart* (Stuttgart: Evangelische Gesellschaft, 1905) who indicates the communalism and political radicalism of the sect at pp. 521 and 125 respectively. Kalb's contention, however, that sects are to be understood primarily on the basis of the larger church from which they separate indicates that he was basically following the traditional pattern of defining the sect in terms of its deviation from the normative church tradition. Ibid., pp. ix-xii and 14. In general, it must be understood, the Germans had a predilection in favor of the church—as opposed to the sect-type. Certainly, by "sect" they did not intend to include the great Protestant *Landeskirchen* of Europe. Sects were schismatics whether from the Roman Catholic Church or from the German Reformed one. This factor is discussed by Paul M. Gustafson in his review of Troeltsch's *Social Teaching* at "Church and Sect or Church and Ascetic Protestantism: Ernst Troeltsch's Problem", *Encounter* 30.2 (1969 Spring): 142-147.

The situation was different elsewhere, however, and that difference provides both the creative impetus and the source of confusion in early sociology of religion. In America, for example, there seemed to be no "church" but only congeries of independent sects. This factor led American writers to the insistence that "the word *sect* is used in no invidious sense, but as a convenient term for the parts into which the Christian body is actually divided or dissected." See William H. Lyon, *A Study of the Sects*, 10th ed. (Boston: Unitarian Sunday-School Society, 1902; first published by the same agency in 1891), p. iv. In other words, the term "sect" could be used to describe equally well the Salvation Army and the Roman Catholic Church. Though this comment was picked up by D. Friedrich Loofs, *Symbolik oder christliche Konfessionskunde*, vol. I (Tübingen: J.C.B. Mohr/Paul Siebeck, 1902), p. 74, its significance seems to have been overlooked until Weber's trip to America impressed upon him the feasibility of seeing the sect as a *sui generis* sociological entity. It was after that trip that he began his writings on the nature of the sects and that Troeltsch's work began to take seriously the types of religious association as independently viable entities. It was primarily Troeltsch, and later and with more clarity, Weber, who began a genuine typological construction of the pertinent characteristics of sects and churches. It is noteworthy that the later development of the typology has largely been the province of American sociologists of religion struggling to find a vocabulary and interpretative scheme which could do justice to the numerous, competing religious groups found there.

4. Max Weber places the sect-church typology in highest relief at his *Protestant Ethic and the Spirit of Capitalism*, trans. Talcott Parsons (New York: Charles Scribner's Sons, 1958), p. 145. The characteristics of the typology, however, emerge throughout his discussion, notably at pp. 132, 144-145, 152, 237 n. 92, and 254 n. 173.

5. Ernst Troeltsch, *The Social Teaching of the Christian Churches*, 2 vols., trans. Olive Wyon (New York: Harper and Row, Publishers; Harper Torchbooks, 1960), pp. 332-333.

6. These elaborated typologies are traced by Ralph B. Potter, "Some Aspects of the Discussion of Typologies of Religious Association since the Work of Ernst Troeltsch" (Seminar paper, Harvard Divinity School, 1959) [Unpublished xero-graph]. One of the more popular and useful elaborations is summarized by Joachim Wach, "Church, Denomination and Sect", in *Types of Religious Experience: Christian and non-Christian* (Chicago: University of Chicago Press, 1951), pp. 187-208.

7. Paul Gustafson, "UO-US-PS-PO: A Restatement of Troeltsch's Church-

Sect Typology", *Journal for the Scientific Study of Religion* 6.1 (1967 Spring): 64-68.

8. Troeltsch discusses these points throughout his lengthy analysis of Christian history, but more specifically at *Social Teaching*, pp. 328-349, 993-1013, and, for the quotation, p. 336.

9. Troeltsch, *Social Teaching*, pp. 347-349, 691ff., 730ff., 800ff., 993-1013, and elsewhere in vol. II, passim.

10. It is precisely such a typological investigation of the world's religious traditions which Weber undertook. He clearly considered the issues raised in his *Protestant Ethic* and the method of analysis which he utilized there to be applicable to the various traditions around the world. This position he made quite clear in the "Vorbemerkung" to his *Gesammelte Aufsätze zur Religionssoziologie*, vol. I (Tübingen: J.C.B. Mohr/Paul Siebeck, 1920), pp. 1-16, which serves as a general introduction to the three volumes in which he explored the religions of India, China, and ancient Judaea. This "Vorbemerkung" has been translated as the Introduction of Weber's *Protestant Ethic*, pp. 13-31, but should rightly be perceived as the Introduction to his overall investigation of the world's religions. Other parts of the single German work, have, unfortunately, been presented in various loci in English, specifically: "The Protestant Sects and the Spirit of Capitalism", "The Social Psychology of the World Religions", and "Religious Rejections of the World and Their Directions", in *From Max Weber: Essays in Sociology*, trans. and ed. H.H. Gerth and C. Wright Mills (New York: Oxford University Press, 1946), pp. 267-359; *The Religion of China: Confucianism and Taoism*, trans. and ed. Hans H. Gerth (New York: The Free Press, 1951); *Ancient Judaism*, trans. and ed. Hans H. Gerth and Don Martindale (New York: The Free Press, 1952); *The Religion of India: The Sociology of Hinduism and Buddhism*, trans. and ed. Hans H. Gerth and Don Martindale (New York: The Free Press, 1958). The extension of this planned analysis to all the world's religious traditions was terminated by Weber's early death, but an attempt to fill the *lacuna* by reconstructing in one place what Weber said about Islam along with what he might have said if he had lived longer has been provided by Bryan S. Turner, *Weber and Islam: A Critical Study* (London: Routledge and Kegan Paul, 1974). When all these various pieces are conceived as Weber himself conceived them—as chapters in one single work, then the outline of a cross-cultural typological study emerges. It should be noted that Troeltsch also discerned the utility of extending his typological analysis beyond the boundaries of Christianity at least as far as the other monotheistic religions. See his *Social Teaching*, p. 340 n. 165b.

11. Weber offered the following description of an ideal type: "An ideal type is formed by the one-sided *accentuation* of one or more points of view and by the synthesis of a great many diffuse, discrete, more or less present and occasionally absent *concrete individual* phenomena, which are arranged according to those one-sidedly emphasized viewpoints into a unified *analytical* construct (*Gedankenbild*). In its conceptual purity, this mental construct (*Gedankenbid*) cannot be found empirically anywhere in reality. It is a *utopia*. Historical research faces the task of determining in each individual case, the extent to which this ideal-construct approximates to or

diverges from reality ..." [Emphases added by Shils and Finch.] See Weber's *Methodology of the Social Sciences*, trans. and ed. Edward A. Shils and Henry A. Finch (New York: The Free Press, 1949), p. 90. The original appeared as "Die 'Objektivitat' sozialwissenschaftlicher und sozial politischer Erkenntnis", in *Archiv für Sozialwissenschaft und Sozialpolitik* 19.1 (1904): 65. Later, Weber attempted to refine his typological method as, for example, in distinguishing the aforedefined *generic* ideal type from *individual* ideal types. See his *Methodology*, pp. 100-101; " 'Objektivitat'," pp. 75-76. Weber's most fruitful formulations, however, and the ones produced by subsequent social scientists have relied on the former *generic* model of typology. This problem has been discussed by J.W.N. Watkins, "Ideal Types and Historical Explanation," *The British Journal for the Philosophy of Science* 3.9 (1952 May), pp. 22-43, who unfortunately attributes Weber's discussion of the *individual* ideal type to Part I of *Wirtschaft und Gesellschaft* when in fact that discussion was presaged by its simultaneous appearance with the discussion of generic ideal types in 1904 at *Methodology*, pp. 100-101; " 'Objektivität'," pp. 75-76. More perceptively is the matter taken up by Thomas Burger, *Max Weber's Theory of Concept Formation: History, Laws, and Ideal Types* Durham: Duke University Press, 1976), pp. 130-135. That author cogently observes that Weber's *individual* type is *not* equivalent to an individual historical event or a particular phenomenon.

12. The most pertinent characteristics, applicabilities, and abuses of typological method are discussed clearly and succinctly in the *International Encyclopaedia of the Social Sciences*, s.v. "Typologies", by Edward A. Tiryakian, pp. 177-186.

13. One discussion of ways in which typological schemes can be made more particular, specific, and constituted into serial continua is that by Paul F. Lazarsfeld, "Some Remarks on the Typological Procedures in Social Research", *Zeitschrift für Sozialforschung* 6.1 (1937): 119-139.

14. The analysis proposed in this paragraph reflects an obvious indebtedness to the work of structural-functionalists, such as Talcott Parsons whose analysis of societal functional requisites and structural pattern variables provides a methodological scheme for cross cultural institutional comparison. Parson's works are voluminous, probably needlessly so, but the basic ideas of his sociological theory can be had from his short book *Societies: Evolutionary and Comparative Perspectives* (Englewood Cliffs: Prentice-Hall, Inc., 1966), especially pp. 1-29.

15. Explanation and prediction as criteria of social scientific procedures are discussed throughout the methodological literature. One instance of their discussion with specific reference to the sect-church-mystic typology is by Howard Becker, "Constructive Typology in the Social Sciences", in *Contemporary Social Theory*, ed. Harry Elmer Barnes, Howard Becker, and Frances Bennet Becket (New York: D. Appleton-Century Company, Inc., 1940), pp. 17-46.

CLASSIFIED BIBLIOGRAPHY

PRIMARY TEXTS IN INDIAN LANGUAGES
(In Kannaḍa unless otherwise noted)

Allamana Vacana Candrike. Edited by L. Basavarāju. Mysore: Nalanisaṅkara Prakaśana, 1960.

Allamana Vacana Candrike. 2nd ed. Ed. L. Basavarāju. Hubli: Moorusaviramath, 1986.

Allamana Vacanagaḷu. Edited by L. Basavarāju. Mysore: Geetha Book House, 1969.

Allama Prabhudēvara Vacanagaḷu. Edited by R. C. Hiremath and M. S. Sunkapur. Dharwar: Karnatak University, 1976.

Allamaprabhuvina Tīkina Vacanagalu. Ed. Immadi Shivabasava Swamy. Mysore: Jagadguru Sri Shivaratreeswara Granthamala, 1986.

Basavaṇṇanavara Vacanagaḷu. Edited by R. C. Hiremath. Dharwar: Karnatak University Press, 1968.

Basavaṇṇanavara Vacanagaḷu (Bhāvārtha Sahita). Hubli: City Book Stall, n.d.

Basavapurāṇa [of Bhīmakavi]. Edited with an Introduction by R. C. Hiremath. Dharwar: Murughā Maṭha, 1971.

Basava Purāṇamu (Dvipada) [of Pālkurike Sōmanātha]. Madras: V. Ramaswamy Sastrulu and Sons, 1966. In Telugu.

Basavarājavijayaṃ [of Mahākavi Saḍakṣridēva]. Edited by R. C. Hiremath. Dharwar: Karnatak University, 1968.

Cannabasavaṇṇavara Vacanagaḷu. Edited by R. C. Hiremath. Dharwar: Karnatak University Press, 1965.

Dēvara Dāsimayyara Vacanagaḷu. Edited by P. G. Haḷakaṭṭi. Bijapur: n.p., 1955.

Hariharana Ragalegaḷu: Samagrasaṃpuṭa. Edited by P. G. Haḷakaṭṭi. Introduction by B. V. Mallāpura. Dharwar: Samāj Pustakālaya, 1968. Originally published at Bijāpura: Śivānubhava Granthamālā, ca. 1930.

Liṅgadhāraṇacandrikā [of Nandikeśvara]. Commentary by Śivakumāraśarmamiśra. Kāśī [Benares]: Medical Hall Press, 1905. In Sanskrit.

Lingadhāranachandrikā of Nandikeshwara (with translation and full notes), History and Philosophy of Lingayat Religion. (being an introduction [there] *to*). Edited and translated by M. R. Sakhare. Foreword by Sir S. Radhakrishnan. Balgaum [Belgaum]: By the Author, 134 Thalakwadi P.O., n.d. [1942]. In Sanskrit.

Liṅgadhāraṇa Candrike (*Kannaḍa*) [of Nandikēśvara]. Edited by Sirsi Guruśāntśāstrigaḷu. Bangalore: Prabōdha Pustakamāle, 1951.

Mahādēviyakkagaḷa Vacanagaḷu. Translated by Armando Menezes and S. M. Angadi. With the original text in Kannaḍa. Dharwar: Shri Manohar Appasaheb Adke, 1973.

Mōḷige Mārayyana Vacanagaḷu. Kannaḍa Adhyayana Saṃsthe, no. 12. Edited by B. S. Saṇṇayya. Mysore: Mysore University, 1969.

Môligeyyana Purâṇa [of Kavigauravâṅka]. Ed. S.S. Bhoosnurmath. Dharwar: Vīrabhadrappa Hâlabâvi, 1951.

Prabhuliṅgalīleya Saṅgraha [of Cāmarasa]. Edited by M. S. Basavaliṅgayya and M. R. Śrīnivāsamūrti. Foreword by B. M. Śrīkaṇṭhayya. Mysore: Mysore University Prasārāṅga, 1970.

Sakalapurātanara Vacanagaḷu. Edited by R. C. Hiremath. Dharwar: Karnatak University, 1972.

Siddhānta Śikhāmaṇi [of Śivayōgi], Śrī Kāśīnatha Granthamālā, no. 30. Edited with a Commentary by Paṇḍita Śrī Kāśīnātha Śāstri. Mysore: Śrī Pañcācārya Electric Press, V. P. Mahādēvayya, 1972. In Sanskrit.

Siddharāmēśvara Vacanagaḷu. Edited by R. C. Hiremath. Dharwar: Karnatak University, 1968.

Śivānubhavasūtraṃ [of Māyidēva]. Edited by V. Nāgēśaśāstrigaḷu. Dharwar: Murughā Maṭh, 1969. In Sanskrit.

The Śrīkara Bhāshya [of Śrīpati Paṇḍita]: *Being the Vīraśaiva Commentary on the Vēdānta Sūtras.* 2 vols. Edited by C. Hayavadana Rao. Bangalore City: n.p., 1936. In Sanskrit.

Śrīkara Bhāṣyaṃ [of Śrīpati Paṇḍita]. Śrī Kāśinātha Granthamāle, no. 36. Edited by Kāśinātha Śāstri. Mysore: Śrī Pañcācārya Electric Press, 1954. In Sanskrit.

Śrīkara Bhāṣya Bhāvapradīpike (*Catussūtrī*) [of Śrīpati Paṇḍita]. Edited by M. G. Nāñjuṇḍārādhya. Ujjain, Karnāṭaka: Śrī Jagadguru Ujjayinī Saddharmasinhāsana, 1968. In Kannaḍa.

Sūnyasaṃpādane [of Gūḷūra Siddhavīraṇāryaru]. Edited by P. G. Haḷakaṭṭi. Bijapur; publisher unknown, 1930.

Śūnyasaṃpādane [of Gūḷūra Siddhavīraṇāryaru]. Edited by S. S. Bhoosnurmath. Unknown place: Ravur and Kalmathadhisvara Swamiji, 1958.

Śūnyasaṃpādane [of Gūḷūra Siddhavīraṇāryaru]. 5 vols. Edited with Introduction, Text, Transliteration, Translation, Notes and Comments by S. C. Nandimath, L.M.A. Menezes, R.C. Hiremath, S. S. Bhoosnurmath, and M. S. Sunkapur. Forewords by D. C. Pavate and A. S. Adke. Dharwar: Karnatak University, 1965-1972.

Śūnyasaṃpādane [of Gummaḷāpurada Siddhaliṅgadēvaru]. Edited by R. C. Hiremath. Foreword by A. S. Adke. Dharwar: Karnatak University, 1972.

Śūnyasaṃpādane [of Halageya Dēvaru]. Unpublished manuscript in the Kannaḍa Institute, University of Mysore, Mysore, India. Catalogue number KA 105.

Śūnyasaṃpādane [of Śivagaṇaprasādi Mahādēvayya]: (*The Dialogues of Allama Prabhu with his disciples in vachana form, unique in Kannada, literature á la mode' Dialogues of Plato*). Edited by L. Basavarāju. Citradurga: Śrī Bṛhanmaṭha Saṇsthāna, 1969.

Śūnyasaṃpādane [of Śivagaṇa Prasādi Mahādēvayyanavaru]. Edited by R. C. Hiremath. Foreword by A. S. Adke. Dharwar: Karnatak University, 1971.

Triśaṣṭipurâtanacâritraṁ. Ed. R.C. Hiremath. Dharwar: Karnatak University, 1978.

Vacana Sāhitya Saṃgraha. Edited by S. S. Bhoosnurmath. Bangalore: Mysore Sarkāra, 1965.

PRIMARY TEXTS TRANSLATED INTO EUROPEAN LANGUAGES

[Allama Prabhul]. *Thus Sang the Veerashaiva Mystics*. Trans. S. Ananthanarayana. Hubli: Moorusaviramath, 1988.

[Basava]. *The Lord of the Meeting Rivers: Devotional Poems of Basavanna*. Trans. & Intro. K.V. Zvelebil. Delhi: Motilal Banarsidass, 1984.

[Basava]. *Sayings of Basavanna*. Ed. & Trans. M. Venkatesa Iyengar. Bangalore: Basava Samiti, 1983.

[Basava]. *Thus Spake Basava*. Translated and edited by A. Sunderaraj Theodore and Devendra Kumar Hakari. Bangalore: Basava Samiti, 1965.

[Basava]. *Vacanas of Basavaṇna*. Taraḷabāḷu Granthamāle

series-2. Edited by H. Deveerappa. Translated by L. M. A. Menezes and S. M. Angadi. Introduction by Śrī Śivakumāra Śivācārya. Sirigere: Annana Balaga, 1967.

[*Basava Purāṇa*]. "Account of the Basava Puran:—the principal Book used as a religious Code by the Jangams." Paraphrased in English by C. P. Brown. *Journal of Literature and Science* (Madras) 12 (1840): 271-291.

"The Basava Purāna of the Lingaits." Translated by G. Würth. *Journal of the Bombay Branch of the Royal Asiatic Society* 8.24 (1865-66): 65-97.

"Channa-Basava Purāṇa of the Lingaits." Translated by G. Würth. *Journal of the Bombay Branch of the Royal Asiatic Society* 8.24 (1865-66): 98-221.

Lingadhāranachandrikā of Nandikeshwara (*with translation and full notes*), *History and Philosophy of Lingayat Religion*, (*being an introduction* [there] *to*). Edited and translated by M. R. Sakhare. Foreword by Sir S. Radhakrishnan. Balgaum [Belgaum]: By the Author, 134 Thalakwadi P.O., n.d. [1942].

[Mahādēviyakka]. *Vacanas of Akkamahādēvi*. Translated by Armando Menezes and S. M. Angadi. Dharwar: Shri Manohar Appasaheb Adke, 1973.

Ramanujan, A. K., ed. *Speaking of Śiva*. A collection of *vacana*-s edited, translated and with an Introduction by A. K. Ramanujan. Baltimore: Penguin Books, Inc., 1973.

[Siddharâma]. *Vacanas of Siddharâma*. Ed., Intro., and Trans. A. Menezes & S.M. Angadi. Foreword by R.C. Hiremath. Dharwad: Karnatak University, 1978.

Songs from the Śaraṇas and other Poems. Edited and translated by Armando Menezes. Dharwar: Karnatak University, 1971.

Śūnyasampādane [of Gūḷūra Siddhavīraṇāryaru]. 5 vols. Edited with Introduction, Text, Transliteration, Translation, Notes and Comments by S. C. Nandimath, L. M. A. Menezes, R. C. Hiremath, S. S. Bhoosnurmath, and M. S. Sunkapur. Forewords by D. C. Pavate and A. S. Adke. Dharwar: Karnatak University, 1965-1972.

Tôṇṭada Siddhaliṅgêśvara]. *Essence of Ṣaṭsthala*. Ed., Intro., and Trans. Armando Menezes & S.M. Angadi. Foreword by R.C. Hiremath. Dharwad: Karnatak University, 1978.

PRIMARY SOURCES: EPIGRAPHIA

Annual Report on Indian Epigraphy for 1953-54. Edited by D. C. Sircar. Delhi: Manager of Publications, 1958.

Annual Report on South Indian Epigraphy for the Years 1939-40 *to* 1942-43. Edited by C. R. Krishnamacharlu and N. Lakshminarayan Rao. Delhi: Manager of Publications, 1952.

A Corpus of Inscriptions in the Kannaḍa Districts of Hyderabad State. Hyderabad Archaeological Series—No. 18. Edited by P. B. Desai. Hyderabad: Director, Archaeological Department, Government of Andhra Pradesh, 1958.

Desai, P. B. *Jainism in South India and Some Jaina Epigraphs*. Number 6 in Jīvarāja Jaina Granthamālā. Scholapur: Jaina Saṁskṛti Saṁrakshaka Sangha, Gulabchand Hirachand Doshi, 1957.

Epigraphia Carnatica. 15 vols. Edited by B. Lewis Rice, R. A. Narasimhacharya et. al. Bangalore, Mangalore, and Mysore: Mysore Government Central Press, Basel Mission Press, and Mysore Government Branch Press; 1886-1919.

———. Vol. III: *Inscriptions in the Mysore District*. Edited by B. Lewis Rice. Bangalore: Mysore Government Press, 1894.

———. Vol. V: *Inscriptions in the Hassan District*. Edited by B. Lewis Rice. Mangalore: Basel Mission Press, 1902.

———. Vol. VI: *Inscriptions in the Kadur District*. Edited by B. Lewis Rice. Bangalore: Mysore Government Central Press, 1901.

———. Vol. VII, Pt. I: *Inscriptions in the Shimoga District*. Edited by B. Lewis Rice. Bangalore: Mysore Government Central Press, 1902.

———. Vol. IX: *Inscriptions in the Bangalore District*. Edited by B. Lewis Rice. (Bangalore: Mysore Government Central Press, 1905).

———. Vol. X: *Inscriptions in the Kolar District*. Edited by B. Lewis Rice. (Mangalore: Basel Mission Press, 1905).

———. Vol. XII: *Inscriptions in the Tumkur District*. Edited by B. Lewis Rice. (Bangalore: Mysore Government Central Press, 1904).

Epigraphia Indica and a Record of the Archaeological Survey of India. [Published serially under various editors and from different places in India since 1894.]

———. Vol. 5 (1898-99). Edited by E. Hultzsch. Calcutta: Office of the Superintendent of Government Printing, India, 1898-99.

———. Vol. 21 (1931-32). Edited by Hirananda Sastri, K. N. Dikshit, and N. P. Chakravarti. Delhi: Manager of Publications, 1931-32.

———. Vol. 23 (1935-36). Edited by N. P. Chakravarti. Delhi: Manager of Publications, 1938.

Gopal, B. R., ed. *Karnatak Inscriptions*. Vols. 5 and 6, Dharwar: Kannada Research Institute, Karnatak University, 1969 and 1973.

Nandimath, S. C. "Studies in Inscriptions." *Journal of the Karnatak University—Humanities* 1.2 (1957 June): 194-227; 2.2 (1958 June): 66-85; and 3.2 (1959 June): 24-29.

Sewell, Robert. *The Historical Inscriptions of Southern India (Collected till* 1923) *and Outlines of Political History*. Madras University Historical Series, No. 5. Edited by S. Krishnaswami Aiyangar. Madras: The Diocesan Press, Vepery, 1932.

South Indian Inscriptions. Archaeological Survey of India publications. D. C. Sircar, gen. ed. Vol. 15, Pt. 2: *Bombay-Karnatak Inscriptions*. P. B. Desai, vol. ed. Delhi: [Government of India] Manager of Publications, 1964.

SECONDARY SOURCES IN INDIAN LANGUAGES
(In Kannaḍa unless otherwise noted)

Bhoosnurmath, S. S. *Śūnyasaṃpādaneya Pāramarśe*. Gulbarga: Rāvūra Śrīsiddhalingeśvaramaṭha and Ādavāniya Kallumaṭha, 1969.

[Chennabasavaraja, Desikendra Shivacharya] J. C. N. *Udaka*. Bangalore: Jagadguru Śrīśaila Niḍumāmiḍi Pustaka Bhaṇḍāra, [ca. 1973].

Chidananda Murthy, M. *Śūnyasaṃpādaneyannu Kuritu*. Foreword by T. N. Śrīkaṇṭhayya. Mysore: Mōhana Prakāsana, 1962.

Diwakar, R. R. *Vacanaśāstrarahasya*. 4th ed. Hubli: Mūrusāviramaṭha, 1968.

Guñjāḷa, S. R. *Basavaṇṇanavara Vacana Padaprayōga Kōśa*. Suyidhāna Sugrantha Māle, no. 32. Dharwar: Jaganmātā Akkamahādevi Āśrama, 1973.

Haḷakaṭṭi, P. G., ed. *Śivānubhava Śabdakōśa*. Dharwar: Samāja Pustakālaya, 1972.

Javaḷi, B. C. *Jagadguru Basavaṇṇanavaru: Vīraśaiva Dharma Sansthāpakare?* Dharwar: Suyidhāna Sugrantha Māle, 1972.

Kabbina, S. S. *Akka Mahādēvi mattu Mīrābāyi*. Upanyāsa Granthamāle, no. 53. Dharwar: Karnatak University, 1971.

Kalaburgi, M. M. *Basavaṇṇanavarannu Kuritu Śāsanagaḷu*. Upanyāsa Granthamāle, no. 72. Dharwar: Karnataka University, 1973.

Kambi, V. S. *Śūnyasaṃpādane*. Upanyāsa Granthamāle, no. 48. Dharwar: Karnatak University, 1973.

Liṅgaṇṇayya, O. N. *Cannabasavaṇṇa*. Pracāra Pustakamāle, no. 166. Mysore: Prasārāṅga, Mysore University, 1969.

Mahānteśa Śāstri, H. T. *Vīraśaiva Navaratna*. Gadag: M. S. Śābādimaṭha, 1968.

[Mailāraśaraṇaru]. *Aśṭāvaraṇagaḷa Mahatva*. Śrī Bālalīlā Mahāntaśivayōgīśvara Granthamāle, no. 69. Dharwar: Murughāmaṭha, 1971.

Māḷavāḍa, S. S. *Hariharana Ragaḷegaḷalli Jīvana Darśana*. Mysore University Viśēṣōpanyāsa Pustakamāle, no. 1. Mysore: Mysore University Prasārāṅga, 1969.

Mallappa, T. N. *Vīraśaiva Ugama Mattu Pragati*. Bangalore: Rao Bahādūr Dharmapravarti Gubbi Tōṭadappanavara Dharmasaṃsthe, 1969.

Malledevaru, Jagadamba. *Ippataidu Vacanakâtriyara Jìvana Hâgū Sâdhane*. Hubli: Murusavira Matha, 1987.

Nâgêṣaśâstrigaḷu, V. *Aṣṭâvaraṇa Vivêka*. Dharwar: Murughamath, 1968.

Nañjuṇḍārādhya, M. G. *Ṣaṭsthala Liṅgapūjāvidhi*. 2nd rev. ed. Mysore: Prabōdha Pustakamāle, 1971.

Nañjuṇḍārādhya, M. G. *Vīraśaivāgama Prayōgaratnaṃ*. Mysore: Prabōdha Pustakamāle, 1968.

Nañjuṇḍārādhya, M. G. *Vīraśaiva Pūrvaprayōga Ratnaṃ* Mysore: Prabōdha Pustakamāle, 1950.

Nañjuṇḍārādhya, M. G. *Vīraśaiva Uttaraprayoga: Antyēṣṭividhi*. Mysore: Prabōdha Pustakamāle, 1970.

Parameśvara Bhaṭṭa, S. V. *Akkamahādevi*. Mysore University Pracāra Pustakamāle, no. 32. Mysore: Prasārāṅga, Mysore University, 1973.

Siddhappārādhya, T. G. *Allama Prabhu*. Pracāra Pustakamāle, no. 115. Mysore: Prasārāṅga, Mysore University, 1972.

Śrīnivāsamūrti, M. R. *Bhakti Bhāṇḍāri Basavaṇṇanavaru*. Bangalore: Central College, Karnaṭak Saṅgha, 1931.

Śrīnivāsamūrti, M. R. *Vacanadharmasāra*. Mysore: Mysore University Prasārāṅga, 1968.

Thipperudraswamy, H. *Anubhava Maṇṭapa*. Sāhityavāhini series, no. 15. Mysore: D. V. K. Murthy, 1971.

Thipperudraswamy, H. *Śūnyasaṃpādane Vivaraṇātmake Paricaya*. Mysore: D. V. K. Murthy, 1973.

Thipperudraswamy, H. *Vananagaḷalli Vīraśaivadharma*. 2nd ed. Mysore: D.V.K. Murthy, 1982.

Venkanayya, T. S. "Shivatattvasara." *Prabuddha Karnatak* 16.2.

Vidyashankar, S. *Vîraśaiva Purânagaḷu: Ondu Adhyayana*. Bangalore: Kannada Sahitya Parishat, 1982.

SECONDARY SOURCES IN EUROPEAN LANGUAGES
Those Dealing Primarily with the Viraśaivas

Allchin, Raymond. "The Attaining of the Void—A Review of Some Recent Contributions in English to the Study of Viraśaivism." *Religious Studies* 7 (1971 December): 339-359.

Anandavardhan Shastri [Helmuth von Glasenapp]. "Die Frage einer Sondervertretung der Lingayats." *Der Neue Orient* 3.3 (1918 May): 135-138. In German.

Artal, R. C. "A Short Account of the Reformed Shaiva or Veerashaiva Faith." *Journal of the Anthropological Society of Bombay* 8.3 (1909): 171-262. An additional note appeared in the same journal 12.7 (1923): 912-913.

Balarama Gupta, G. S. "The Lesson of the Master—A Note on Basavanna." *Journal of the Karnatak University—Humanities* 20 (1976): 50-54.

Basavalingiah, M. S. "Conception of Brahma in Vīraśaiva Philosophy." *Proceedings and Transactions of the All-India Oriental Conference* 8 (1935 December): 312-321.

[*Śrī*] *Basavēśvara: Eighth Centenary Commemoration Volume*. Edited by Government of Mysore, State Level Committee: Eighth Centenary Celebrations of Śrī Basaveśvara. Introduction by Sadashiva Wodeyar. Bangalore: Government of Mysore, 1967.

———. Chidananda Murthy, M. "Śrī Basavēśvara and His Modern Outlook on Life." Pp. 109-115.

———. Dikshit, G. S. "Social and Religious Conditions of Karnāṭak before Basava." Pp. 117-132.

Karnāṭak Hiremath, R. C. "Śrī Basavēśvara: A Biography." Pp. 3-30.

———. Hondius, J. M. "Significance of Śrī Basaveśvara's Teachings to the World." Pp. 83-84.

———. Shapeti, S. B. "The Buddha and Śrī Basavēśvara." Pp. 171-179.

———. Shivarudrappa, A. L. "Vīraśaivism and Advaita." Pp. 363-368.

———. Sunkapur, M. S. "Śrī Basaveśvara: A Social Reformer." Pp. 133-137.

Brown, C. P. "Essay on the Creed, Customs and Literature of Jangamas." *Journal of Literature and Science* (Madras) 11 (1840 January-June): 143-177.

Chandrasekhariah, K. "A Sociological Analysis of Virasaivism." Ph.D. dissertation, Johann Wolfgang Goethe University, Frankfurt am Main, 1955.

Chidananda Murthy, M. *Basavanna.* National Biography series. New Delhi: National Book Trust, India, 1972.

Clabeaux, John J. "Basavavacanas." Course paper, Harvard University, 1977.

Das Gupta, Surendranath. "Vīra-śaivism: History and Literature of Vīraśaivism." In his *A History of Indian Philosophy*, vol. 5, pp. 42-64. Cambridge at the University Press, 1969.

Desai, P. B. *Basavesvara and His Times.* Foreword by D. C. Pavate. Dharwar: Kannada Research Institute, Karnatak University, 1968.

Egnor, Margaret T. "The Lingayats of Mysore: A Study in the Acquisition of Power and Prestige." Senior Honors thesis, Harvard University, 1970.

Encyclopedia of Religion and Ethics. S. v. "Lingayats," by R. E. Enthoven.

Greene, Roland, "Heart, Form and Worship in the Lyrics of Basavaṇṇa." Course paper, Brown University, 1978.

Hallisey, Charles S. "Basavaṇṇa and Kabīr: Ideas of Interior Religion." Course paper, Harvard Divinity School, 1977.

Hiremath, R.C. *Sri Channabasavesvara (Life and Philosophy).* Dharwad: Karnatak University, 1978.

Hunashal, S. M. *The Lingāyat Movement: A Social Revolution in Karnatak.* Dharwar: Karnatak Sahitya Mandira, 1947.

Ishwaran, K. *Religion and Society Among the Lingayats of South India.* Leiden: E.J. Brill, 1983.

[Jaṅgamavāḍi Maṭha]. *An Extract from the Judgement in the Benares Sri Jagadguru Vishwaradhya Simhasana Math Case.* Śrī Śivadharma Granthamālā series, no. 19. Edited by the Manager of the Jangamawadi Math. Benares: By the editor, 1965.

Kalghatgi, T. G. "Satsthala and Gunasthana (A Comparative Note)." *Philosophical Quarterly* (Amalner) 36.1 (1963 April): 101-110.

Kambi, V. S. *Philosophy of the Sunyasampadane*, Vol. 1. Dharwar: Kumaresha Granthamale, 1973.

Kashinatha Shastri. *Shakti-Vishistadvaita or the Philosophical Aspect of Virasaivism.* Sri Kashinathagranthamala series, number 37. Edited and translated by R. Chakravarti. Mysore: Sri Panchacharya Electric Press, 1957.

Kashinatha Shastri. *Speeches on Veerashaiva Religion.* Sri Kashinathagranthamala series, number 12. Mysore: Sree Panchacharya Electric Press, 1969.

Kavirāj, Gopī Nāth. "Some Aspects of Vīra Śaiva Philosophy." *Princess of Wales Sarasvati Bhavana Studies* 2 (1923): 137-158.

Kittel, F. *Über den Ursprung des Lingakultus in Indien.* Mangalore: Basel Mission Book and Tract Depository, 1876. In German.

Kumar Swami. "The Linga in Veerashaivism." *Prabuddha Bharata* 47 (1942): 181-185.

Kumara Swamiji. *Mirror of Virashaivism.* Dharwar: Navakalyana Math, 1960.

Kumaraswamiji. "Vīra-Śaivism." In *History of Philosophy Eastern and Western*, vol. 1, pp. 393-400. Edited by S. Radhakrishnan. London: George Allen and Unwin, Ltd., 1952.

Kumaraswamiji. "Vīraśaivism." In *The Cultural Heritage of India*, 2nd ed., vol. 4, pp. 98-107. Edited by Haridas Bhattacharyya. Calcutta: Ramakrishna Mission, 1956.

Kumaraswamiji. *The Virashaiva Philosophy and Mysticism.* 2nd ed. Foreword by Paul Brunton. Introduction by J. M. Holmes. Dharwar: Navakalyana Math, 1960.

Kumara Swami. "The Veerashaiva Weltanschauung." *Prabuddha Bharata* 46 (1941): 311-316.

Kumaraswamiji. *The Virasaiva Weltanschauung.* Dharwar: V.R. Koppal, 1954.

Lakshmi, V. T. "The Lingayatas: Their Religion and Literature." *Triveni* n.s. 9.11 (1937 May): 43-51.

Michael, R. Blake. "Laicization of the Ascetic Ideal: The Case of the Vīraśaivas." Pp. 405-441 in *Monastic Life in the Christian and Hindu Traditions: A Comparative Study.* Ed. Austin B. Creel & Vasudha Narayanan. Lewiston, NY: The Edwin Mellen Press, 1990.

Lingananda (né Sangamesh). *Emblem of God.* Suyidhana Publication Series, no. 38. Translated by S. M. Angadi. Dharwar: Suyidhana Sugrantha Maale, 1973.

McCormack, William. "Forms of Communication in Vīraśaiva Religion". In *Traditional India: Structure and Change,* pp. 119-129. Edited by Milton Singer. Philadelphia: American Folklore Society, 1959.

McCormack, William, "Lingayats as a Sect." *The Journal of the Royal Anthropological Institute of Great Britain and Ireland* 93 (1963 January to June): 59-71.

McCormack, William. "On Lingayat Culture." In *Speaking of Śiva,* pp. 175-187. Translated with an Introduction by A. K. Ramanujan. Baltimore: Penguin Books, Inc., 1973.

Madtha, William. "Vīraśaivism and Christianity: An Ecymenical Dialogue on Doctrine." *Journal of the Karnatak University—Humanities* 20 (1976): 30-41.

Mahādevi (né Ratnamma) *A Guide to Lingayatism.* Brief Sketch of the Authoress by S. R. Gunjal. Dharwar Suyidhana Sugrantha Maale, Jaganmata Akkamahadevi Ashrama, 1973.

Mahādevi (né Ratnamna). *Revolution in Kalyana.* Suyidhana Publication series, number 32. Translated by S. M. Angadi. Dharwar: Suyidhana Sugrantha Maale, Jaganmāta Akkamahādevi Āśhrama, 1973.

Malledevaru, H. P. *Essentials of Vīraśaivism.* Bombay: Bharatiya Vidya Bhavan, 1973.

Manjappa, Hardekar. *Basava: The Dimension of Universal Man.* Translated by A. Mylar Rao. Foreword by Venkatesh Bheemarao Alur. Dharwar: Hardekar Manjappa Smaraka Granthamale, 1966. [Kannaḍa original published ca. 1924.]

Marro, Clement. "Role and Position of the Guru and of the Jangama in Lingayatism." *Bangalore Theological Forum* 6.2 (1974 July-December): 28-51.

Marro, Clement A. "Shri Basaveshvara: A Social Reformer."

Bangalore Theological Forum 5.1 (1973 January-June): 81-93.

Menezes, Armando. "Basavanna: Mystic and Poet." *Journal of the Karnatak University—Humanities* 20 (1976): 52-49.

Michael, R. Blake. "Ascetic Protestantism and Vīraśaivism: A Comparison with Respect to the Spirit of Capitalism." Course paper, Harvard University, 1973.

Michael, R. Blake. "Foundation Myths of the Two Denominations of Vīraśaivism: *Viraktas* and *Gurusthalins.*" *Journal of Asian Studies* XLII.2 (1983 February): 309-322.

Michael, R. Blake. "'*Liṅga*' as Lord Supreme in the *Vacanas* of Basava." *Numen* 29.2 (1982 December): 202-219.

Michael, R. Blake. "To Burn or To Bury: Funerary Practices among the Liṅgāyatas. Monograph in progress. Preliminary form presented at Association of Asian Studies annual meeting, Chicago, Illinois, 1982 April.

Michael, R. Blake. "Women of the *Śūnyasampādane:* Housewives and Saints in Vīraśaivism." *Journal of the American Oriental Society* 103.2 (1983 April-June): 361-368.

Michael, R. Blake. "Work as Worship in Vīraśaiva Tradition." *Journal of the American Academy of Religion* L.4 (1982 December): 101-115.

Nandimath, S. C. *A Handbook of Vīraśaivism.* Foreword by R. D. Ranade. Dharwar: S. E. Association, 1947. [Subsequently reprinted with supplementary materials and altered pagination at Delhi: Motilal Banarsidass, 1979.]

Nandimath, S. C. "Śaivāgamas: Their Literature and Theology." *Journal of the Karnatak University—Humanities* 6 (1962 June): 1-34 and 7 (1963): 1-48.

Nandimath, S. C. "Śrī Basaveśvara." *Journal of the Karnatak University—Humanities* 8 (1964): 209-224.

Nandimath, S. C. "Theology of the Śaivāgamas, being A Survey of the Doctrines of the Śaiva Siddhānta and Vīraśaivism." Ph.D. dissertation, University of London, 1930. (Microfilmed.)

Nilakanta Sastri, K. A. "A Note on Virasaivism—Its History and Doctrine." *Proceedings and Transactions of the All-India Oriental Conference* 18 (1955 December): 386-391.

Paraddi, Mallikarjun. "Vīraśaivism in Sanskrit Literature." *Journal of the Karnatak University—Humanities* 20 (1976): 161-167.

Parvathamma, C. *Politics* and *Religion: A Study of Historical*

Interaction between Socio-political Relationships in a Mysore Village. Foreword by Prof. I. Karve. New Delhi: Sterling Publishers (P) Ltd., 1971.

Parvathamma, C. *Sociological Essays on Veerasaivism*. Bombay: Popular Prakashan, 1972.

Parvate, S. D. *Vīraśaiva Philosophy of the Śaivāgamas*. Hubli: [publisher unknown], 1927.

Ramanujan, A. K. Introduction to *Speaking of Śiva*. Edited and translated by A. K. Ramanujan. Baltimore: Penguin Books, Inc., 1973.

Ramanujan, A. K. "Men, Women, and Saints." Lectures given at Harvard Divinity School, 1977 April.

Ramaswami Shastri, K. S. "Shaivism and Veerashaivism." *Prabuddha Bharata* 48.6 (1943): 287-291.

Ranaganna, S. V. "Religion and Kannada Literature." *Journal of the Karnatak University—Humanities* 20 (1976): 6-14.

Rao, Parvati N. "Basaveśwara and George Herbert as Practical Mystics." *Journal of the Karnatak University—Humanities* 20 (1976): 55-60.

Rathinasabapathy, V. *Perspectives in Virasaivism from Tamil Sources*. Dharwad: Karnatak University, 1982.

Sadasivaiah, H. M. *A Comparative Study of Two Vīraśaiva Monasteries: A Study in Sociology of Religion*. Mysore: Prasaranga, Manasa Gangotri, 1967.

Sakhare, M. R. *History and Philosophy of Lingayat Religion*, (*being an introduction to*) "*Lingadhāranachandrikā*" *of Nandikeshwara* (*with translation and full notes*). Foreword by Sir S. Radhakrishnan. Balgaum [Belgaum]: By the Author, 134 Thalakwadi P.O., n.d. [1942].

Sakhare, M.R. *History and Philosophy of Lingâyat Religion*. Dharwad: Karnatak University, 1978.

Sakharpekar, S. D. "Agamic Vīraśaivism." *Proceedings and Transactions of the All-India Oriental Conference* 7 (1933): 399-404.

Saletore, B. A. "The Vīra Śaivas and their Contribution to Vijayagara." *Karnāṭaka Historical Review* 4.1-2 (1937 January-July): 57-60.

Samartha, Michael Prakash. "The Compassionate Basava." Ph.D. dissertation, Hartford Seminary Foundation, 1972.

Samartha, M. P. "Basava's Spiritual Strugle." *Religious Studies* 13 (1977 September): 335-347.

Sargant, N. C. *The Lingayats: The Vira-saiva Religion.* Bangalore: Christian Institute for the Study of Religion and Society, 1963.

Schrader, F. Otto. "Lingāyats and Metempsychosis." *Wiener Zeitschrift für die Kunde des Morgenlandes* 31 (1924): 313-317.

Sharma, Arvind. "Vīraśaivism." Course paper, Harvard Divinity School, n.d.

Shintri, Sarojini. "A Mystic's Message: An Interpretation of Akkamahadevi's Life." *Journal of the Karnatak University—Humanities* 20 (1976): 61-68.

Shivamurthy Shivacharya Mahaswamiji. *Vīraśaiva View of Man and Woman in Relation to God.* Sirigere: Sri Taralabalu Jagadguru Brihanmath, 1985.

Srikantan, K. S. "Basava, the Founder of Veerashaivism." *Prabuddha Bharata* 48.5 (1943): 237-240.

Thipperudraswamy, H. *Basaveshwara.* Makers of Indian Literature series. New Delhi: Sahitya Akademi, 1975.

Thipperudra Swamy, H. *Toward Perfection (A Novel on Allamaprabhu).* Trans. C.N. Hiremath. Hubli: Moorusaviramath, 1985.

Thipperudraswamy, H. *The Vīraśaiva Saints: A Study.* Translated by S. M. Angadi. Mysore: Rao and Raghavan Publishers, 1968.

Uttangi, C. D. *Anubhavamantapa: The Heart of the Lingayat Religion.* Dharwar: Karnatak Sahitya Mandira. 1955.

Vail, Lise F. "The Lingayat Gurusthala Matha: An Investigation into the Nature and Role of the Household Monastery in South India." Ph.D. dissertation, University of Pennsylvania.

von Glasenapp, Helmuth. *Die Philosophie der Inder: Eine Einführung in ihre Geschichte und ihre Lehren.* Stuttgart: Alfred Kröner, 1949. Pp. 288-292. In German.

Wolf, Herbert C. "The *Liṅga* as Center: A Study in Religious Phenomenology." *Journal of the American Academy of Religion* 46.3.K.2 Supplement (1978 September): 365.

Yaravintelimath, C. R. "Muktayakka." *Journal of the Karnatak University Humanities* 20 (1976): 68-76.

SECONDARY SOURCES IN EUROPEAN LANGUAGES

Ethnographs, Censuses, and Gazetteers

[Bombay] *Gazetteer of the Bombay Presidency.* Vol. I, pt. II: *History of the Konkan Dakhan and Southern Maratha Country*

Volume edited by James M. Campbell. Bombay: Government Central Press, 1896.

Census of India, 1921. Vol. XII, pts., i and ii: *Madras*. Edited by G. T. Boag. Madras: Superintendent, Government Press, 1922.

Census of India, 1931. Vol. VIII, pts. i and ii: *Bombay Presidency*. Edited by A. H. Dracup and H. T. Sorley. Bombay: The Government Central Press, 1933.

———. Vol. XIII: *Coorg*. Edited by M. S. Mandanna. Madras: Government of India Central Publication Branch, Calcutta, 1932.

———. Vol. XIV, pts., i and ii: *Madras*. Edited by M. W. M Yeatts Calcutta: Government of India Central Publication Branch, 1932.

———. Vol. XXV, pts., i and ii: *Mysore*. Edited by M. Venkatesa Iyengar, Bangalore: The Government Press, 1932.

———. Vol. XXIII, pts., i and ii: *H. E. H. the Nizam's Dominions (Hyderabad State)*. Edited by Gulam Ahmed Khan. Hyderabad, Deccan: The Government Central Press, 1933.

Census of India, 1971. Series—14, pt. II-A: *Mysore*. Edited by P. Padmanabha. Mysore: Director of Census Operations, n.d.

Dubois, Abbé J. A. *Description of the Character, Manners, and Customs of the People of India: and of their Institutions, Religious and Civil*. Translated from the French manuscript. London: Longman, Hurst, Rees, Orme, and Brown, 1817.

Dubois, Abbé J. A. *Hindu Manners, Customs and Ceremonies*. 3rd ed. Translated from the Author's later French MS and edited with Notes, Corrections, and Biography by Henry K. Beauchamp. Prefatory Note by F. Max Müller. Oxford: Clarendon Press, 1906.

[Steele, Arthur]. *Summary of the Law and Custom of Hindoo Castes within the Dekhun Provinces Subject to the Presidency of Bombay, Chiefly Affecting Civil Suits*. Bombay: Courier Press, 1827.

Thurston, Edgar, assisted by K. Rangachari. *Castes and Tribes of Southern India*. Vol. IV—*K to M*. S. v. "Lingāyat," pp. 236-291. Madras: Government Press, 1909.

SECONDARY SOURCES IN EUROPEAN LANGUAGES

Those Dealing with Vīraśaivism's Immediate Context— Vijayanagara, Mysore, and Karnāṭaka

Beals. Alan. "Leadership in a Mysore Village." In *Leadership and Political Institutions in India*, pp. 427-437. Edited by Richard L. Park and Irene Trinker. Princeton: Princeton University Press, 1959.

Desai, P. B. "Ballāḷa III and Vijayanagara." *The Journal of Karnatak University—Social Sciences* 7 (1971): 119-130.

Desai, P. B. "The Foundation of Vijayanagara." *The Journal of Karnatak University—Social Sciences* 6 (1970): 175-194.

Desai, P. B. "The Legendary Origin of Vijayanagara." *The Journal of Karnataka University—Social Sciences* 8 (1972): 61-69.

Hayavadana Rao, C. *History of Mysore* (1399-1799 *A. D.*). 3 vols. Bangalore: Superintendent of the Government Press, 1943-1946.

Heras, H *Beginnings of Vijayanagara History*, Bombay: Indian Historical Research Institute, 1929.

Kittel, F. *A Kannaḍa-English Dictionary*. Mangalore: Basel Mission Book and Tract Depository, 1894.

Kuppuswamy, G. R. *Economic Conditions in Karnāṭaka* (A. D. 973-A. D. 1336). Dharwar: Karnatak University, 1975.

McCormack, William. "Sister's Daughter Marriage in a Mysore Village." *Man in India* 38.1 (1958 January-March): 34-48.

MacKenzie, J. S. F. "On the Rules which Govern Kanarese Poetry." *Indian Antiquary* 2 (1873): 109-112.

Mahalingam, T. V. *Administration and Social Life under Vijayanagara*. Madras University Historical Series, no. 15. General editor: K. A. Nilakanta Sastri. Madras: University of Madras, 1940.

Mugali, R. S. *History of Kannada Literature*. (New Delhi: Sahitya Akademi, 1975).

Muthanna, J. M. *History of Karnataka: History, Administration and Culture*. Mysore: Usha Press, 1962.

Mysore, India: Tourist Road Map. Based on Survey of India Road Map. Designed by Ashwinee, Bangalore. Bangalore: The Mysore State Tourism Development Corpn. Ltd., n.d.

Narasimhacharaya, R. *History of Kannada Literature*. Mysore: Wesley Press and Publishing House, 1940.

Nilakanta Sastri, K. A. *A History of South India from Prehistoric Times to the Fall of Vijayanagar*. 3rd ed. London: Oxford University Press, 1966.

Ranade, R. D. *Pathway to God in Kannada Literature*. Bhavan's Book University, no. 72. Bombay: Bharatiya Vidya Bhavan, 1970.

Rice, Edward P. *A History of Kanarese Literature*. The Heritage of India Series. Calcutta: Association Press, [ca. 1915].

Saletore, B. A. *Karnaṭaka's Trans-Oceanic Contacts*. Dharwar: Karnatak University, 1956.

Saletore, B. A. *Social and Political Life in the Vijayanagara Empire* (A. D. 1346—A. D. 1646). 2 vols. Foreword by S. Krishnaswami Aiyangar. Madras: B. G. Paul and Co., Publishers, 1934.

Sewell, Robert. *A Forgotten Empire* (*Vijayanagara*): *A Contribution to the History of India*. London: Swan Sonnenschein and Co., Ltd., 1900.

Singh, Ram Bhushan Prasad. *Jainism in Early Medieval Karnataka* (*c.* A. D. 500-1200). Foreword by A. L. Basham. Delhi: Motilal Banarsidass, 1975.

Srinivasachari, C. S. "A Great Contribution of Vijayanagara to the Tamil Country: The Conquest of the Madura Sultanate and the Restoration of Hindu Orthodoxy." *Karnāṭaka Historical Review* 4.1-2 (1937 January-July): 6.14.

Venkata Ramanappa, M. N. *Outlines of South Indian History: With Special Reference to Karnataka*. 2nd ed. Delhi: Vikas Publishing House Pvt. Ltd., 1975.

Venkata Ramanayya, N. *Vijayanagara: Origin of the City and the Empire*. Bulletins of the Department of Indian History and Archaeology, no. 4. General editor: K. A. Nilakanta Sastri. Madras: University of Madras, 1933.

Vijayanagara Sexcentenary Commemoration Volume. Dharwar: Vijayanagara Empire Sexcentenary Association, 1936.

———. Heras, H. and V. K. Bhandarkar. "Vijayanagara Empire: A Synthesis of South Indian Culture." Pp. 29-38.

———. Iswara Dutt, K. "Telugu Literature under the Vijayanagara Empire." Pp. 53-68.

———. Narasimha Char, D. L. "Kannada Literature under Vijayanagara." Pp. 347-366.

———. Raghavacharlu, K. "Krishna Raya, The Man." Pp. 181-190.

———. Rama Rao, R. "Hinduism under Vijayanagara Kings." Pp. 39-52.

———. Saletore, B. A. "Theories Concerning the Origin of Vijayanagara." Pp. 139-159.

———. Shrikantaya, S. "Vijayanagara and Vidyaranya." Pp. 161-168.

———. Srikantha Sastri, S. "Development of Sanskrit Literature under Vijayanagara." Pp. 295-328.

———. Venkat Rao, Nidhathavolu. "Krishnadevaraya and his Literary Circle." Pp. 231-239.

PRIMARY AND SECONDARY SOURCES IN EUROPEAN LANGUAGES

Those Dealing with Vīraśaivism's Broader Context—Other Indian Traditions

Appasamy, A. J., editor. *Temple Bells: Readings from Hindu Religious Literature*. Calcutta: YMCA Publishing House, n.d.

Basham, A. L. *The Wonder That Was India: A Survey of the Culture of the Indian Sub-Continent before the Coming of the Muslims*. First Evergreen edition. New York: Grove Press, Inc., 1959. First published at New York: The Macmillan Co., 1954.

Bhandarkar, R. G., *Vaiṣṇavism, Śaivism and Minor Religious Systems*. Strassburg: Karl J. Trübner, 1913.

Briggs, George Weston. *Gorakhnāth and the Kānphaṭa Yogīs*. Religious Life of India series. Calcutta: Y. M. C. A. Publishing House, 1938.

Chandidās. *Love Songs of Chandidās: The Rebel Poet-Priest of Bengal*. Translated with an Introduction and Notes by Deben Bhattacharya. New York: Grove Press, Inc., 1967.

Dumont, Louis. *Homo Hierarchicus: An Essay on the Caste System*. Translated by Mark Sainsbury. Chicago: University of Chicago Press, 1970.

Dumont, Louis. "Le renoncement dans les religions de l'inde," *Archives de sociologie des religions* No. 7 (1959 January-June): 45-69.

Eck, Diana Louise. *Banaras, City of Light*. New York: Alfred A. Knopf, 1982.

Elmore, Wilber Theodore. "Dravidian Gods in Modern Hinduism: A Study of the Local and Village Deities of Southern India." *University Studies* (University of Nebraska) 15.1 (1915 January): 1-149.

Farquhar, J. N. *An Outline of the Religious Literature of India*. The Religious Quest of India series. London: Humphrey, Milford, Oxford University Press, 1920.

Hacker, Paul. "Zur Geschichte und Beurteilung des Hinduismus: Kritik einiger verbreiteter Ansichten." *Orientalistische Literaturzeitung* 59.5-6 (1964): 231-245. In German.

Ingalls, Daniel H. H. "Cynics and Pāśupatas: The Seeking of Dishonor." *Harvard Theological Review* 55 (1962): 281-298.

[Jayadeva]. *Love Song of the Dark Lord: Jayadeva's GĪTA-GOVINDA*. Edited and translated by Barbara Stoler Miller. New York: Columbia University Press, 1977.

Joseph, P. *The Dravidian Problem in the South Indian Culture Complex*. New Delhi: Orient Longman Ltd., 1972.

Kabīr. Vol. I. Translated and edited by Ch. Vaudeville. Oxford: Clarendon Press, 1974.

Kane, Pandurang Vaman. *History of Dharmaśāstra* (*Ancient and Mediaeval Religious and Civil Law in India*). Government Oriental Series, class B, no. 6. Vol. V, Pt. I: *Vratas, Utsavas and Kāla etc*. Poona: Bhandarkar Oriental Research Institute, 1958.

Kingsbury, F., and G. E. Phillips, ed. and trans. *Hymns of the Tamil Śaivite Saints*. The Heritage of India Series. Calcutta: Association Press, 1921.

Krishnaswamy Aiyangar, S. *Some Contributions of South India to Indian Culture*. Calcutta University Readership Lectures series. Calcutta: University of Calcutta, 1923.

Krishnaswamy Aiyangar, S. *South India and Her Muhammadan Invaders*. New Delhi: S. Chand and Co. (Pvt.) Ltd., [1921].

Lahovary, N. *Dravidian Origins and the West*. Bombay: Orient Longmans Ltd., 1963.

Lorenzen, David N. *The Kāpālikas and Kālāmukhas: Two Lost Śaivite Sects*. Berkeley: University of California Press, 1972.

Mandelbaum, David G. *Society in India*. 2 vols. Berkeley: University of California Press, 1970.

Pandey, Raj Bali. *Hindu Saṁskāras: Socio-Religious Study of the Hindu Sacraments*. 2nd rev. ed. Delhi: Motilal Banarsidass, 1969.

Renou, Louis. *Religions of Ancient India*. First Schocken edition. New York: Schocken Books, 1968. First published at London: Athlone Press, 1953.

Sacred Books of the East. 50 vols. Gen. ed. F. Max Müller. Oxford: Clarendon Press, 1879-1910.

———. Vol. 2: *The Sacred Laws of the Āryas* (*as Taught in the Schools of*) *Āpastamba*, *Gautama*, *Vāsishṭha*, and *Baudhāyana*, Pt.

1: "Āpastamba and Gautama." Translated by Georg Bühler. Oxford : Clarendon Press, 1879.

———. Vol. 14: *The Sacred Laws of the Āryas (as Taught in the Schools of) Āpastamba, Gautama, Vāsishṭha, and Baudhāyana*, Pt. 2: "Vasishṭha and Baudhāyana." Translated by Georg Bühler. Oxford: Clarendon Press, 1882.

———. Vol. 25: *The Laws of Manu*. Translated by G. Bühler. Oxford: Clarendon Press, 1886. Subsequently reprinted separately at New York: Dover Publications, Inc., 1969.

———. Vol. 29: *The Grihya-Sūtras: Rules of Vedic Domestic Ceremonies*, Pt. 1: "Śāṅkhāyana-Grihya-Sūtra, Āśvalāyana-Grihya-Sūtra, Pāraskara-Grihya-Sūtra, Khādira-Grihya-Sūtra." Translated by Hermann Oldenberg. Oxford: Clarendon Press, 1886.

Srinivas, M. N. "A Note on Sanskritization and Westernization." *Far Eastern Quarterly* 15.4 (1956): 481-496.

Srinivas, M. N. *Religion and Society among the Coorgs of South India*. Foreword by A. R. Radcliffe-Brown. New York: Asia Publishing House, 1952.

Stevenson, Mrs. Sinclair. *The Rites of the Twice-Born*. 2nd ed. Foreword by A. A. MacDonell. New Delhi: Oriental Books Reprint Corporation, 1971. First published at London: Oxford University Press, 1920.

Sullivan, Herbert P. "A Re-Examination of the Religion of the Indus Civilization." *History of Religions* 4 (1964): 115-125.

Tiruvalluvar. *The Kural: or The Maxims of Tiruvalluvar*. 2nd ed. Translated by V. V. S. Aiyar. Sheramadevi, South India: The Bharadvaja Ashrama. [ca. 1925].

Tiru-Valluvar. *Kural: The Great Book of Tiru-Valluvar*. Bhavan's Book University, 125. Translated and with Notes by C. Rajagopalachari. Bombay: Bharatiya Vidya Bhavan, 1975.

Tulsī Dās. *The Petition to Rām: Hindi Devotional Hymns of the Seventeenth Century*. Translated with Introduction, Notes and Glossary by F. R. Allchin. London: George Allen and Unwin Ltd., 1966.

Weber, Max. *The Religion of India: The Sociology of Hinduism and Buddhism*. Translated and edited by Hans H. Gerth and Don Martindale. New York: The Free Press, 1958.

Whitehead, Henry. *The Village Gods of South India*. 2nd ed., rev. and enl. The Religious Life of India series. Calcutta: Association Press, 1921.

Wilson, H. H. *Mackenzie Collection: A Descriptive Catalogue of the Oriental Manuscripts and Other Articles Illustrative of the Literature, History, Statistics and Antiquities of the South of India—Collected by the Late Lieut.-Col. Colin Mackenzie, Surveyor General of India*, Calcutta: Asiatic Press, 1828.

SECONDARY SOURCES IN EUROPEAN LANGUAGES
Those Dealing with Methodological Issues

Friesen, Duane Keith. "The Relationship between Ernst Troeltsch's Theory of Religion and His Typology of Religious Association." Ph.D. dissertation, Harvard University, 1972.

Gusfield, Joseph R. "Tradition and Modernity: Misplaced Polarities in the Study of Social Change." *American Journal of Sociology* 72.4 (1967 January): 351-362.

Gustafson, Paul M. "Church and Sect or Church and Ascetic Protestantism: Ernst Troeltsch's Problem." *Encounter* 30.2 (1969 Spring): 142-147.

Gustafson, Paul. "UO-US-PS-PO: A Restatement of Troeltsch's Church-Sect Typology," *Journal for the Scientific Study of Religion* 6.1 (1967 Spring): 64-68.

International Encyclopedia of the Social Sciences. S. v. "Typologies," by Edward A. Tiryakian.

Michael, R. Blake. "A Note on the Origins of the Sect-Church Typology: The American Connection." Paper presented at the annual meeting of the Ohio Academy of Religion, Westerville, Ohio, 1980 April.

Lazarsfeld, Paul F. "Some Remarks on the Typological Procedures in Social Research." *Zeitschrift für Sozialforschung* 6.1 (1937): 119-139.

Parsons, Talcott. "An Outline of the Social System." In *Theories of Society: Foundations of Modern Sociological Theory*, pp. 30-79. 2 vols. Edited by Talcott Parsons, Edward Shils, Kaspar D. Naegele, and Jesse R. Pitts. New York: The Free Press of Glencoe, Inc., 1961.

Parsons, Talcott. *Societies: Evolutionary and Comparative Perspectives*. Foundations of Modern Sociology Series. Englewood Cliffts: Prentice-Hall, Inc., 1966.

Potter, Ralph B. "Some Aspects of the Discussion of Typologies of Religious Association since the Work of Ernst Troeltsch."

Seminar paper, Harvard Divinity School, 1959 April 2. (Xerocopied.)

Smith, Wilfred Cantwell. "Methodology and the Study of Religion: Some Misgivings." In *Methodological Issues in Religious Studies*, pp. 1-30. Edited by Robert D. Baird. Chico, CA.: New Horizons Press, 1975.

Smith, Wilfred Cantwell. *Religious Diversity: Essays by Wilfred Cantwell Smith*. Edited with an Introduction by Willard G. Oxtoby. New York: Harper and Row, Publishers, 1976.

Troeltsch, Ernst. *The Social Teaching of the Christian Churches*. The Cloister Library. 2 vols. Translated by Olive Wyon. Introduction by H. Richard Niebuhr. New York: Harper and Row, Publishers; Harper Torchbooks, 1960.

Troeltsch, Ernst. *Die Soziallehren der christlichen Kirchen und Gruppen*. Tübingen: J. C. B. Mohr (Paul Siebeck), 1912. In German.

Watkins, J. W. N. "Ideal Types and Historical Explanation." *The British Journal for the Philosophy of Science* 3.9 (1952 May): 22-43.

Weber, Max. *Gesammelte Aufsätze zur Religionssoziologie* 3 vols. Tübingen: J. C. B. Mohr (Paul Siebeck), 1920-1921. In German.

Weber, Max. *Methodology of the Social Sciences*. Translated and edited by Edward A. Shils and Henry A. Finch. Foreword by Edward A. Shils. New York: The Free Press, 1949.

Weber, Max. "Die 'Objektivität' sozialwissenschaftlicher und sozialpolitischer Erkenntnis." *Archiv für Sozialwissenschaft und Sozialpolitik* 19.1 (1940): 22-87. In German.

Weber, Max. *The Protestant Ethic and the Spirit of Capitalism*. Translated by Talcott Parsons. Foreword by R. H. Tawney. New York: Charles Scribner's Sons, 1958.

Weber, Max. "Die protestantische Ethik und der 'Geist' des Kapitalismus," *Archiv für Sozialwissenschaft und Sozialpolitik* 20 [n. s. vol. 2] (1904); 1-54 and 21 [n. s. vol. 3] (1905): 1-110. In German.

Weber, Max. *Wirtschaft und Gesellschaft: Grundriss der Verstehenden Soziologie*. Revised edited by Johannes Winckelmann. Köln: Kiepenheuer and Witsch, 1956. In German.

INDEX

Author Index of *Vacana* Quotations

(Author, text, chapter &/or *vacana* number, page)

Maḍivāḷa Mācayya
ŚS Gū., 9: 21— 42
Mahādēviyamma
ŚS Gū., 13: 44— 47
Muktāyi
ŚS Gū., 2: 35— 33
Nīlamma
ŚS Gū., 21: 40— 58
Nuliya Candayya
ŚS Gū., 14: 2—118
ŚS Gū., 14: 7— 48

Siddharāma
SRV 25— 5
SRV 453— 8
ŚS Gū., 3:131— 35
ŚS Gū., 10: 1—100
ŚS Gū., 10: 7— 42
ŚS Gū., 10: 36—151
ŚS Gū., 10: 50— 43
ŚS Gū., 10: 53—114

Text-Source Index of *Vacana* Quotations

(Text, chapter and/or *vacana* number, author, page)

ŚS Gū.,	8: 55	Allama Prabhu	109
ŚS Gū.,	8: 64	Allama Prabhu	109
ŚS Gū.,	8: 65	Cennabasava	40 & 107
ŚS Gū.,	8: 66	Allama Prabhu	108
ŚS Gū.,	8: 75	Cennabasava	40
ŚS Gū.,	9: 5	Allama Prabhu	41
ŚS Gū.,	9: 21	Maḍivāḷa Mācayya	42
ŚS Gū.,	10: 1	Siddharāma	110
ŚS Gū.,	10: 7	Siddharāma	42
ŚS Gū.,	10: 10	Allama Prabhu	149
ŚS Gū.,	10: 12	Cennabasava	111
ŚS Gū.,	10: 14	Allama Prabhu	112
ŚS Gū.,	10: 16	Cennabasava	148
ŚS Gū.,	10: 17	Cennabasava	147
ŚS Gū.,	10: 29	Cennabasava	149
ŚS Gū.,	10: 36	Siddharāma	151
ŚS Gū.,	10: 48	Allama Prabhu	113 & 161
ŚS Gū.,	10: 50	Siddharāma	43
ŚS Gū.,	10: 53	Siddharāma	114
ŚS Gū.,	10: 63	Cennabasava	115 & 129
ŚS Gū.,	10: 98	Cennabasava	115
ŚS Gū.,	11: 2	Basava	116 & 130
ŚS Gū.,	11: 8	Cennabasava	44
ŚS Gū.,	11: 9	Cennabasava	117 & 162
ŚS Gū.,	12: 1	Āydakki Mārayya	46
ŚS Gū.,	13: 2	Basava	159
ŚS Gū.,	13: 44	Mahādēviyamma	47
ŚS Gū.,	14: 2	Nuliya Candayya	118
ŚS Gū.,	14: 7	Nuliya Candayya	48
ŚS Gū.,	14: 43	Allama Prabhu	120
ŚS Gū.,	14: 45	Allama Prabhu	121
ŚS Gū.,	14: 46	Cennabasava	119
ŚS Gū.,	15: 4	Ghaṭṭivāḷayya	49
ŚS Gū.,	15: 10	Ghaṭṭivāḷayya	151
ŚS Gū.,	15: 18	Allama Prabhu	153
ŚS Gū.,	15: 27	Ghaṭṭivāḷayya	152
ŚS Gū.,	15: 52	Cennabasava	49
ŚS Gū.,	15: 56	Basava	50
ŚS Gū.,	16: 4	Akkamahādēvi	154
ŚS Gū.,	16: 9	Basava	155
ŚS Gū.,	16: 14	Akkamahādēvi	51
ŚS Gū.,	16: 15	Allama Prabhu	156
ŚS Gū.,	16: 17	Allama Prabhu	51
ŚS Gū.,	16: 33	Akkamahādēvi	52
ŚS Gū.,	16: 39	Akkamahādēvi	156
ŚS Gū.,	16: 41	Allama Prabhu	157
ŚS Gū.,	17: 24	anonymous	52
ŚS Gū.,	17: 33	Basava	53
ŚS Gū.,	18: 9	Basava	54
ŚS Gū.,	18: 15	Allama Prabhu	54
ŚS Gū.,	19: 22	Cennabasava	55
ŚS Gū.,	19: 46	Allama Prabhu	122
ŚS Gū.,	19: 68	Basava	123
ŚS Gū.,	19: 78	Basava	55
ŚS Gū.,	19: 82	Cennabasava	124
ŚS Gū.,	19: 92	Allama Prabhu	125
ŚS Gū.,	20: 51	Cennabasava	56
ŚS Gū.,	21: 8	Allama Prabhu	57
ŚS Gū.,	21: 12	Allama Prabhu	58
ŚS Gū.,	21: 40	Nīlamma	58

Kannaḍa First-Line Index of *Vacana* Quotations

(First line in Kannaḍa, text, chapter and/or *vacana* number, page)

English First-Line Index of *Vacana* Quotations

First line in English, text, chapter and/or *vacana* number, page

Index with Glossary

ERRATA

Page:	*Line:*	*For:*	*Read:*
4	6	puring	pouring
4	18	period	periods
4	21	*Śūnyaṣampādane*	*Śūnyasaṃpādane*
4	23	Śūnyaṣampādane	*Śūnyasaṃpādane*
7	10	Mārkendeya	Mārkeṇḍeya
7	11	Māṅdōdari	Mandōdari
13	32	Protestantism (*sic*)	Protastantism (*sic*)
19	44	Murugha	Murughā
20	2	December).	December): 202-219.
20	5	Siddhavīranāryaru	Siddhavīraṇāryaru
21	9	person	personal
22	3	*nēmaniṣthe*	*nemaniṣṭhe*
23	5	February).	February): 309-322.
23	28	Martindate	Martindale
26	2	tolerence	tolerance
26	19	suzerian	suzerain
29	34	non-	not-
30	1	*Gūlūru*	*Gūḷūru*
30	34	*Twenty*	*Twenty One*
37	31	abhorrant	abhorrent
39	23	lead	led
50	37	acceded	accede
53	5	*saraṇa*	*śaraṇa*
56	19	Animiśa's	Animiṣa's
56	36	Twentyone	Twenty One
58	28	throns	thorns
59	19	Ghaṭṭivālayya's	Ghaṭṭivāḷayya's
60	4	1345 1646-*A.D.*)	(*A.D.* 1346-*A.D.* 1646)
60	47	Saletere	Saletore
61	44	empire Heras	empire. Heras
61	45	14-8 Heras	14-8. Heras
65	28	Siddhavīranāryaru	Siddhavīraṇāryaru
79	10	idea.sl	ideals.
80	3	ond	and

109	26	saṃsāric	samsaric
110	24	tign	sign
113-127	headers	*Sūnyasaṃpādane*	*Śūnyasaṃpādane*
141	26	next	text
154	37	Mahādeviyakka	Mahādēviyakka
159	17	nurtue	nurture
178	36	Pennsylvania.	Pennsylvania).
182	16	(*States*)	(*State*)
191	42	αιρεσιs	α'ι'ρεσιs
192	33	αιρεσιs	α'ι'ρεσιs
198	39	*Sūnyasaṃpādane*	*Śūnyasaṃpādane*
200	36	Tōṇṭada	[Tōṇṭada
207	21	Ecymenical	Ecumenical
208	23	S.E. Association	L.E. Association